John Matthews has sper
Western Mystery traditio
acknowledged authority
legends. Recently, he has begun to work with men's
groups, which led to the editing of this collection.
He has contributed widely to literary journals such
as *Temenos,* the *Literary Review, New Celtic Review,* and
From Avalon to Camelot and his many books include
At the Table of the Grail (Arkana, 1987), *The Grail,
Quest for Eternal Life* (Thames and Hudson, 1981),
and *Gawain, Knight of the Goddess* (Aquarian, 1990).

M
A
N
D
A
L
A

CHOIRS OF THE GOD

Revisioning Masculinity

EDITED BY JOHN MATTHEWS

Mandala

An Imprint of HarperCollins*Publishers*

Mandala
An Imprint of GraftonBooks
A Division of HarperCollins*Publishers*
77-85 Fulham Palace Road,
Hammersmith, London W6 8JB

Published by Mandala 1991
1 3 5 7 9 10 8 6 4 2

A catalogue record for this book
is available from the British Library

ISBN 1 85274 110 4

Typesetting by MJL Limited, Hitchin, Hertfordshire
Printed in Great Britain by Mackays of Chatham, Kent

CONTENTS

DEDICATION

To the memory of Frank Hudson Keep (1907-1965) who knew when to know, to dare, and to keep silent.

Whoever holds fast the great archetype,
  to him the world comes.
It comes and is not wounded,
  in peace, in equality and in bliss.
Music and enticement:
  indeed, they make the wanderer pause upon his way.
Meaning comes forth from the mouth
  mild and without flavor.
Thou glancest at him and seeth nothing remarkable.
Thou listenest to him and hearest nothing remarkable.
Thou reachest toward him and – findest no end.

Tao-Teh-King (trans. Richard Wilhelm)

INTRODUCTION: REVISIONING MASCULINITY

Friend of souls inspired by the god
Enraptured one, living in caverns,
Thou playest the harmony of the world
with jesting song of the flute...
tending the race of men
over the immeasurable earth.

Orphic Hymn

These days we hear a great deal about the feminine principle of deity known to most people simply as 'the Goddess'. Drawing on ancient accounts of matriarchal worship, many distinctive groups have claimed her for their own: feminists, witches, shamans are all Goddess-worshippers. What, then, shall we say about the God?

In all cultures since the earliest recorded times there have been deities who played a central role in the working of society. Theories abound which have indicated a kind of pendulum-swing from Goddess to God and back again. We hear less of the balanced, polarised cultures which worshipped male *and* female principles jointly. But if we are ever to see a return to that balanced state, which is reflected at all levels of society and could point the way towards the healing of the breach between men and women in our own time, there needs to be more work done on the rebalancing of the masculine. In other words, we need to hear from the God.

This can and does lead to some sensitive and unduly neglected areas. It is a well-attested fact that women are more naturally in tune with the spiritual way of life than are most men. In the monotheistic religions male priests serve masculine deities and their attitudes to women have tended to take on a harsh or unresponsive tone. For many generations the clear voices of women have been silenced, and it is not surprising that there is currently a greater preponderance of feminine mystery teaching, and that many of the voices are raised in anger.

The intention of the collection which follows is not, however, to be divisive but to emphasise that there is a place for both the male *and* female principles in the world, and that only a balanced and polarised acknowledgement of both aspects will suffice. The collection as a whole is essentially about ways in which men can break out of the kind of stereotyping which our culture and/or time have imposed upon us. Of course, this reflects upon everyone, regardless of gender; but just as women have been working, over the past 40 years especially, to break down the kind of stereotypes which made them slaves of the bedroom and the kitchen, so too, in more recent times, an increasing number of men have begun to examine the kind of self-produced, self-perpetuating images which have made them recognisably male!

There is, of course, still a large majority who are happy to regard themselves as naturally superior to women, to view themselves as kings and heroes to whom the rest of the world — particularly their own wives and children — should look up. That this kind of cultural situation is at last beginning to break down is as much the result of the women's movement as of the men's. Some men have actually *listened*!

However, the problem really only begins here. If you take away the image of the dominant male, what remains? The New Age wimp? The consciously bisexually-minded male whose recognition of his own femininity has actually weakened his position, both in society (which still, by and large, recognises men as superior) and in personal relationships?

Of course, the use of the term 'stereotype' brings its own problems. All men, as are all women, are individuals first: the most blatant macho-male may have hidden elements of sensitivity in his character, of which a cursory glance reveals nothing. Equally, an apparently sensitive man may be a tyrant in his own home. It is difficult to judge the truth, and we should be wary of trying to categorise men, just as we should avoid doing so to women.

What, then, are the answers? Or, if we are unable to offer something so concrete, in what direction should we be looking? One course that seems to offer a valid and powerful series of insights is the world of myth and ritual, which has already been extensively explored by modern feminists. Here, all barriers are broken down and we enter an area where stereotypes either will not hold, or are shown to be hollow in various ways and at various levels.

The differences between men and women go very deep — deeper, certainly, than mere gender, sexuality or cultural background. This is nowhere more clearly demonstrated than at the archetypal level, in the magical imagery of gods and goddesses. A man who, for instance, chooses to work with the figure of Zeus will almost certainly discover that the all-powerful male deity has much to tell him about the uses and misuses of power. While if you choose to work with Ares, an aspect of deity which strongly reflects the nature of two masculine concerns, love and war, you will assuredly discover that neither of these things is sufficient in itself to keep you either balanced or satisfied.

Of even greater interest is the study of the hero-figure. We have only to look at the writings of the mythographer Joseph Campbell, in particular his book *The Hero With A Thousand Faces*, to see just how wide the spectrum of male experience can be, and just how many gradations of strength and sensitivity exist within this one archetype.

Yet here, just as in many other areas of the esoteric, we have to guard against a kind of nostalgic, backward-looking exploration of old ideals such as heroism, chivalry or the wild man. All of these aspects of masculinity are there within us, but they are aspects only, not the whole picture. Against them, we have to set others: the estranged son with the overbearing father, the competitive child, the mother's boy, and the tyrant in the high chair, whose cries of 'I want! I want!' echo trought the lives of so many adult males.

As the men's movement gains momentum, these fragmented selves will doubtless begin to be reunited, until a point is reached where we are able to see ourselves whole again. That this wholeness must, in time, include women is beyond question — but we still have a long way to go before we can be proud of being men without feeling that we have reached this position at the expense of the other sex.

Meanwhile, the sense of lost masculinity, of being somehow disempowered by women, has turned many men to anger. Thus, unable to express themselves in any other way, they turn to the old stereotypes of bully-boy and macho-tyrant. For such people the sense of being whole and united again is especially hard to recover.

We are told how, in the Dionysiac mysteries of ancient Greece, at a certain point all the men withdrew into a dark room adjacent to the main temple area, leaving the women to celebrate the mysteries there, while the men did so in the darkness and silence of an artificial womb. This is a paradigm for our own recent past, where men have tended to withdraw into silence, leaving women to celebrate the mysteries of the Goddess alone. It also bears out well the dictum of the great esotericist Dion Fortune, who declared that men were active in the outer world but passive in the inner, while women were the reverse.

This is still true today. Men lack a sense of inner mythology, and this leaves them often with a sense of futility and rootlessness which is one of the most basic aspects of male disempowerment. If we are to discover a way to balance ourselves, to become whole again, we have to try to get in touch with our inner selves, so that we become active there also.

One of the primary reasons for the sense of disempowerment felt by many men today is a general failure to recognise the importance of ritual in our lives. Men have no rite of passage to take them out of childhood into manhood — unlike women, who leave childhood behind when they begin menstruating. The ability to discover or create ritual awareness is one of the first steps which the mythically aware man can take towards wholeness.

Many of us (women as well as men) carry wounds within ourselves which we received in childhood and for which we have never had the opportunity to seek healing. At a very deep level this has everything to do with our sense of sexual identity. By seeking out and identifying these wounds, and by working with them in the context of myth, we can come to terms with ourselves in a way that is both natural and enspiriting.

All of these themes are expressed, in one way or another, in the essays which go to make up this book. From Robert Lawlor's powerful, sometimes controversial overview of 'Male Power on Earth', to Greg Stafford's personal evocation of his own struggles against 'The Monsters' which lurk within everyman, to the rich and energising account of working with magical aspects of the God in R J Stewart's 'The God in Western Magical Arts', and to John Rowan's stimulating description of working with men's groups, the emphasis is on the practical response to the problem of masculinity, and to our being able to revision ourselves and our life roles, both through the acknowledgement of the God within, and through working with the aspects of male energy discoverable within all aspects of myth and deity.

THE HAWK, THE HORSE AND THE RIDER

By

ROBERT BLY

Robert Bly writes here about male initiation, a subject so hedged about with taboos that it is refreshingly good to read something which cuts across the fears and shadows experienced by most mature males when they attempt to break free of their stereo-typed roles. Here we may enter a place from which it is poss-ible to see what we have all lost, first of all, by not practising initiation rites at puberty, and secondly, by our inability to separate ourselves from our own parents in a way that enables us to retain familial links while learning independence and free-dom in the world. There is simply no escaping the gender traps of our modern society; perhaps by following Robert Bly's wise advice we may begin the long journey back to an understand-ing of what it means to be men.

1

THE HAWK, THE HORSE AND THE RIDER

We know so little of initiation that the very word is bewildering, sending the mind along a hundred byways as soon as it hears this latinate word. For some it means a simple passage through a door, as when one says, 'She initiated me into meditation,' or, 'She initiated me into sexuality.' For others, it suggests a slow elaborating of spiritual awareness, as in 'My whole life has been an initiation.' By initiation, anthropologists usually mean a rite of passage, which involves mythical stories, painful rituals and ceremonial dances. Finally, some writers consider the word to betoken intricate and occult descents or ascensions that happen to a soul when it is out of the body.

It is fair to say that there is female initiation, male initiation and human initiation. Each gender has its own practices and rituals, particularly around those processes that begin at puberty; and there is also an initiation into human warmth and community which has nothing to do with gender.

The essay that follows, continuing the emphasis of this book, concentrates on the initiation of men. Almost all cultures we know of have practised male initiation, and in certain contemporary societies, for example, highland tribes of Papua New Guinea, Gisu and Masai tribes of Africa, and aboriginal societies in Australia, male initiation enthusiastically continues.

It should be said that, even though I will refer at times to contemporary initiations in New Guinea or Australia, I do not put them up as models. The New Guinea cultures, enmeshed for centuries in tribal warfare, enforce harsh initiations that apparently produce warlike but not particularly resilient adults. Among the eighty or so tribes we know of who carry out male initiation in New Guinea, some initiatory work is brilliant, some disgusting and mad. Even if all initiation in New Guinea were brilliant, men in the West could not adopt the methods wholesale because we no longer live in their matrix of nature and necessity.

By talking of initiation, I do not mean to imply that we should reinstitute initiation for Western men at once. I suspect it will be years before we understand the process of initiation well enough to offer valuable ceremonies. An essay such as this one amounts to speculative play, an attempt at reremembering, a tentative glance at forgotten territory.

I INITIATION OF THE RIDER

The traditional rites of ancient initiation were complicated and subtle experiences which we can imagine better as a continual spiral than as a walk down a road. But, taking an elementary view of male initiation, we can imagine it as a road or stair with four stages.

The four stages in this scheme are: bonding with the mother and separation from the mother; bonding with the father and separation from the father; the appearance of the male mother; and finally, the interior marriage or marriage with the Swan Woman.

ONE Bonding with the Mother and Separation from the Mother

This first event goes well in some families, poorly in others; we can distinguish as well between a solid bonding at birth and a later, more problematical bonding. The medical profession in the West has adopted birth practices involving harsh lights, steel tables, painful procedures and the infant's isolation for long periods, all of which work to damage the birth bond. Joseph Chilton Pearce has written of that sort of damage in *The Magical Child*. Mothers can sometimes repair a defective bonding later by careful attention to their sons' needs, by praise, carrying, talking, protecting, comforting — and many mothers do exactly that. We can say that bonding with the mother goes relatively well in the West. It is the separation from the mother that doesn't go well.

When a boy first experiences competition, coldness, punishment and expertise with adult men, it seems to the boy that cool tension lies there, and warm excitement with the mother; money with the father, food with the mother; anxiety with the father, assurance with the mother; conditional love with the father, unconditional love with the mother. All over the industrial world, we meet

15

women whose thirty-five year-old sons are still living at home. One such woman told me that her divorce brought her a welcome release from the possessiveness of her husband, who did not want her to leave the house. But she remarked that her son, still living at home, said to her recently, 'Why are you going out so much in the evenings?'

In recent years, the percentage of adult sons still living at home has increased, and we can see much other evidence of the difficulties a young man feels in separating from the mother: the guilt he feels if he parts from her; the constant attempt, usually unconscious, to be a nice boy; his lack of close male friends; his absorption in boyish flirtation with women; his attempt to carry feminine pain; his tendency to change his own wife or girlfriend into a mother; his reluctance to become self-disciplined, and his preference for 'softness and gentleness'; and a general confusion about maleness. These qualities all belong to simple human imperfection and yet, when they, or a number of them, appear together, they point toward a failure in the very first stage of initiation.

Ancient initiatory practices, still going on in many parts of the world, solve this first problem decisively. The old men actively intervene. Typically, when several boys in the tribe have reached the proper age, which is somewhere between eight and twelve, a group of old men will appear and take each boy away from the house of his mother, from whom he will be separated for a year or more. After the initiatory period spent with the old men, the boys return to the village, their faces covered with ash, to indicate that they are now 'dead' to the mothers, who cry out in mourning when they see their sons again. The mothers, playing their part, ask to be reintroduced, because they maintain that they can no longer recognize their sons. In this way each mother learns her son's new name, which he has received in his 'second birth'.

TWO Bonding with the Father and Separation from the Father

The second stage of initiation we will call bonding with the father and separation from the father. In our culture, it is possible that a son and father may not bond until the son has reached his late forties, and then separation still has to take place. Bonding with the father seems to happen slowly in any case. It requires much physical closeness. In pre-Industrial times, father and son would typically sit, stand, or work close to each other for long periods.

During these times the boy's body, one might say, learnt to tune to the father's frequencies, or, more accurately, learnt to tune to the vibratory rate of the adult male body. The times for this slow, lazy, extended tuning are not as available for contemporary sons. Newspapers report that the father of a twelve-year-old boy spends an average of ten minutes a day with the son. While that son is an infant, the average time is fifty-six seconds.

We know that an infant's mind thinks magically — that is, it attributes vast powers to itself. The infantile mind attributes a parent's death or absence to the child's own behavior, or will. 'If I had been a worthy child, my father would still be here.' A son's psyche then interprets the father's absence from the home — an absence which has lengthened during the Industrial decades — as evidence of the son's own unworthiness. When the father works out of the house, then, the son's sense of unworthiness hampers any bonding that might take place when the father does spend time with the son.

Bonding also requires exchange of feeling. Throughout the nineteenth century, the vast majority of American men were immigrants learning a new language. When people speak their original languages, we can say that certain feelings 'get said' — it's as if the language itself says them. But the immigrant father found himself required to learn the new language called English; and the loss of old ways of speaking affected the ability of these men to talk to their daughters and their sons, and it has, consequently, affected the ability of those sons to talk to their sons and so on. We notice that in all frontier situations, the men, urgently attending to new weather, crops, soils, animals, effectively turned over to women almost all cultural activities — novel reading, music appreciation, library activities, literary societies, and so on. The frontier boy then learnt discrimination of feelings almost entirely from his mother. If bonding requires conversations in which feelings and longings can come forward, and verbal situations in which the young male can feel care for the soul, then it's clear the son will bond with the mother, not the father.

The average son feels, particularly in these post-immigrant times, abandoned by his father as far as soul-talk goes. Uncles and grandfathers sometimes gave that soul-talk during the nineteenth century. But now, the grandfather having gone to retirement homes, the father typically returning exhausted and late to his suburban house, the son receives very little soul-talk from men of any age.

For good bonding, we add that the son needs to see the father at work. The German psychoanalyst Alexander Mitscherlich, in his *Society Without the Father*, notes the change that takes place in the son when he no longer sees where the father works, with whom he works, what his job actually is. Mitscherlich observes the son fantasizing that his father is a participant in evil. Unobserved work is demonic work. A hole appears in the son's psyche, Mitscherlich says, and into that hole pour the demons of suspicion, suspicions of all older men, of 'Darth Vader,' the Dark Father, the evil patriarch. A magnetic repulsion then exists between son and father. The son feels he must, through asceticism, meditation, or feminist doctrine, purify himself from the father's corruption. The ground of suspicion then is not good ground for bonding.

But if bonding with the father has not taken place, how can separation take place? Most sons in this century live in limbo, neither bonded nor separated. There are many exceptions to this generalization of course; but most of those who have bonded have worked in physical trades with their fathers as, for example, carpenters, woodcutters, musicians, or farmers.

For most sons, the bonding with the father, following the break characteristic of modern adolescence, stagnates for several decades, then starts up again around the age of forty or forty-five. This delayed bonding with the father slows up the separation as well, so that the contemporary man is often fifty or older before the first two events of initiation have taken place completely enough to be felt as events.

THREE Appearance of the Male Mother

A third event in traditional male initiation is the appearance of the male mother, and most initiations regard that as an essential event. John Layard, who gained much of his knowledge of male initiation from his years with the Stone Age tribes of Malekula, describes Arthur — in his study called *The Celtic Quest* — as a male mother. 'Arthur' may have been a name traditionally given to an old male initiator centuries before the cycle calls him King Arthur. We discover in the ancient Mabinogion story called 'Culhwch and Olwen', that Arthur's kingdom, Layard says, 'has to be "entered" as though it were a woman.' Layard continues: 'This entry into the male world which is a "second mother" is what all initiation rites are concerned with.' When Arthur has accepted Culhwch, he details the things he will not give to the young man, namely ship, cloak, sword, shield, dagger and Guinevere, his wife. He then asks the boy, 'What do you want?' Culhwch says, 'I want my hair trimmed.' Then 'Arthur took a golden comb and shears with loops of silver, and combed his head.' The younger man has placed his head, or his consciousness, into the hands of a nurturing older man, whom he trusts; and by that act, he has been symbolically freed from his obsession with both his mother and father. The one who combs and cuts his hair — Arthur — is not his personal father; so through this 'head-care' the young man passes into a third realm.

It is Arthur's kindness, his 'savvy', his willingness to nurture and guide the young man, his spiritual energy, his store of psychic knowledge, that does the work. Pablo Casals did similar work with younger cellists. Most great black jazz musicians in this century have had male mothers. There are always a few teachers or mentors who understand the concept of the male mother and embody it, but not many. If a young man today accomplishes the first two tasks — bonding with and separation from the mother, bonding with and separation from the father — he may still have difficulty with the third. The concept of male mother actually implies a second birth. It continues the insistence on that birth.

The Australian aboriginal initiators to this day make a sort of vagina of sticks and brush twenty to thirty feet long, and send the boys in at one end. At the other, the old men, the air around them fragrant with the piercing sound of the bull-roarers, receive the boys and declare them now to be born again a second time from the male womb, being born this time not from female body but from male spirit.

We recall that Jesus insisted on the importance of the second birth. The Church usually assumes that the metaphor refers to a religious conversion, but that interpretation may miss the true meaning of this image, which has been a vibrant one since the Stone Age. Jesus may have been providing a second birth to young men in his secret ceremonies.

In certain tribes, such as the Kikuyu, the emphasis around the male mother does not fall on birth so much as on nurturing. One vivid Kikuyu ritual illustrates the teaching offered by the old men. Young initiates, having been taken only recently from their mothers, gather one night around a fire, together with the older men, following several days of little or no food. These old men, one by one, open their arms with a knife and let the blood flow into a gourd, which passes around the circle and is then offered to the young men. By this ritual the old men announce themselves as male mothers. The boy is asked to end his obsession with female milk and move to male blood, and to taste in the blood the depth of the older men's love for him.

Young men in the West do not experience a ritual of that sort. We give the initiating power into the hands of the peacetime army, or the Church, or the corporations, but all three have become public or commercial entities, no longer trusted by young men. The mass lecture system, used in the universities, does not offer the face to face experience of the older initiation, and does no better in its care for soul.

Finally, we notice that the mentors or old men in the traditional initiations administer various kinds of 'tests' to the young man. These tests may include dangerous cattle raids or horse raids, or they may involve pain, or times of hunger, deprivation and solitude.

The story called 'The Drummer', collected by the Grimm Brothers, suggests the sort of trials that initiators in Northern Europe asked for. As the story starts, a young man, a drummer, picks up a piece of white linen on the shore. The linen turns out to belong to a swan-woman, who has been enchanted, and whom the young man offers to help. But in order to free her he has to sleep on a pine of tanbark, learn to refuse food, overcome his fear of giants, brood in solitude for a year in a hut at the foot of the mountain, steal what he needs, 'rob the robbers', and so on. After these sufferings and trials he can at last meet the Swan Woman on the mountain top where she lives.

FOUR   Marrying the Swan Woman

In the old Celtic initiation, described in 'Culhwch and Olwen', Arthur guides Culhwch toward marriage with a mysterious feminine figure called Olwen, which means 'White Track' or 'Trace of the Moon on the Water'. The Goose Girl at the Well, whom we meet in the Grimm Brothers' story of that name, and 'The Woman at the Well', with whom Christ speaks in the New Testament, preserves the memory of this mysterious water woman. 'Faithful John', another story collected by the Grimm Brothers, describes her as a beautiful woman who lives on the other side of the water and can be enticed into the human world by showing her objects made of gold. The Russian fairy stories call her 'The Maiden Czar', a woman who is a virgin but also a being of great authority, a czar.

The fourth stage, then, represents an astonishing leap into the other world. We glimpse a connection between the Swan Woman and Mona Lisa in Leonardo's psyche, and 'Diotima' is Socrates' psyche, and the lunar substance that contributes to the creation of gold in alchemy.

The being who appears in the fourth stage is the Woman Who Loves Gold, or Helen, or Elena the Wise, as some Russian fairy tales call her: and it is the young man's task to marry her. Edward Schieffel, in his *Rituals of Manhood*, about contemporary male initiation in New Guinea, mentions that in the Kaluli tribe the young boys being initiated dive for stones in a pool below a waterfall. A boy may find in the pool a certain stone called 'The Stone Bride', which he can identify because it moves on its own. We see here the ritual appearance of a secret, powerful and helpful being who is not an ordinary or physical woman. The initiating process, then, does not end in machohood, or brutality, but rather moves toward complication, a deepening of feeling, and an openness to the feminine, inside the soul and outside.

When most men imagine initiation today, they imagine it as a continuous development of isolated masculinity, but we recall that most fairy stories end with a 'marriage'. The twentieth century Spanish poet, Antonio Machado, retained a very lively memory of Elena, or the Hidden Woman, about whom he wrote a number of poems. This poem he wrote around 1900:

> *Close to the road we sit down one day.*
> *Our whole life now amounts to the mystery of time, and our*
> *   sole concern*
> *the attitudes of despair that we adopt*
> *while we wait. But she will not fail to arrive.*

This fourth stage, then, the marriage with 'The Swan Woman', suggests that the old men call in 'The Other World' and the feminine at the same time. The young man learns to deal with both. At the close of the Grimm Brothers' story, 'Iron John', which I believe sums up initiatory practices in Europe over many centuries, three events happen almost simultaneously: the young man receives a ritual wound in the thigh, the kingship comes to him, and the Wild Man, earlier a primitive being, reveals himself as a Lord. The events are interrelated in this way. Only an initiated, or adult, man can become a King. But to become a King means that one sits down with a Queen, that is, lives without undermining her power. To receive a wound 'in the thigh' helps with this process, for one knows then how the woman experiences her wound, from which she recovers each month. Once the young man has experienced this dual being in his emotional body, it is safe and proper for the Wild Man, the carrier of the grief of nature itself, to rise in his soul. At this point the Wild Man gives 'all his treasure' to the young man.

Initiation of the sort we have been describing amounts to a development or building up of the emotional body. Genetic inheritance, play, and sports of all kinds give the young man his physical body; he develops that himself, but it is up to the old men to help the young man develop his emotional body. For example, the old man, Hamlet's father, urges Hamlet to let go of his naïveté, and to build an emotional body capable of anger, combat, tricksterhood, loyalty, and intensity. Each time Hamlet listens he is brought one step closer to the clarity and danger of the father's house.

Geneticists now know that the male fetus, though already destined to be male, shows no distinction from the female fetus until the fifth week. At that point, about 250 orders come in from the DNA, ordering changes in the fetus that is destined to be a boy. Both body and brain change from female to male. Men, then, are an experimental species. We could say that this extensive alteration, or rebuilding, or transformation remains unfinished at the moment the boy emerges from the womb. The girl child can 'be herself', but the boy child is still not himself. The old men's initiation advances the masculinization process begun in the womb, and that is the labor. At the same time, if the initiators allowed the development to produce a savage man, a man isolated in his masculinity and out of touch with the feminine, the old men's labor would have failed. The initiators work to produce a lively and compassionate member of this basically experimental species.

Successful initiation in these four stages, whenever it is achieved, results in what we might call conscious masculinity. It builds up an emotional body open to depth of feeling, open to receive the power of 'The Queen', capable of warriorhood or tricksterhood when necessary, and able to contain and endure several sorts of ecstasy, among them the ecstasy of leadership and of Eros.

We need to repeat once more that the ancient view of emotional initiation implies a spiral movement rather than a linear passage. A man spirals through defined stages, and a given stage is not finished once and for all. We go through all stages in a shallow way, then go back, live in several stages at once, go through them all with slightly less shallowness, return again to our parents, bond and separate once more, find a new male mother, and so on, and so on. The old initiation systems having been destroyed, and their initiators gone, a given step is rarely accomplished cleanly, or accomplished at an early age. A quality of male initiation as we live it now is a continual returning.

II INITIATION OF THE HORSE

For our purposes in this essay, we will imagine the man — or the woman — as made up of a horse and a rider. Our opening section has concentrated on the initiation of the rider. By the rider we understand that changeable part born to specific parents, flexible, even whimsical, capable of altering course quickly: the reader of books, the self-transformer, owner of rapidly changing opinions, embedded in family life. The rider's mind is fresh and excitable; he or she endures setbacks and sufferings, becomes educated, or 'drawn out' of the childhood state, learns how to go around or through family wounding, aims at wholeness, enters seminars with persistence and hopefulness, gains knowledge, grows, and 'develops'. Developmental psychology, self-psychology, transcendental psychology, depth psychology...all have been invented by the rider to initiate himself.

By the term 'horse', we understand the more instinctual part, more wilful than the rider or less obedient to the rider's will, associated more with the physical, instinctual, muscular, hormonal body than with its alert and inventive rider. The 'horse' is less open to change; the horse retains patterns known for thousands, perhaps millions of years. We could say that the 'horse' is utterly absorbed by the ancestors, hardly aware of any inventions since the flint arrowhead; the horse is slow, conservative, powerful, unheeding, many times stronger than the rider.

At a certain moment in traditional initiatory practice, the old men put the young men in touch with the horse. We can glimpse this moment, metaphorically, in the Celtic fairy story called 'Conn-Edda', which is included in W B Yeats's collection of Irish fairy tales. A young prince, Conn-Edda, experiencing the hostility of his 'stepmother', finds himself on a quest likely to result in his death. The mysterious old man whom he consults tells him to mount 'a shaggy horse' near the old man's house, and 'let the reins fall'. A bird 'with a human head', an ancestral figure uniting animal and human worlds, gives further instructions: he and the horse are to follow an iron ball wherever it goes. The man and horse traverse painful countrysides together. They go through dragonish, tormenting, underwater, volcanic landscapes that cause suffering, distress, lacerations and misery. The horse asks, 'Are you still with me?' after the rider has been burned and scarred.

We are in the area now of tooth-breaking, scarring with nettles, tattooing, being put upside down below ice, living without food or water in the desert, having a finger cut off, seeing others pack salt into one's open wounds, experiencing a cutting of the penis, enduring sleepnessness, feeling a rib broken. Mircea Eliade reports that these sufferings are a part of the traditional initiations all over the world. These painful trials are intended to catch the attention of the 'horse'.

As we read these old accounts, disguised as stories, we have a sense that a derangement of some sort takes place whenever the horse is contacted. The horse is so wilful and the rider so pampered that both must suffer a deep shock if old patterns are to be effectively disturbed. A little later in 'Conn-Edda', we can feel the rider's shock when the shaggy horse tells the young man to kill him and flay him. The young rider responds by refusing, adducing principles from loyalty vows, humane traditions, knightly customs, family instructions, and community allegiances. The shaggy horse says, 'Forget all that.' After the rider changes his mind, the knife moves on its own towards the horse's throat. The mind of the civilized rider is deranged by this event. We could say that the rider's characteristic hunger for life has received a shock.

During a late scene in the Grimm Brothers' story 'Iron John', the wild man's student, a young man, while riding on 'the black horse', takes a wound, as we mentioned, in the thigh. That thigh wound connects him to thousands of boar woundings that took place in ancient Crete, in Greece, and in Celtic countries; we sense that our culture has lost sight of the significance of those woundings long ago.

The young man in 'The White Bear — King Valemon', a Norwegian tale, has to endure, without making a sound, a darning needle that a witch drives straight through his arm during her attempt to find out if he is asleep or not. He has to endure this wound before he can reunite with the feminine being from which he has been separated for years.

I mention these stabbings and burnings to concentrate on the horse, whose attention it is so difficult to get. We are talking metaphorically, and we know the horse is not identical with the body, no more than the rider is identical with the brain. Each is a being so complicated it can only be described by metaphor or image.

We are not doing well during this century in contacting the horse. We have concentrated on the initiation of the rider, and often the concentration has been brilliant. Therapists, who do some of the initiation of the rider, hope that the rider's new insights will drift downward, be absorbed by the physical body, show themselves as increased body awareness, as changed posture, and a muscular system less rigid and fossilized.

But to do 'body work' well does not mean that you have contacted the horse. On the contrary, one could say that in recent decades the horse has drifted away, wandered farther and farther out of range. It does not hear when called to and has forgotten the meaning of the verbal instructions that it does hear. It turns aside to eat grass whenever it feels like it, throws its rider in the ditch when irritated and, in general, ignores the highly articulated rider who urges it to proceed down the road toward 'individuation'.

We are not likely to be successful in any reinstatement of initiatory practice until we understand the idleness and deafness of the horse. I prefer not to use psychological jargon in order to define the horse more clearly — that would merely be to ignore the whole problem by letting the rider control the argument.

III   INITIATION OF THE HAWK

We have not yet exhausted the traditional range of initiatory practice. To take one more step we might imagine a hawk or a falcon perched on the rider's shoulder. This predatory bird stands for that part of us which frees itself from both rider and horse, flies high into the clouds, sees the countryside from afar, lives in air. Rumi says: 'He is made of air and has gone into air.' This is the Traveller, who visits distant places while we sleep, ascends into the air around the moon, goes to Tibet, dives down to earth and glides out over the sea, pays a visit to the dead, and flies back down to sit on the wrist.

The Traveller is easily distinguished from the rider, who takes on a coloring from the family into which he or she is born. The Traveller does not seem to exhibit incest longings, shame, father-anger, abuse, or rage. All those emotions, and the painful living-out of them, belong to the rider.

A number of ancient teaching stories, or 'hearth stories', describe the Traveller as a bird: a raven; a falcon; an eagle; a goose. In the Grisons' tale called 'The Raven', the raven, having been enchanted, has to exchange his castle for the dark wood. He lives in the dark wood, and advises a young virgin who offers to help him that she is to fill a jar with her tears, and then sprinkle his feathers with it. She is not to let even a single drop fall to the ground.

In other words, something from the dark world and the night and the realm of tears has to be carried over into the day, and into daylight consciousness. The initiation of the Traveller has something to do with sleep, and with bringing back forces or information to the waking self. When the waking self deals with the 'ten thousand things', that is, our exhausting ordinary life, its thought energy becomes dispersed. The concentrated thought energy or power that we experience in deep sleep then needs to be carried back — in a carefully managed jar — and brought up into daylight consciousness without spilling a drop.

We recall many reports of a mysterious sleep in the old tales. For instance, we recall Snow White's sleep, and the sleep the Drummer experiences on the tanbark, and the Bear King's three-night sleep on top of the mountain. The King and Queen in 'The Goose Girl at the Well' fall into a deep sleep shortly before they find their daughter again. The young man in 'The Water of Life', also a Grimm Brothers tale, having entered the castle and found there the Water of Life, falls into a deep sleep, from which he has to awaken at just the right moment in order to get out of the castle by midnight. Some ancient Christian texts maintain that Jesus himself administered the three-day sleep, known from many Mediterranean traditions, and the texts say further that he was giving exactly that initiation to the young man wearing the seamless robe of One About to Sleep when the soldiers broke in. It says in Mark: 'And there followed him a certain young man, having a linen cloth cast about his naked body; and the young men laid hold on him: And he left the linen cloth and fled from them naked.'

The initiatory sleep surfaces vividly in *Cymbeline*,[1] whose storyline and language refers over and over to initiation practices, as well as to alchemical themes. Iachimo, for example, recognizes Imogen as 'The Arabian Bird', that is, the Phoenix, the goal of

[1] Readers interested in pursuing *Cymbeline* should consult Wendy Macphee's fine summation of alchemical, initiatory and plot patterns in *Cymbeline*, published by the Theatre Set-Up, 41 Colne Road, Winchmore Hill, London N21 2JJ.

alchemy. Leonatus Posthumus is the *lion* of alchemical work and Imogen the *air*. As the play proceeds, Imogen is led into a cave where she dresses as a man, and there she later falls into a long initiatory sleep. When she awakes, she is confronted with the severed head of Bran, the Raven King, who is, in the alchemical texts, a strong symbol of alchemical death.

We notice that it is Belario who stands at the mouth of this cave. That detail suggests that the initiation of the Traveller in Britain took place under the guidance of the Celtic sungod Bel, just as in the Greek temples it took place under the guidance of Apollo.

Later in the play, Posthumus enters into his initiatory death or magic sleep as well. I mention the Shakespearean details to remind us that it was during the Renaissance that the ancient initiation material began to appear once more, through the work of Bruno, Raymond Lull, the Kaballah, Robert Fludd and John Dee. These details in *Cymbeline* also suggest that Shakespeare, toward the end of his life, found the 'hawk' information so valuable that he attempted to bring it forward in dramatic form, where it presents itself, half open, and half hidden.

Those Renaissance writers who spoke of the third initiation did well to keep the premises at least half hidden, because the connection of hawk initiation with alchemy made it heretical for the Church. Uneasy tensions developed around these issues; and we know that Church officials repeatedly threatened alchemists with death for their heresy, and did burn Giordano Bruno to death.

During Shakespeare's lifetime, Jacob Boehme embarked on an immense literary labor attempting to reconcile theological and alchemical language. Jung has continued this struggle; and many theologians continue to accuse him of heresy.

More recently, English students of Celtic initiation, among them R J Stewart, Gareth Knight, Eleanor Merry, John and Caitlín Matthews have done much helpful work in recovering some of the old initiatory knowledge in the 'hawk' tradition.

We are trying to remember what initiation was and is. We notice that those men and women who study initiation in our culture usually choose one of the three roads I've mentioned, and ignore the other two. The 'Occult', or 'New Age', or Magician students long most of all to initiate the hawk through magical practices; that will not do unless the young man's or young woman's airiness, mother attachment, father-anger, passive aggression and brutality are dealt with first. Similarly, if a young man labors to release his emotional body from maternal attachments and father abandonments, he will still not arrive if his 'horse' is left alone to get deafer, lazier and more wilful year by year. That would be equally true for women. Working to discipline the 'horse' in a man, while caring nothing for the rider or the hawk, would probably produce a highly evolved brute like Savonarola, Calvin, or General Patton.

We've said as much as we have space for here about these three methods, or roads, or countrysides of initiation. I think the moment we are living in is a fruitful moment for brooding on these matters. It is as if we have been content with unconscious manhood and unconscious womanhood for centuries. Boys developed into men — or did they? — and girls developed into women 'involuntarily', 'without intending to', 'growing like weeds'. But two questions remain: If we grow without direct intent, is it unconscious men and women we grow into? And secondly, why has this involuntary process begun to fail?

There must have been some substratum of consciousness in uncles, grandmothers, grandfathers, worthy elders, that once helped the process along. Now, with grandparents devalued or sent to geriatric communities, we are truly 'on our own', without guides, wandering in uncharted lands. No one is going to do initiation for us. That recognition could lead us into hopelessness; but on the other hand I think it is clear by now that when we fall away from doctrine or guidance we do not regress into chaos. If we descend into the soul, we descend into a structure, not into emptiness or disorganization. The farther we go down into the psyche, the more order we find. We have the right to say that there is a deep structure to a man's psyche, as there is a deep structure to a woman's psyche. It is the psyche's structure that all initiatory thought aims to discover, for it will hold us up.

MALE POWER ON EARTH

By

ROBERT LAWLOR

*In his searching overview of historical patriarchy, Robert Lawlor
sees this male-dominated phase of history as coming to its end
— according to Hindu belief with the end of the age of Kali Yuga
in 2442 AD. Looking beyond this at the possibility of a world
where masculine energies can be revitalised and where men and
women can work together in harmony, he seeks to find a way
of adjusting to this new era by re-examining some of the myths
of patriarchy.*

*From this emerges a new way of looking at history itself —
its causes, its casualties and its almost invisible but ever-present
tides, reflecting human thought and belief systems.*

*By this process a number of masculine stereotypes are shown
for what they are — hollow images which can be shattered.
Among these are the militaristic, hero-centred figures of the
dominant male, and the life-denying, self-castrating ascetic who
renounces the world and the process of birth in order to reach
a point of exclusive power.*

*In the process of this, Lawlor presents us with a most per-
suasive and subtle account of the transition from matriarchy
to patriarchy — as a natural outcome of the change from hunter-
gatherer to agriculturally oriented societies. The prediction of
a gradual reversal of this — not to a backward-looking, nostalgic matriarchal world but to an integrated, genderless state of
being — is something to which both sexes should look forward
with growing awareness.*

2

MALE POWER ON EARTH

THE ORIGINS AND END OF THE MALE-DOMINANT WORLD ORDER

In my recent book, *Earth Honouring*, I have developed the theme that the ancient concepts of the cycles of time, such as the Hindu concept of Yugas, can be associated with an alternation between the domination of matriarchy succeeded by the domination of male power or patriarchy, followed by the re-emergence of a new matriarchy. The theory that, during the Stone Age, the world lived in peace, was woman-centred, maintained the sacred value of the Earth and the pre-eminence of the Earth Mother, and polytheistically worshipped goddesses and gods who were humane, life-generating and supportive, has been developed by the eminent archaeologist Dr Marija Gimbutas. According to Dr Gimbutas' view of history, the ascendency of the feminine principle and matriarchal world view was shattered approximately 5000 to 6000 years ago by patriarchal invaders, who first installed war-like male Gods in the place of the Goddesses.[1] With the rise of the Hebrew (and then Christian) movements they erected an all-powerful monotheistic male Creator, which remains the metaphysical paradigm upon which our present society is built.

To understand how the patriarchal structure was implanted within our psychology and sexuality and how it is retained in men, women and our institutions of today is of primary importance in releasing the creative power of human imagination. The ability to imagine from a position outside the present system is the most potent option in coping with the impending termination of the male-dominant world order, as well as for envisioning the forms of a new phase of human history which must follow.

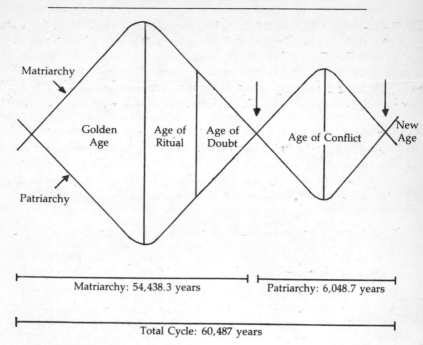

Matriarchy: 54,438.3 years   Patriarchy: 6,048.7 years

Total Cycle: 60,487 years

Fig 1. The Yugas and the Patriarchal/Matriarchal cycle
The Hindu cycles are based on a vast cycle of 54,438.3 years with a rising
or 'golden age' followed by two phases of decline: the 'age of ritual' and
the 'age of doubt'. I have assimilated this larger cycle with the Matriarchal age which fits approximately with the continuous hunting and gathering culture of the Australian Aborigines. In the closing phase of the
Matriarchy, we have the beginning of agriculture, which coincides with
excavations in Anatolia. The rise of Patriarchy can be assimilated with
the Kali Yuga which is the 'age of conflict and destruction' following the
Matriarchal cycle. According to the traditional Hindu calendar, Kali Yuga
commenced in 3012 BC, the middle of Kali Yuga is 582 BC, the beginning
of the twilight is 1939 AD, and the end of the twilight of Kali Yuga 2442
AD. The imbalance of masculine energy is a necessary phase in the destruction and decomposition of the old forms before the new forms emerge.
The entire oscillation is 60,487 years.[2]

HISTORY AND THE TRANSFORMING WORLD VIEW

I would like to begin this exploration by first establishing the guide-
lines for our use and understanding of history. History, as Owen
Barfield points out in *Speaker's Meaning*, is a rather recent concept.
History in the form we know today emerged in Europe in the

course of the 17th century. At the beginning of the 17th century, both history and natural science were considered sub-classes of philosophy and from there grew as separate academic disciplines, as well as becoming new and different ways of approaching experience and understanding life. By the 19th century, the power of science has ascended to such a degree that it was assumed that the scientific method was the only reliable way of investigating history or, for that matter, any other avenue of human enquiry — with the possible exception of the arts. There are obvious considerations which should have, but unfortunately did not, prevent the total subjugation of the study of history to the proof-orientated, chronological methodology of rational science. I list a few of these considerations:

1. We have no direct empirical access to the past.

2. Historical events are immaterial and cannot be observed or experimented with.

3. All records and memories of history are dependent upon subjective, interpretive and linguistic mind processes, founded on individual perceptions and containing limited or precommitted perspectives.[3]

I would like to avoid the constrictions and contentions of the 19th century approach to history and return to that sense of history which existed 300 to 400 years ago: *history not separate, distinct or different from the present*.

We exist in bodies which have been developed, shaped and organised — with blood, bones, breath, flesh and nerves — in the past. The past is not only the entirety of our physical nature but is also ever-present in our minds as language. Words acquire shared meaning only from past use. Every word which we speak or write fuses our thoughts to every other past occasion and mind that used the same word for a similar expression. Therefore we are, in body and mind, never disassociated from the past. History is the structural tissue of every moment. The present and future are only the residues of the past; what is and will be are only explorative variations of that which originally was and has always been. The past is womb, Mother and grave of all that exists. History, the feminine aspect of time, is the immaterial matrix out of which the temporal and specific emerge. If we look beneath the atom there are invisible fields, forces, powers, pulsations, which are in turn synchronised with rhythms and patterns of ever larger fields and forces of order. The visible drama of events emerges and submerges into history in much the same way as matter does from immaterial fields of force.

Let me give a living example of this theory of history. I presently live on a remote island off the coast of Tasmania. The windswept stretch of water which surrounds this island, the Bass Strait, connects the Indian Ocean with the Pacific Ocean and separates the island state of Tasmania from the southernmost shores of mainland Australia. Here, in 1835, in this lonely and beautiful environment, a hideous genocide reached its culmination. The last tribal people of the oldest continuous culture, the Tasmanian Aborigines, were brought here as captives by British convict colonialists and exposed to conditions which caused them to perish. Recently, the remaining descendents of the Tasmanian Aborigines made application to the government for land rights to the small site where their last tribal ancestors were buried. The island population of Anglo-Saxon sheep farmers predictably protested loudly against even the *suggestion* of returning this land to the Aborigines. The Aboriginal graves were, for the most part, unmarked and grown over beyond recognition. The ensuing public row led to a scientific verification of exactly where the graves were located. A governmental scientific team arrived and employed a device which accurately recorded the electromagnetic field flowing through the subsoil of the entire grave site. When these records were fed through a computer, a graphic image was obtained showing exactly where the excavations were originally made. The earth, in over a century and half, had not compacted in the same way as the virgin soil and the electromagnetic flow remained sufficiently altered that the energy fields maintained the image of the violation. The earth's memory had not forgotten the atrocity.

Biologist Rupert Sheldrake has devoted his life's work towards postulating a scientifically verifiable theory for an active interdependent exchange between the forms/processes of nature and a pattern image within an invisible field level of organisation. In Sheldrake's theory, these morphic and biomorphic fields act informatively, even causatively, in the structures, forms and developmental processes of our natural and intelligible world. The interplay, transferral and transmission between the forms of this world with their respective morphic fields, which Sheldrake refers to as 'morphic resonance', constitute a memory factor inherent at the very basis of form and substance.[4] Sheldrake's idea of morphogenetic fields is strikingly comparable to the ancient concept of an archetypal realm and mythic preformative powers. Based on this similarity, I propose that the concept of history should evolve more towards a method of describing the alternative emergings and submergings of forms and their related fields.

In addition to Sheldrake's postulated morphic fields, there exists a range of subtle intermediate fields surrounding living organisms, some of which are now detectable and have an electromagnetic character. The renewed investigation of bio-electric currents and fields is giving rebirth to the ancient concept of energy-medicine. I believe the understanding of the interrelationship between visible and invisible realms should also reshape our understanding of time and history. As events recede in time, they become understandable in relation to the energies and characteristics of the archetypal fields from which they emerged. For example, in the Pintupi language of the Australian Aborigines, there is no division between past and present. Things which are being or have actually been seen or experienced perceptually, including happenings in dreams, trance and visions, are contrasted to events which have not been seen, such as things that have been told to one second-hand through language. History, myths, and stories are experienced first in language, then enter an unseen internal image or belief system, or enter into our visible dreams and sometimes realities. The passage may also be reversed, but in Aboriginal thought this division is of primary importance.[5]

Our language does not make the distinction between events which exist for us in the visible or perceivable world and those which exist only in language. I shall throughout refer to the linguistic advantages of replacing the past/present division with the division between the imperceivable/perceivable. I believe our understanding of history is facing a revolution similar to that which occurred in physics at the turn of the century. As we become more aware of the actual effects and influences that myths and invisible archetypal fields have in the movements of human history, we can perhaps look forward to a day when the 'bone peddlars' will no longer lay claim to the bottom line of historical interpretation.

In tests conducted during shuttle flights in 1989, crystals grew in the micro-gravity environment in the spacecraft, pure and more symmetrical than those from corresponding experiments on Earth. Also protein crystals grew larger and more uniformly. This could be interpreted as demonstrating that the pollution and disturbances of the electromagnetic fields on Earth are disrupting the communication of form/substance in its capacity to mirror the clarity and symmetry of its archetypal formative fields. We should note that these experiments include the protein crystals of our own bodies.[6]

One other example which I feel it is necessary to include is of a more personal nature. I recently became ill for months on end with a group of symptoms: exhaustion, depression, mucous inflammation and severe pain in my upper arms. Orthodox medicine could only diagnose my illness as a new syndrome. Through a series of treatments from a brilliant young homoeopath, it was revealed that the surface symptoms were caused by a sodium imbalance, which he rebalanced through an energy-medicine technique. The second phase of treatment revealed a closure of energy flow in the heart centre and heart meridians caused by childhood vaccinations. This second diagnosis surprised me. However, I then recalled a previously blocked experience which occurred between seven and nine years of age. I was suffering from allergies and hayfever and was forced by my parents to receive weekly inoculations in my upper arms. The inoculations were supposed to alleviate my allergic sensitivities. The treatment, of course, never worked, but the pain and trauma of the injections at this impressionable age caused a loss of trust in my parents as well as in the world around me. The energy obstructions acquired at this time have affected, to this day, my way of relating to the world. Like the Aboriginal graves, physical traumas at one stage of development can be imprinted into the field level as psychic energy obstruction. In many ancient languages, the word for 'earth' and the word designating the human body are the same. The identity of our bodies with the earth is an essential component in this reconceptualisation of history.

MALE SEXUALITY AND THE SHAPE OF HISTORY

With these remarks to guide our general approach to history, I shall begin the search for the origins of the present male domination of society, religion, myth and intellectual processes at the midpoint or zenith of the patriarchal development; that is, 2000 to 2500 years ago in the centuries prior to and just following the birth of Christ. At this moment of history, in the formation and emergence of Christianity as a world movement, the idea of male celibacy (in the extreme, male castration) was associated with the achievement of spiritual purity and power.

The imposition of this idea on the sexual imagination of the masses in the Middle East at that time was not only a powerful religious motivation, but also an effective political mechanism. These events are documented in Barbara Walker's *The Woman's*

Encyclopedia of Myths and Secrets and Elaine Pagels' *Adam, Eve and the Serpent*. To summarise some of the attitudes which solidified out of this concept, I shall focus on Paul, whose fanaticism for male celibacy and repulsion against women are clearly announced in his Letters and Epistles, along with his veiled references to castration as a means of obtaining perfect celibacy.

> Paul hinted that he was one of the 'new creatures' in Christ, neither circumcised or uncircumcised. A man would have to be one or another, unless he altogether lacked a penis. Paul made an oblique reference to a mutilation: 'I bear in my body the marks of the Lord Jesus' (*Galatians 6:17*). He scorned the 'natural' (unmutilated) man for his lack of spirituality: 'The natural man receiveth not the things of the Spirit of God; for they are foolishness unto him' (*1 Corinthians 2:14*). Paul wrote to the Galatians: 'I would they were even cut off which trouble you' (*Galatians 5:12*). The world rendered 'cut off' also meant 'castrated'. Paul spoke 'after the manner of men,' as if he were not one, because his hearers' flesh had an 'infirmity' that he didn't share. He asked them to crucify and destroy 'our old man,' a common Middle Eastern epithet for the phallus. 'He that is dead is freed from sin' because he could no longer serve the 'uncleanness of women'.
>
> (Barbara Walker, *The Woman's Encyclopedia of Myths and Secrets*, San Francisco, Harper and Row 1983, pp776 and 777)

According to Gnostic texts, both Paul and Jesus were educated and initiated in the radical Jewish ascetic communities at Qumaran called the Essenes. The Essenes were an extremist group captivated by Eastern theories of the cycles of time. These milleniumist philosophies prophesied that the final judgement and destruction of human civilization was approaching and that a new age and a new world order were to prevail. There are statements in the Gospel attributed to Jesus which show that he had absorbed the association of sexual denial with the achievement of a 'new spiritual age'. Jesus himself advocated castration: 'There be eunuchs, which have made themselves eunuchs for the Kingdom of Heaven's sake. He that is able to receive it, let him receive it.' (*Matthew 19:12*) (ibid p146).

In spite of the similarities, there were differences between the teachings of Paul and Jesus which may be attributed to the fact that they each received a different initiation into the esoteric doctrines of the Essenes. The Jews and the Essenes, like all developed societies of the time, followed the basic fourfold structure of the caste system, similar to that of Indian culture. Jesus' lineage, according to text, was one of the ruling aristocracy. He was of a genealogy of kings whose function, like all royalty, was to look after the domestic law and the social and commercial interactions of the society. Paul, on the contrary, was of the priest caste and hence had a more austere view of the role of sexual energy and sexual restraint in the formation of individuals and society.

A number of interpretations of the Gnostic texts now regard Jesus as the leader of a breakaway faction of the Essenes who gained great popular appeal by advocating, not only the overthrow of Roman rule, but the breakdown of the Judaic caste structure. The liberalism of Jesus would allow worthy members from all levels of society to receive the highest initiation and spiritual achievement, which until then had been reserved only for the priest caste. Jesus is seen by some Gnostic interpreters as 'a sort of spiritual socialist' whose egalitarian ideals finally angered the Essenes. Dr Barbara Thuring, archaeologist at Sydney University, interprets the 'last temptation' of Christ as a dialogue, not between Jesus and the Devil, but as a refusal by Christ to accept a deal with the priestly zealots. The Essenian priests, perhaps Paul himself, recognised that Jesus' popularity amongst the peasantry could be used as the front for establishing the ascetic aims of the Essenian vision of a 'new world'. The New Testament states that Jesus' death occurred, not from Roman persecution, but from a conspiracy amongst the Jews themselves.[7] The Gnostic texts indicate that perhaps the priestly zealots may have masterminded this conspiracy. Perhaps it was felt that Jesus was more inspirational as a martyr than as a living radical. Paul may have realised, upon his trip to Rome after the death of Christ, the efficacy of the Jesus story as a popular myth to gain the groundswell support neccesary to sweep Christianity into the existing hierarchical structure of the Roman Empire. After the death of Jesus, the discontent and rebellion that he had sown amongst the peasant villages throughout Galilee ignited and drew members from all castes into a Jewish insurrection against Rome. This insurrection was violently put down by Titus, the Roman Emperor, leading to the annihilation of Jerusalem politically, and the destruction of the Jewish Temple which was replaced by an edifice to the pagan gods of Rome. This jolt to Judaism caused a splintering which eventually reformed into the present Rabbinical structure. The Christians who arose from the Essenes, while maintaining some of the Jewish tradition, went their own way. Jesus and his Christian followers endorsed from his ascetic background the rejection of family, marriage and procreation, which were so cherished and fundamental to traditional Jews. Voluntary celibacy for the sake of following Christ into a 'new age' was unacceptable for conservative Jews.[8]

With this platform, Christianity spread throughout the Mediterranean and Middle Eastern world like a plague of locusts until, under enormous pressure in the 4th century, the Roman Emperor Constantine converted to Christianity, the long persecuted Church becoming a state religion.[9] Thus, the idealistic dream of the desert ascetics of centuries before — 'the kingdom of God on earth' — was paradoxically realised in the Holy Roman Empire; an empire in which the celibate priest caste, headed by an omnipotent Pope, would come to rule the world.

Gnostic texts have increased the possibility of New Testament interpretations, but the factuality and details of the above account have been, and will continue to be, argued indefinitely. It is not, therefore, the contentions surrounding the various historical fabrications which are of interest, but instead the outlines of an historical process. It is certain that the energy derived from sexual repression and denial, incited by the zealot preachers of celibacy and castration, fanned the flames of this incredible world movement. Young minds, discontended with a degenerating Roman Empire, were infected with a doomsday prophecy and idealistically grasped for personal immortality by rejecting a dying world: through the renunciation of sexuality, procreation and, in effect, the power of women. Accounts show that young Christian converts flocked to Roman doctors by the thousands for the castration operation.[10] Along with castration, martyrdom grew as an expression of devotion to the new spiritual age.[11] Death, not life, powered the dynamic rise of the Christian world.

Jung and his followers opened up Western psychology to a cosmological premise which had long existed in the East: human sexual energy emerges out of deep mythic and archetypal fields that associate mankind with the invisible forces which interplay in ordinary life. The formation and emergence of Western Christianity resulted from consciously and unconsciously tapping into mythic fields and archetypal powers, particularly the image of the castrated or crucified male.

Participation in the historical transition that is upon us requires, I believe, an awareness of how archetypal fields and mythic patterns shape history, as well as an understanding of the traumas and distortions which have developed historically and are maintained in the intermediate fields that surround us psychically and biologically. The Christian attempt to achieve a new world order and a 'new age' failed because of two major points of ignorance. I would like to deal with each of these separately as both hold important lessons for our present aspirations for the advent of a new age:

1.   The Christians and Essenes were ignorant of the mythic and historic implications and sources of the ascetic ideals and associated sexual powers which they adopted.

2.   The Christians had no essential understanding of their enemies — the Roman Empire — and, as the adage goes: when one destroys and devours that which one does not understand, one simply becomes it.

THE ORIGINS OF THE MALE POWER MYTH

We can reach further back into the shadows of prehistory to find the mythic field from which the image of the castrated male emerges. By the time it was employed by the Christian fathers it had been long activated in the human imagination.

I first encountered the image of castration as a young man in my early twenties, while searching through mouldering books on yoga in the Sri Aurobindo library in Pondicherry, India. One volume contained an old photograph showing a Jain yogi who, through ascetic practices and physical mastery, had drawn his penis and scrotum into his lower abdomen, leaving only folds of skin covering the introjected organ. The text stated that the Jain monk could expect his body to naturally dissolve his genitals completely in about seven to twelve years and that, from that time onward, he would be freed from the burden of sexuality and all sexual desire. In addition, he would obtain clairvoyance and other supernatural powers. This image was for me at that time intriguing and even inspiring. I had recently left behind the moral and political collapse of the early 1960s in America; the Vietnam war, the assassinations of Martin Luther King and the Kennedys, and Marilyn Monroe's suicide. I had survived the early blush of hallucinogens and free sex while living as a young painter amongst the artist community of the East Village in New York. The corruption and confusion of the time had set me on a search for the so-called new age. From the available Eastern philosophies I had adopted ascetic practices such as meditation, fasting, and celibacy. I was completely unaware that this personal pattern was recapitulating the cycle of emergence of Christianity 2000 years earlier, including the practice of austerities and renunciation inherited from the Jains.

> Perhaps the earliest sectaries to regard asceticism as the key to heaven were Jain Buddhists whose theology influenced Persian patriarchs, who in turn influenced Jewish eremites like the Essenes. Jain Buddhist monks had already penetrated the courts of Syria, Egypt, Macedonia and Epirus by the 4th century BC and were glorified in legend for the alleged magic powers they developed through prodigies of self-denial.

> (Barbara Walker, *The Woman's Encyclopedia of Myths and Secrets*, San Francisco, Harper and Row 1983, p63)

Who were the Jains and how did their philosophy come to contain such a profound nihilism that it infected the world with a life-denying vision? To speculate on this we must return to the matriarchy/patriarchy theme of Dr Gimbutas. Perhaps because matriarchy had reached great heights of social and spiritual expression in India, its collapse there may have been interpreted, particularly in the male psyche, as the end of the world. Jainism arose in Northern India amongst the populations that bore the brunt of this radical transition following the Aryan patriarchal invasions. The disillusionment and despair inherent in Jain philosophy may reflect a reaction like that of a hurt child who has been abandoned by its mother. Indeed, Jain cosmology views the world as being in a constant cycle of decline from an original golden age.[12] Spiteful of the Great Mother who had either failed or deserted them, the Jain philosophers saw that patriarchy must control the world and impose structures, laws and prohibitions upon a hopelessly degeneration humanity. Women, the Mother figure, and nature itself must be subjugated and transcended.

> Some of the ascetics openly despised sexuality and motherhood. The *Mahabharata* anticipated St Augustine's remarks about the nastiness of birth: 'Man emerges mixed with excrement and water, fouled with the impurities of woman. A wise man will avoid the contaminating society of women as he would the touch of bodies infected with vermin'. Some advertised their renunciation of sex by castrating themselves or affixing large metal rings in the flesh of the penis. (ibid, p63)

These historical events crystallized as emotional components of the collective male psyche. Men came to believe that, in disavowing themselves from the desires and needs of their physical bodies, they could enact a spiritual escape from the natural world. In this view, the pursuit of sexual and physical mastery would raise men above nature and result in the acquisition of supernatural powers. This male psychology, which arose in yogic ascetism, today haunts the entire enveloping field of the collective male psyche. Body-builders, athletes, soldiers, all the death-defying heroes, are driven by the internalised belief that physical mastery can attain to the status of immortality.

The emergence of this psychological configuration was in association with a cultural formation. Culture presently means opera or art galleries or literature, etc, but culture originated from the way in which a particular human society related to the Earth. The present scientific dictionary definition of culture sheds more etymological light: 'culture is a growth process occurring in a prepared nutritive medium'. The medium in the broader sense is the Earth and the Earth nourishes man in four distinct cultural modes: 1 hunting and gathering; 2 herding of livestock; 3 agriculture, and 4 industrialism. Joseph Campbell in *Historical Atlas of World Mythology Volume 1* relates that the earliest 'Homo sapiens' graves found in Iran and dating back 40,000 to 50,000 years seem to represent the forerunners of a racial group which, expanding eastward and westward in the Northern latitudes, moved very early from hunting and gathering into the herding and controlled grazing of domestic livestock.[13] These Northern cultures are associated with the Caucasian racial type and were perhaps the forefathers of the Aryan culture. Every organism at birth receives, with the gift of life from the mother, a programme which, throughout its life, leads it toward dissolution and death. We may assume that Aryan culture represents that programme for this cycle of time.

Ancient myths from Anatolia state that the herding and domestication of animals was the only craft, of all the technologies basic to civilisation, which was contributed to by men. Evidence suggests that patriarchy developed almost exclusively among nomadic herders and graziers. This cultural foundation forms the basis of male-dominant society.[14] It can also be argued that industrialism is the final or degenerate phase of patriarchy. Machines and mechanical inventions are the natural outgrowth of the subjugation of animals. Automobiles, tractors and tanks are mechanical contrivances replacing the energy derived from enslaved animals.

I believe hunting and gathering is the natural cultural growth of matriarchy. No other way of life demonstrates such a reverence and respect for the feminine principle of the Earth. No other way of life draws humanity into a more intimate rapport with the Earth Mother goddess Gaia and the life-creating biosphere. True matriarchy is not domination by a hierarchy of women but an order which enhances the continuity of life and sustains the nourishing power of nature. In addition, matriarchy allows men and women to have distinctly different religious and metaphysical beliefs and spiritual powers, as well as different life patterns and prerogatives. The respect for, and amplification of, sexual differences represent, in society, the universal polarity upon which the manifest world relies. All these characteristics were present in the pure matriarchy of the Australian Aborigines which existed as a hunting and gathering society for 40,000 to 60,000 years or more.[15]

Prehistorians now assume that, 10,000 to 12,000 years ago, there were 10 to 12 million people on Earth; *all*, with the possible exception of Northern herdsmen, were hunters and gatherers. Now there are 5 billion people on Earth and only one-hundredth of 1% are hunters and gatherers.[16] This population explosion and radical cultural shift is primarily the result of the invention of agriculture. Evidence from excavations in Anatolia show that agriculture emerged in the final declining phase of the perhaps 60,000 year cycle of matriarchal hunters and gatherers. Perhaps, due to scarcity and pressure from surrounding patriarchal herders, Anatolian women collected seeds and began to rely on controlled cultivation.[17] In these early agricultural societies, only women tilled the soil and soil fertility became associated with the procreativity of the female body.

> Just as menstrual blood was a source of fertility, so it was believed that it brought about fertility of crops. Democritus recommended that women run barefoot with hair let loose three times around the perimeter of the fields in order to produce a fruitful harvest. Pliny believed that if menstruating women walked through the fields barefoot, their hair loose and their skirts lifted up to their thighs, harmful insects would be exterminated. Medieval peasants believed that the crops grew faster if women walked around the edge of the fields or exposed their sexual organs.
>
> (Resit Ergener, 1988, *Anatolia Land of the Mother Goddess*, Hitit Publications, Ankara, p17.)

42

Agriculture, as the basis for human society, had a difficult and sometimes disastrous beginning. In 'self-fertilising' river flood plains such as the Nile and Indus, agriculture formed stable and enduring cultures. But in many regions it was a sporadic or gradually declining economic and social foundation. Many of the regions which were first cultivated are now deserts. Total reliance on yearly harvests brought famine in the poor years and overpopulation in the bountiful. Since new life in a woman's body results from the flow of menstrual blood, so earthly fertility was associated with blood and blood sacrifice. In Catalhoyuk and other Anatolian excavations of 'Earth Mother' cultures, there is evidence of animal and human sacrifice associated with agricultural fertility rites.[18] It is in this cultural context that we discover again the image of the castrated male.

The adoption of agriculture 7000 to 12,000 years ago had vast, perhaps unseen, metaphysical and psychic implications. Populations became geographically fixed, their survival dependent upon regional fertility and regional weather. The sky, source of rain and weather conditions, came to dominate the religious imagination. 'Weather Gods' of the sky became predominant along with the desire for a static cosmic order which behaved in a regular periodic manner.[19] In Anatolia and Mesopotamia, Chronos, the male god of time and re-occurrence, merged with Zeus the cloud-gathering thunder god. The idea of blood sacrifice was incorporated into the worship of the celestial weather gods and is depicted in a very ancient and important myth from Western Anatolia. Cybele, the great Earth Mother goddess of fertility, is angered because her younger lover/son Attis is to marry the daughter of King Midas. Before the wedding the jealous and lusting Cybele (Earth hungry for rain) causes Attis to become demented with passion so that he castrates himself. The castration causes Attis to ascend to heaven with his celestial father. The flow of blood from his wound waters the Earth and plants spring up. Cybele's fertility is thus regenerated through the castration sacrifice. Pine trees grow from the Earth to symbolise Attis' sacrificed phallus.[20]

Attis is directly comparable to other castrated weather gods such as Tammuz and the Egyptian Osiris. In all cases these are male deities responsible for recurring vegetation cycles and all are sons of a celestial father. In the case of Osiris, he is the son of Ra. In all these myths the son is transfigured, by the father, into a 'Lord of Heaven'.[21] The castration of Attis occurred in the city of Menisa in Western Anatolia where a major cult and temple to the goddess Cybele developed.

The priests of Cybele, Aphrodite and other mother goddesses used to castrate themselves in imitation of Attis
and Adonis. Their severed penises would be tossed into
houses to bring fertility, or buried in a basket in the innermost and most sacred section of the temple after being
painted and varnished. A great pine trunk represented
the god's organ of reproduction, and temples to Cybele
were invariably situated near pine forests.

(ibid. p22)

In 90% of the churches in England built before the 12th century,
a statue of a severed phallus was found buried underneath the
altar.[22]

Let us speculate on how the mythic field of this phase in the
transition between matriarchy and patriarchy may have manifested
in the historical world. Early agricultural communities were completely dominated by women who held not only the power of
human procreation but also the knowledge and skills of agriculture, as well as all the other crafts such as weaving, pottery and
metallurgy. In both human and animal populations, excess males
are the most expendable and it was males, both human and
animal, that were ritually sacrificed in fertility rites. During the
lean years surplus males were expelled from the agricultural community by the ruling women and by the selected males who were
retained for breeding.[23] The brutality of older men toward young
males in ancient Middle Eastern society, as well as the power older
men have in modern society in despatching young males to war
and death, are resonations from the same mythic pattern. Older,
established males, preserving their positions of power in society,
ostracised young men from the community. Freud and Reich,
thousands of years later, uncovered the shadow of this history in
the psychology of modern males. Again we observe the historical trauma imprinted in the invisible field of the collective psyche.

The exiled males lived in marginal, semi-arid regions surrounding the fertile agricultural land. They herded animals, traded,
pirated, and waged war, occasionally winning plunder and kid-
napping women from settled communities whom they enslaved.
After thousands of years the herding nomads became powerful
and, following the Aryan invasions of India, the nomadic patriarchal societies began to over-run the matriarchal centres, taking
control of agriculture and the crafts, while simultaneously adapt-
ing to fixed settlements. The story of Mithra, a male fertility god,

illustrates this transition. Mithra's ascendency to heaven does not require self-castration as with the earlier Attis and Osiris, but occurs immediately after he slays a bull, symbol of the termination of his herding, nomadic past.[24]

The Greek version of the Attis myth adds another insight into the evolution of the modern male psyche and power structure. Adonis is the Greek equivalent of Attis. Adonis was the lover of Aphrodite and suffered a castration fate similar to that of Attis. In the Greek myth, Adonis' detached penis becomes Priapus, the male fertility god famous for the enormous size of his genitals and his insatiable appetite for sexual gratification. James Wyly, in *The Phallic Quest*, develops the idea that the Priapus/Adonis polarity is an apt metaphor for the polarisation in modern day male sexuality. The Priapus male, with his detached sexual organ as well as his sexual energy detached from any psychological, metaphysical or spiritual meaning, is capable of using sexual energy for purely physical and material inflation of his ego. Through the sublimation of raw sexual energy the Priapus male is constantly searching for more power, wealth and self-aggrandisement.[25] The contemporary businessman and entrepreneur, the life-endangering drives of soldiers, athletes and labourers, are all representatives of the Priapus male type. The opposite is Adonis, the sexually neutralised male: the priest, the academic, the over-intellecutalised scientist, or the man of excessive scholarship, religiousness or ethical propriety. Paradoxically, the inflated, externalised Priapus male tends towards unconscious self-castration (sexual debilitation) through the excessive use of alcohol and tobacco, or excessive strenuous work, or the anxieties and responsibility associated with obsessive ambition. On the other hand, the Adonis type of male very often attempts to rid the world of the projection of his own sexual repressions. J Edgar Hoover, an apparently disturbed, repressed homosexual, tried with the obsessiveness of a medieval bishop to puritanically control, through blackmail, the morality of America.[26]

The story of Attis/Adonis has such power in the human imagination that, like so many other ancient myths, it was swallowed up by Judeo-Christian theology. Modern Jewish ceremonies use the ancient Semitic word for God, Adonai (meaning 'Lord of Heaven'). The date of Christmas, 25th December, was decided in the 4th century AD and is the exact date of the rebirth of Attis and Adonis in the ancient myth. Pine trees, the phallus of Attis, were decorated for thousands of years by the castrated priests of Cybele, both in Anatolia and later in Rome. Christianity adopted the same custom.

The glossy decorations on Christmas trees are derived from the age-old practice of decorating pine trees in the temples of Cybele with painted and varnished reproductive organs of the castrated priests.

(ibid p23)

Castration, as a fertility sacrifice, evolved in some regions into crucifixion. During the years of severe famine the communal headman ('the king') would be fixed to a cross and wounded so that his blood spilled on to the fields. To rational minds blood sacrifice for agricultural fertility is a distasteful, primitive superstition, yet we need only observe ourselves ingesting food to realise that death is the generator of life. Agricultural society, in establishing a mutual wounding relationship between humanity and Mother Earth, structured itself upon fixed, religious moralities. Hunting and gathering requires a deep, flowing, empathetic ritual identification with the totality of nature. In this way, humanity gains the perception and knowledge of species required for the successful, ever-moving hunt. On the other hand, agriculture divides the natural world into a fixed 'good and evil'. Those elements, organisms and conditions are 'good' which enhance the growth of crops, while the factors which destroy or inhibit are regarded as 'evil'. Fixed morality is the mutilation of the wholeness of human nature just as agriculture is a mutilation of the wholeness of the Earth Mother. The identity between our bodies and the Earth impels us to self wound in reciprocity for the wound to the Earth caused by agriculture.

Castration symbolises what is perhaps a universal male tendency: the need to 'cut-off' from physically experiencing feelings and emotions at their deepest levels. This need has been implemented in some cultures through the practice of adolescent male circumcision, and in our culture through infant circumcision, often supplemented later by socially encouraged alcohol abuse. Alcohol allows for the unconscious release of deep feelings or it deadens the capacity to feel at all.

As male took control of an agriculture-based society, the need to see themselves as the creators of life and fertility was reflected in the transformation of Chronos/Zeus, the great weather god, into the Creator, God the Father.[27] The male Creator God replaced the primacy of the Earth Mother. In the old matriarchy, women priests conducted and presided over all the rituals, sacred dance and initiatory practices. Males, in order to acquire the image of religious authority, had to dress as women.

In almost all human society the transferral of divine authority from women to men was achieved by dressing the priests like women priestesses.

(ibid, p106)

The cassocks, scarves and high bishop hats of Christianity, as well as the whirling skirts of Islamic dervishes, are all variations of women's garments. In the high Christmas mass in Jerusalem, the priest performs the service behind an altar; between his feet, under the altar, lies a statue of the newborn Christ, as if the priest had given birth to him from beneath his long skirts.

The relationship between femininity and spiritual authority can also be found in older hunting and gathering societies. Medicine men, shamans, men of high degree, and all males who attained to spiritual authority in tribal society did so through an identification with the female principle. In Aboriginal initiations, older men wearing female adornments have the neophyte boys crawl out from between their legs.[28] The boys are covered with blood and fat, symbol of the birth fluids. Likewise, the Yakut shamans wore women's clothing and ornaments with female breasts painted on their chests. The Mongol shamans of central Asia had to be ritually sodomised by other men in order to open the bodily energy channels which allowed them direct communication with the spirits of nature.[29]

Unlike early agricultural societies, these more ancient shaman rituals did not represent an envy or desire to usurp life-giving feminine powers. Instead they enacted a respect for the omnipotence of the female principle.

The numerical and geometric philosophy of Pythagoras, like so many mystic teachings, contains residues of ancient matriarchal thought. The Pythagoreans believed that the simple laws of form metaphorically contain the image of the natural order of the world. The Pythagoreans revered the golden mean, or creative division of unity, as the *fiat lux* of creation. The golden mean divides unity into two parts so that the small part is proportional to the larger part, as the larger part is to the whole. The larger part, from which the smaller part is derived, is associated with the female and the smaller part with the male. Therefore male is in relationship to female as female is to the creative unity or God. This formula is perhaps the simplest means by which our abstracted minds can describe the fundamental basis for the male/female relationship in most indigenous tribal cultures.

ROME REVISITED

The Roman Empire, as depicted in Christian history, is one of the most maligned and distorted entries. I believe it is important to re-evaluate the legacy of Rome in relation to the great historical drama of matriarchy/patriarchy. The ancestors of Romulus, founder of Rome, go back to Anatolia and it appears that he attempted on the seven hills of Rome to establish a matriarchal order after its fall in Anatolia.[30] The Sabine people, who at that time inhabited the area of Italy surrounding Rome, were also strictly matriarchal. Romulus required all of his followers to marry with Sabine women and to adopt their social structure. One of the initial goals of Rome was to make a secure place for the worship of ancient gods and goddesses as the destruction of matriarchal polytheism at that time was relentless throughout Anatolia, North India and the Middle East. The Romans considered the severe monotheism of the Middle East to be atheistic. They were appalled at the defilement and denial of the physical body as practised by Eastern ascetics. Ecstatic ritual, magic, animism and nature worship, polytheism, sexual freedom, aesthetic and humanistic values, all residues of ancient matriarchy, were the vital core which the clumsy, chauvinistically armoured Roman Empire attempted to preserve.

> If a man were called to fix the period in the history of the world during which the condition of the human race was most happy and prosperous, he could, without hesitation, name that which elapsed from the death of Domitian to the accession of Commodus (ie the reigns of the emperors Nerva, Trajan, Hadrian, Antoninus Pius, and Marcus Aurelius)...the labours of these monarchs were overpaid by the immense reward that inseparably waited on their success; by the honest pride of virtue, and by the exquisite delight of beholding the general happiness of which they were the authors.
>
> (Gibbon, as quoted in Elaine Pagels, *Adam, Eve and the Serpent*, New York, Random House 1988, p53.)

Rome's attempt to protect aspects of ancient Anatolian matriarchy and Homerian polytheism allowed for a pluralism which, more than internal corruption, eroded its ambitions for world empire. The Christian devastation of Rome, the smashing of its extensive public art and architecture, the burning of its vast libraries, contributed to the advent of the Dark Ages.[31] The conscious motivation of Christianity was a social and religious revolution but, unconsciously, its aggression was a continuation of the worldwide destruction of the ancient matriarchy and it achieved the crowning imposition of male dominance on Earth. Certainly Christian claims of the barbarousness of Rome are belittled by the bloodthirsty record of subsequent Christian rule, including the 4.5 million women and children who were brutally tortured and burned by the 'good Fathers' of the Roman Church. It is modestly estimated that 60 million people were put to death in the Christianising of the world. This includes the numerous Inquisitions, the Crusades against Islam, and the Church-supported destruction of indigenous peoples during the colonialist period in North and South America and Australia.[32] The number increases if one wishes to acknowledge that both Hitler and Stalin were brought up and educated by Christian families and schools.[33] When one considers European history and that of its colonies after the rise of Christianity — with its plagues, wars, famines, social injustice, harsh primitive industralisation, the disease of spiritless materialism and environmental pollution — Gibbon's view of the Roman Empire seems somewhat justified. In any case, with the fall of Rome, imperialism, centralised wealth and power, and social inequality were not obliterated by Christian zealotry, but polytheism and the residues of matriarchal cultures certainly were.

MALE DOMINANCE TODAY

In order to consider the present state of male sexuality, one must first regain an understanding of the difference between *phallus* and *penis*. The phallus is a symbol of the metaphysical power of the universal masculine principle, that is, male creative energy in its absolute, archetype form.[34] As such, the phallus is not the exclusive possession of men. Women, in all known ancient cultures, perform purely feminine rites associated with the phallus. The serpent, or phallic energy, was ritually available to women directly from the Earth's rocks, trees, thunder, fire, and star light. The life-giving feminine body, cyclic and intuitive, when ritually raised to excitation by phallic energy, could become an instrument in tuning the course of human society to the larger geophysical cycles of the planet.[35] With the rise of patriarchy the phallus became the exclusive possession of men and was associated with the penis.

Women who practised phallic rites were destroyed as being witches.

The penis, of course, is a frail organ and, except for occasional erections, is flaccid most of the time. In order to validate male supremacy, the penis must masquerade as phallus. This deception manifests first in language such as 'Eve being born from the side of Adam', in other words woman is an extension of man. The disguise continues in the structures and technologies of male-dominant society in the form of spears, swords, guns, church spires, rockets, airplanes, skyscrapers, automobiles. The glamorous models in automobile commercials and beautiful airline hostesses support the idea that women are an extension of phallic technology. It is evident again in our male-concocted economic system, based on the illusion of indefinite growth and expansion. With this male-dominant mind set, coitus with a woman is experienced, not as penis submerged in vagina, but woman as an extension of the penis.[36] All these power facades are part of the attempts to inflate the penis, or physical man, into the image of the universal phallic power. The denial of the metaphysical aspect of male sexuality is the subscript to dogmatic material rationalism.

The culturally dominant male psychology is revealed in the body language of the most commonly accepted position for sexual intercourse. The locked buttocks of the surmounting, thrusting male block the experience of full and diffused sensual pleasure, isolating it in the external and imaginatively extended penis. These sexual attitudes, and this method of copulation, we as a culture are finally accepting from Tantric and other erotic literature to be only one among many options for heterosexual intercourse.[37]

Beneath the penis/phallus complex lies the mytho of Adonis/Priapus which is an active field of consciousness-energy influencing the psychic and neuro-muscular formation of the contemporary male image. Christianity retains the same field in the form of the crucified obedient son (Adonis/Christ) and the all-powerful creative father (Priapus). Both these male deities result from an unresolved love/hate relationship to the feminine principle, the Great Mother (Cybele/Gaia).

Every historical event, like every individual, has an inside as well as an outside. We are dealing here with a deeply internalised belief system concerning male sexual identity on social, physical, psychological and metaphysical levels. Our image of masculinity, its origins and historical convolutions, as well as its meaning, has become invisible to the men who possess it.

Male dominance and the status of women in present day Middle Eastern countries, where patriarchal religious law controls civil justice, is, in many ways, similar to that of Christian Europe before the colonial period. The civilising and stabilising roles that women played on the frontiers of the developing 'new world' released feminine energy, modifying European patriarchy at least on the institutional and social levels. The European world wars of this century also provided disruptive opportunities for women to advance into positions, functions and identities previously denied them. Yet, in subliminal psychological and linguistic layers, recently enhanced by insidious manipulation of the electronic media, the patriarchy of America and Europe maintains its base. Lexical studies reveal the number of English word meanings that have changed from the 17th century onwards so as to support and apparently universalise the male-dominant world view.[38]

The collapse in the late 1980s and early 1990s of clandestine socialist centralised bureaucracies and the degeneration of centralised hierarchies in religion and government throughout the Western world are an optimistic barometer of the terminal condition of the patriarchy. The environmental crisis is beginning to give increased meaning and clarity to the feminist movement but, as world issues intensify, the fundamentalism of patriarchy will continue to retaliate. The upsurge of fundamentalist Christianity in the United States predictably made its priority anti-abortion policy in an attempt to re-establish the subjugation of the female body. The Roman Church, clinging to its policy of subjugation of women through unwanted pregnancy, refuses to condone contraception in spite of the threat of the AIDS epidemic. Meanwhile, the traditional male institutions of profanity and pornography plus domestic violence spew forth in popular culture virtually unchecked. The demise of the patriarchy may be a long and vicious struggle, yet an essential first step is to make visible its domain within ourselves and in the social structures surrounding us.

MALE POWER: LANGUAGE AND REALITY

Visibility requires contrast and the greatest contrast to present day male sexuality, I believe, is to be found by reaching beyond the agricultural phase of our development (where the disturbance and castration began) to the male nature as it was in hunting and gathering societies. Traditional hunting is, in many ways, the most balanced culture for men. It activates the basic male needs to protect, fortify, subdue and heroically utilise his body aptitudes his body aptitudes for survival.

In almost all known tribal communities it is understood that women are born from nature and that men are formed by culture. The first prority of all indigenous hunters and gatherers is 'the making of men'. Amongst African tribes it is said that everyone is born from, and as, a woman. Through initiation, society 'makes its men'. The rituals, ceremonies, initiation rites, and male scared knowledge, all of the methods of making men, exist and persist solely through language. The male spermatozoa also function biologically as a naming activity. The sperm activates, or names, regions of the DNA of the female ovum, thereby defining the basis of the new organism. The difference between the contribution of the female and that of the male in the creation of life is similar to the difference between the thing that is named and the name. The seminal or creative power of the word is a motif found in Judeo-Christian, Egyptian and Hindu cosmologies. The Australian Aborigines expressed this notion in a male initiatic image of a nose and mouth directly adjoined to the phallus.

The capacity to create through naming or language is the basis for male power in the world. Patriarchy is based on the symbolic power of words and has misused this power to disavow itself from the obvious biological superiority of women and even deny its dependency upon the physical Earth which nourishes and supports its very existence. A father is only a father by name while a woman is a mother in body. Names and words are not physical things: they only *name* physical things.[39] Children, and unfortunately all of us who are frozen in the linguistic hypnotics of modern patriarchy, are unable to distinguish between the language systems that have been spliced between ourselves and our physical world. Accounting, financing and economics, the more abstract the language the more binding is its reality in the (lethal) paper tiger that is modern patriarchy.

Through language ancient Jain ascetics implanted an internal image which split mind from body for the purpose of mastering the sensations of pain and pleasure. In so doing they adopted a self-delusion in which pain and pleasure, life and death, were external to a self-mastered, invulnerable male body. The result is a form of hypnosis. The invulnerability of the body was extended to matter through materialistic science and the mechanical manipulation of the physical world. Life appeared to be controllable and death ceased to be an inevitability. Death as a threat rather than a reality explains the basis of masculine courage as well as the entire dynamic of the male competitive social structure. Men walk on to battle fields or into boxing or football arenas in the belief that death or defeat are only a possible threat which courage and self-mastery can overcome. Likewise, every time we step into an aeroplane or motor car, we are seduced by the idea that, through male mechanical mastery, death has become somehow avoidable. Every time we confront the threat of death armed with this illusion, we are reinforcing the idea that death can be eventually eliminated. Genetic engineering, nano-technology and so many other male thought projections are based on the illusion that the manipulation of nature can allow him to rise above death like the resurrected body of Christ. The 'high' that comes from confronting and rising above the threat of death, pain and defeat underlies the whole of our society. The risks that provide enjoyment and interest in our society, such as the boom or crash financial structure of the stock market, the use of toxic substances such as tobacco or alcohol, the stockpiling of nuclear arms, an industrial system which survives on destruction of the environment, populations coping daily with the pollutants and dangers of the urban environment; all these are a means of evoking the threat of death and destruction so as to reinforce an illusory invulnerability to it.

MALE POWER: LOVE, DEATH AND MEANING

In my book *As On The First Day*, I have examined the culture of traditional Australian Aborigines as a means of contrasting many aspects of our contemporary life patterns with a society that can make visible to us our fundamental hidden assumptions. I believe the understanding of the relationship of the male psyche to death is of the utmost urgency. In the Aboriginal world the menstrual blood of women is viewed not only as a substance but as an energy or force which brings new life into the world. Complementarily, male blood is a force which carries souls from this world into the realm of the dead. Death is male business in Aboriginal society and male initiations impart a knowledge of the transition which we call dying.[40] In tribal thought, dying begins the moment life leaves the body and can take longer than the period of pregnancy which is required in the formation of a new life. Men learned the science of dying through male initiation and it is believed that men can only come to know the nature of life through knowing the nature of dying. Hunting and the empathetic trance through

53

which the hunter identifies with the prey is the foundation for the understanding of the process of dying. Higher initiations enable men to die 'while yet alive' and thus they come to know the transitional modalities of the spirit passage following life.

At the onset of adolescence a tribal Aboriginal boy enters the initiatic phase of life which can last for 20 years or more. From that moment he may see his mother only rarely and/or in a ceremonial context. The initial circumcision requires the mother's acceptance that the son's initiatic death effectively terminates the mother/son interdependency. The Aboriginal boy immediately after the circumcision ordeal ceremonially confronts his mother. The mother perceives that the effeminate adolescent son (Adonis) has been absorbed into a transforming manhood. At that moment she relinquishes even the idea of a continuing, celibate intimacy with her beloved son. A stark modern contrast to this ritual can be found in an interview with Mother Theresa in which she states that her self-sacrificing service to the poor was motivated by an unquenchable love for Christ. She describes that she saw the face of her crucified lover (castrated or circumcised son) in the eyes of every Calcutta beggar.[41] Aboriginal ritual prevents the feminine psyche from remaining fixated in the subliminated love of mother/son — Aphrodite/Adonis. After the experience of motherhood, an Aboriginal woman, through participation in this male initiation, recentres her psyche on relationships with mature, initiated males in which the depth and power of sexuality prevails throughout life, both ritually and personally. In this way the mother/son complex depicted in the Attis/Cybele myth does not develop in traditional Aboriginal society.

Attis, the castrated son/lover, as well as his shadow side, Priapus, symbolise the blight of modern males in which the mother remains a primary relationship during and long after puberty. The dominant presence of the mother in the life and psyche of young males tends towards the repression and/or sublimation of the sexual aspect of his relationship with women. From Attis' attachment to the mother he learns not to sexually desire the woman whom he loves. The inverse 'Priapus male', on the contrary, finds he cannot love the woman he sexually desires.

An Aboriginal initiated male, by ritually confronting both death and the separation from the mother, transfers his relationship to both from the physical to the metaphysical level. The Earth, the sacred ceremonial grounds, and the ancestral goddesses, all absorb the connotation of the mother. Only initiated men in traditional Aboriginal society marry and, through initiation, the male is able to separate his deepest fears, those of maternal abandonment and death, from his love for women.[42]

In our society the actuality of death and post-death transition are psychologically blocked or denied. The constant presence of the threat of death or demise in war, business and sport replace the true basis of male knowledge. Lost is the initiation which allows men an internal experience of the entire passage from life to the realm of the dead. The loss of the knowledge and understanding of dying is at the marrow of our present dilemma as a race. The deterrents that modern male society has built (its industrial economy and war machine) cannot deter what they are supposed to deter. The threat of death is other than the reality of death itself. Hence, as Barbara Walker has stated in her book *The Crone*, the human species has impaled itself in a mad illusionistic dilemma; 'We must be willing to destroy ourselves in order to escape destruction.'[43]

CONCLUSION

Let us return to the island where the oldest and perhaps purest matriarchal or earth-honouring society perished. The oceans around Tasmania have warmed considerably in the last four or five years and the tides have pushed higher than any previously recorded. Bushes and sag grass along the ocean's edge topple as the sandy group beneath them is washed away. Both figuratively and actually, the male-dominant world is built on the coastline existence. The Mother ocean has already begun abruptly, or gradually, eroding the base from beneath the fortifications of the patriarchal world order. The transition we are confronting will not be accomplished simply through human designs or human will, but through the forces of an underlying metaphysical dimension. If we are to participate, I believe, with Barbara Walker, that the most effective means is for women, and men who have broken patriarchal conditioning, to refuse completely the male metaphysics and all its implications. The Father God and his obedient, crucified son are early agricultural archetypes that have been for millenia misunderstood and misused; they must be allowed to return to their mythic field in order to be resuscitated. Whatever else the energy associated with this mythic image may have accomplished, it has undeniably contributed toward the torment, represssion and destruction of the feminine principle, human sexuality, and the earthly environment. Women and indigenous peoples, those who have been most victimised by Christian patriarchy, are beginning to turn away from seeking solace in the image of the victim-Son/God. Through an understanding of the deep identity of the human body with that of the Earth, women may break their dependency on men and the patriarchal structure and begin to recover the grounds of an ancient female religion. They may begin to take possession of their roles which have so long been denied them; those of Priestess, Physician, Moral and Social Legislator, and the Guardians of Earth and Life.

The work of Margo Anand, *The Path of Sacred Sexuality*, is a hopeful indication that women are again assuming one of their most important roles; that of teacher of erotic arts. Through the ecstatic, men may regain the confidence and skills to receive and give pleasure and also to experience the self-abandonment which is the preliminary to initiatic death. Perhaps through the rebirth of female spirituality, its dance, mystic ceremonies and ecstatic rites, humanity will regain the courage to accept the beauty and mystery of life and of death and regain the sacred value of the Earth.

REFERENCES

1. Gimbutas, M (1982) *Women and Culture in Goddess-Oriented Old Europe*. Thames & Hudson, London.
2. Lawlor, R (1989) *Earth Honouring; The New Male Sexuality*. Millennium, Newtown.
3. Barfield, O (1967) *Speaker's Meaning*. Rudolf Steiner Press, Letchworth.
4. Sheldrake, R (1988) *The Presence of the Past; Morphic Resonance and the Habits of Nature*. Times, USA.
5. Myers, F (1986) *Pintupi Country, Pintupi Self-sentiment; Place and Politics among Western Desert Aborigines*. Smithsonian Institute Press, Washington & London.
6. *Science News*, Volume 136.
7. Thuring, Dr B *Dead Sea Scrolls*. ABC Film Special (1990).
8. Pagels, E (1988) *Adam, Eve, and the Serpent*. Random House, New York.
9. ibid.
10. Walker, B (1983) *The Woman's Encyclopedia of Myths and Secrets*. Harper & Row, San Francisco.
11. Pagels, E. op. cit.
12. James, E O (1969) *Creation and Cosmology; A Historical and Comparative Inquiry*. E J Brill, Leiden.
13. Campbell, J (1988) *Historical Atlas of World Mythology Vol 1: The Way of the Animal Powers*. Harper & Row, New York.
14. Ergener, R (1988) *Anatolia — Land of the Mother Goddess*. Hitit Publications, Ankara.

15. Tonkinson, R (1978) *The Mardudjara Aborigines; Living the Dream in Australia's Desert*. Holt, Rinehart & Winston, New York.
16. Maturana, H R & Varela, F J *The Tree of Knowledge; The Biological Roots of Human Understanding*. New Science Library, Shambhala, Boston.
17. *Science News*, op. cit.
18. op. cit.
19. James, E O, op. cit.
20. Ergener, R, op. cit.
21. James, E O, op. cit.
22. Walker, B, op. cit.
23. Ergener, R, op. cit.
24. James, E O, op. cit.
25. Wyly, J (1989) *The Phallic Quest; Priapus and Masculine Inflation*. Inner City Books, Toronto.
26. *The Secret Files of J Edgar Hoover*. ABC Film Special (1990).
27. James, E O, op. cit.
28. Walker, B, op. cit.
29. Ergener, R, op. cit.
30. op. cit.
31. Walker, B, op. cit.
32. Wilson, R A *(1989) Ishtar Rising*. Falcon Press, Las Vegas.
33. Walker, B, op. cit.
34. Monick, E (1987) *Phallos, Sacred Image of the Masculine*. Inner City Books, Toronto.
35. Redgrove, P (1987) *The Black Goddess and the Unseen Real, Our Unconscious Sense and their Uncommon Sense*. Grove Press, New York.
36. Easthope, A (1986) *What a Man's Gotta Do; The Masculine Myth in Popular Culture*. Paladin, London.
37. Anand, M (1989) *The Art of Sexual Ecstasy; The Path of Sacred Sexuality for Western Lovers*. Jeremy P Tarcher, Los Angeles.
38. Barfield, O, op. cit.
39. Easthope, A, op. cit.
40. Tonkinson, R, op. cit.
41. Jean Huston, *Search for Meaning* by Caroline Jones, ABC National Radio.
42. Lawlor, R (1991) *As on the First Day*. ITI, Vermont.
43. Walker, B (1985) *The Crone; Woman of Age, Wisdom and Power*. Harper & Row, San Francisco.

THE MONSTERS

By

GREG STAFFORD

Shamanism is probably the oldest form of spiritual practice in the world. While there are many recorded instances of female shamans (shamankas) the majority seem to have been males — and this has continued to be the case until fairly recently, when shamanism has become increasingly popular as it is recognised as a totally current and practical way of living one's life.

Greg Stafford has been consciously involved in shamanism for over ten years, self-admitted victim of it previously. His own life-pattern has moved in and around this aspect of knowledge in a unique fashion. The description of that weaving is both moving and passionate: it shows us one man's struggles which touch upon the struggles of all men. It demonstrates that the practicalities of shamanism are, as they ever were, of utterly current value.

The archetype of the Monster, of our 'evil self', is a further problem with which all men must deal. Just how deeply our own personal monsters are buried in our conscious or unconscious selves is a matter of endless speculation and the cause of considerable pain. It is important to note that the solution lies neither in denial nor in projection of this aspect of ourselves. Although most of us will not be driven to the lengths or depths to which Greg has gone, he offers hope and encouragement to all who determine to take the struggle into the enemy camp, and who are equally determined to come forth victors.

3

THE MONSTERS

We must consciously interact with mythology in our lives, or else it will interact with us unconsciously. The two archetypes which I shall discuss here are the Magus and the Warrior. Conscious interaction with both was denied to me, but they interposed themselves anyway, to my detriment at first but eventually to my benefit. The Magus was supposed to be thrown out because there was no place for the irrational in my life. The Warrior was discarded because we had been raised in a supposedly peaceful society.

Interacting with these two has saved my life, and improved it beyond what it had previously been. I do not expect your journey to be the same as mine, or have the same results. But maybe my story can help.

God gave me a few good gifts, and I have to use them or go nuts. One is to tell stories at the correct times, and so now I am telling this one. Another is that from the earliest times I had 'quite an imagination'. Another is that sometimes I can see invisible things, and hear them. And this is a story about that.

When I was young I had no idea what was going on or what I was doing. I just heard the voice, and followed it through the strange places that it led me, even eventually unto death. When I tried to explain something, like the little deer-guy who watched me from the sumac forests by the railroad tracks, I was laughed at, complimented on my imagination, or ignored.

I learned that everyone did not see what I saw or hear what I heard. I learned not to speak of it. Eventually, I decided that I was either mad or making it up, and so I stopped talking about it and tried not to see what I saw. I became an expert at denial, just to save my young mind and soul.

As a result I lived in a lonely, cursed world. Where other people got sad, I was surrounded by a palpable black mist which obscured everything around me. When other kids felt left out they cried, but I formed a thin hard shell over my skin. Where other kids had vague fears about walking home from school, I was stalked by a great bloodthirsty, eight-legged monster. I had a recurring nightmare for years in which I was pursued by a lion which I escaped only at the last moment by leaping into a sapling which bent over as the lion hurtled overhead into a river and was washed away.

My youth was not aided by spirituality. I was sent to a Catholic school, whose nuns filled me with the dogma that we are all evil and can do nothing about it. We were bad boys and would be bad men. They filled my life with unrelenting horror.

I lived in a world of ruins. The wasteland appeared whenever I walked alone. Those were the days when television broadcast daily advertisements about building your own fallout shelters to survive the coming war. As I ran from the monster's shadow, I saw only ruins — house roofs fallen in, cars rusted out on the overgrown streets. A great gloom lay upon me and the land.

When I was in first grade, one of the nuns had the whole school line up to be fingerprinted. In class she told us what the procedure was to be, that the cards would be later filed in City Hall, and that we must be sure to wash our hands afterwards. Precocious me; as we waited in line in the hallways afterwards, I asked her *why* this was being done. She said: 'It is so that after the atomic bomb, if you forget who you are you can go to City Hall and look it up. Stay in line.'

Even at the age of six, I didn't buy that line of bullshit, but at age six a small boy does not confront the Black Lady after being told to stay in line. After that the desolated ruins were populated with corpses of children, too.

When I was little my mother taught me not to fight. My father was away in the Navy, in the war, so he never said anything. I scrapped with my brothers constantly. Other than that, though, I was a very, very good boy most of the time. I coloured inside the lines, ate everything (except my vegetables), sat quietly (though squirming) at church, and did whatever Mom told me to do. I was a good boy. And so later, when the Fightin' Guy woke up in me, I usually squashed it down and said it wasn't there. 'We don't do that.'

I found escape in reading. After I discovered myths I read them voraciously. The heroic Arthurian tales were another favourite of mine. But a knowledge of legendary things did not give me a clue on how to settle my internal turmoil, and as the illness of denial filled me I got crazier.

When I reached adolescence, the Age of Hormones, I became a trouble-maker. I didn't know why, but I felt it necessary, somehow. I felt neglected and ignored, and I had to do *something*. Lots of my spare time was spent doing mischievous, but not hurtful things. For instance, one time we went around and switched the For Sale signs on everyone's lawns. Another time we stole all of the neat little white letters off peoples' mailboxes and left them on the road spelling obscene things.

When I was about 13 I blew up all the plastic models which I had so lovingly constructed for the past seven years. One wall of the bedroom I shared with my brother was covered with adjustable pegboard shelves, each with a carefully glued, painted and rigged model ship displayed on it.

My big brother brought home the explosives. It was not without emotion and thought that I surrendered the fleet to be scuttled. I started with the oldest model, a crudely painted aircraft carrier with crooked decals, and felt almost no regret or loss. The most dramatic was the motorised PT-109, drenched in gasoline, which chugged down the local stream with Black Cat one-and-a-half-inchers hissing into the water all around it until one lucky throw obliterated it in a great gout of flame and noise. The orgy of naval destruction ended with a cherry bomb vaporising my favourite ship, a perfectly constructed destroyer escort without a drop of glue showing, with guns that moved, and whose flags spelled out something real (my father, a former Signal Officer in the Navy, arranged them).

During adolescence I was filled with an exuberance and energy which did not know any bounds. I had to do *something* with it. Being a minor swimming champion was not enough. It took only the chance to meet the right people for me to take up the 'outlaw' life.

My right people were my parents' wrong people. We learned to smoke cigarettes (for which I was arrested), drink alcohol (for which I was arrested), vandalise property (for which I was arrested), and skip school (for which I was suspended).

We also got into fights. Usually with guys from the next town up the road who came to the local rock and roll place and got stupider than we were. Not deadly fights, but enough to know the thrill and hurt of violence.

And through it all I still passed the tests in school and turned in the class reports on time, and my grades never went below a solid B average. I still kept reading, and after a Latin course indulged regularly in mythology. By this time, instead of just reading stories and tales, I had begun to read *about* myths too. I was fascinated by their structure and inner workings.

About two weeks after I was arrested for smoking a cigarette in public, I got ill. Though sometimes subject to bouts of asthma, I was generally healthy, if somewhat skinny and awkward. But several times during my childhood I got deathly ill, each time with diseases which the doctors could not diagnose, and this was one of those times. It was a mouth infection which lasted for about a week. When I first got sick I decided to read some mythology with the intention of writing a story about a gang war between Odin's guys and Zeus's. But I could not drink or eat without great pain, and so ate and drank very little. As a result I spent the time semi-conscious, thinking of gods, and got well just in time to attend the trial for smoking. Weak and wan, I attended, and viewed dissected lungs.

I loved being crazy like that, and it was yet to get me in the deepest trouble of my life. The crisis of denial turned to defiance, especially of my father. He never accepted me as me, and it was a big problem. It was as if I had been condemned to eternal childhood, and I didn't like it. I didn't know if I was a man, or what to do if I was.

One day I got into a fist fight with my father. It was late at night, too late for a teenager to be out and too late for a father to be up drinking while he waited. I was rebellious and defiant, he outraged and defensive. And so in the middle of the night we got into a fight, and the son of a bitch smashed me good. I swear to God I could have smashed him back, and knocked him good and hard on his ass — I know because all my brothers did it. But I didn't. I just didn't because, well, he was my father.

It wasn't the first fight I was in (or backed down from), and it wasn't the last either. But it was the Big One. After that, I figured, if I can get beat up like a man I can begin to be one. Of course, I was wrong.

The invisible voice kept talking to me. Now I knew where it would take me: into excitement and danger. By this time my father and I hated each others' ways of life. Determined to find some way better than my father's, I reversed all his social values and got much more crazy.

The summer after I graduated from high school I hitchhiked to California to be a hippie. I succeeded, and entered the world of 'sex, drugs and rock and roll'. It was a great time to be young, adventurous and courageous. It convinced me that I needed very little to live, and little to be happy. After a summer full of various types of ecstacy I returned home to attend college.

In school again, I read everything in the library about mythology, often at the expense of the classes which I found boring. I began to write stories. They were legends and myths of an imaginary world called Glorantha, where the gods were real and magic worked for everyone. It was strictly for my own entertainment, and to satisfy my inner needs. And I told stories too, to whoever would listen. It was a great way to entertain girls.

During this time I encountered the works of Joseph Campbell. I decided that my life would be a quest, though I did not know what the object was to be. I just wanted to answer the call which had been beckoning me since as early as I could remember. I was pained not to know, and pained even more not to know where to find out. I had no teachers.

When the Vietnam war began I was initially interested in it, in an academic way. By the time that I reached draft age, this had turned into horror. I was horrified by the danger and when a former girlfriend's brother (poor Harry) was killed, it became a fear instead. At first the political implication of our wrong involvement provided an excuse to avoid it, and then a growing knowledge of politics which heretofore had been dormant in my mind. But mainly, it resulted in a great and total rejection of the Warrior way. I'm a lover, not a fighter, after all. Peace and love, man. Fuck the hypocrisy of the government of our great 'peaceful' nation. *We* don't do that.

I became more deeply involved in the hippie movement. The political outlet of protesting the Vietnam war was important, but not enough to satisfy my needs. The ecstatic experience became my goal. I'm an adventurer, and adventure I did. Into realms where no sane person dared to go. Not just the usual hippie stuff, but right down into the dirty and nasty stuff too. Thus I was one of the many victims of drugs, flunking out of the psychedelics and into hard drugs.

When it caught up with me, I died. I contracted hepatitis during my stint as a speed freak, and it progressed to the clinically terminal stage. No one told me it was the end, but I knew. My nightmares told me I was dying, and taking a damn slow time about it, too.

One day my father came into the hospital. I longed for some human contact, even from him. I was terrified and desperate for any comfort. Instead, he gave me hell. It was a list of my sins, spat out in a torrent of rage. I turned over and pretended to go to sleep, but he kept on. When he left I cried. Fine parting words: thanks for nothing. I swore that I'd never do such a thing.

A few days later I passed over, and in the invisible realms of the Other Side I met spirits and was shamanically initiated. The details diminish on paper, so I can't write of it. But when I woke that day, nine mornings before Easter, everything had changed, and has remained different ever since. One of the things which became different is that I have to tell you of this now. But at that time I had no clue, and misunderstood one of the greatest moments of transformation of my life. I thought that a peaceful resolution of my internal conflict would be found by working in the world, and ignoring all the craziness I loved so much.

I went right into the straight life. I got a job at an employment agency, did everything they told me to do, and after 12 months was interviewed for a spot as office manager. I knew by then, however, that I no longer wished to work at that kind of job, and soon quit.

For several more years I held odd jobs and travelled widely throughout the US. It was another bout of the nomadic life. I knew I was lonely, and finally became adjusted to that fact. I thought I could endure it for all my life. Then I met a fine, kind woman. Within no time I was married and living in California. It was a great life, and we were all incredibly happy for years.

I thought then, that the way to manhood lay in fatherhood. I would be able to make the world a better place if I did what my father did not do. And so I stayed home and helped with the diapers, and shared in the house work, and did as much as I could to share all such burdens. My record was not perfect, but I maintained a good communication with my children as they grew.

I delved into some of the weird cults of the San Francisco Bay area, and settled on attending the seasonal celebrations of the local witches and druids. It was very unsatisfactory, but in the moments of meditation I felt calm the way I never had felt before. But I had trouble with most of the people, who were so unusual that I liked them, but so flaky that I could never consider myself one of them.

About this time I invented a fantasy board game. I had been trying to be a freelance writer of fantasy fiction, and after a particularly nasty rejection letter I decided to create a do-it-yourself epic. It came out as a fantasy board game in which I supplied the setting and characters, and the play of the game determined the plot. I used every trick I could muster from mythology to make it work, and it did. Unfortunately, I could not find a publisher because no one in those days was publishing fantasy games.

One day I experienced a very strange feeling, not unlike those which I had had while taking drugs. But I wasn't taking anything. I decided to cast the *I Ching* to see what it said about how I felt, but instead sat down with the Tarot cards and read them. They said I should begin my own company, and check back in seven years. I started a game company. It was called Chaosium, because my life was a coliseum of chaos at that time.

I slowly assembled a team of other men who helped out, and we were soon roaring along at the crest of the growing fantasy roleplaying game business.

Fantasy roleplaying is a unique sort of social activity which is now about 16 years old. It began with a game called *Dungeons & Dragons*, a great game for beginners and people who have to work out their issues with violence. We published games for more mature people who wished to deal with other aspects of life as well. *RuneQuest* was our pride, set in the magical world of Glorantha which I had begun creating in college many years earlier. It was very well received by the game-playing public, and successful enough to be still popular today, ten years later.

In fantasy roleplaying the players construct an imaginary persona who participates in a story which is outlined by another player called the gamemaster. The outcome of the gamemaster's story is determined by the actions of the player characters, who might choose whatever outcome they wish, often in contrast to the gamemaster's plan. Thus, for instance, in an Arthurian roleplaying game your character is presented with choices which are similar to those found in the stories, but you have a chance to decide what occurs. It is a harmless, vicarious adventure which exercises imagination and allows engagement with archetypes through an enjoyable social event. At last I had found the natural outlet for my talents, and soon the company was prospering.

Although years had passed I was still not accepted by my father. I still refused to follow his agenda. To him, I was still just a big kid. Six years after I had started my game publishing company he asked me, with scorn, when I would get 'a real job'. I was so angry that I could not speak, and left the room.

During this time I continued working not to be an absentee father like my dad had been, and to be the best father I could for my children. I played with them, listened when they talked, and made time for them. I also thought, wrongly, that I could erase my own agony over a lost, fatherless childhood by supporting theirs.

I tried my best with my wife, but I had too little information on what a husband was supposed to do. Quite unconsciously, I moved from a position of sharing everything into a position of sharing unequally. My life was full of good things and events, but after a time I thought that the good was not coming from me at all, except through the relationship. I thought, for instance, of the nuns' message that I was no good at all. Thus if the relationship was good, it had to be coming from my wife.

Seven years passed, and things seemed to be going so well that I was afraid to check with the Tarot cards and have to risk making a change. Abruptly, my life got more difficult and I became more unhappy. The pressures of business and family life got too complex for me. I was overwhelmed, and at one point just went to bed and did not get up except to eat and shit. I stopped talking. At dinner I looked around at my frightened family, and was unable to say anything to them about what I was feeling. It was terribly frightening for them, and I was helpless to do anything about it.

Then I got a letter in the mail which reminded me that I was supposed to go to a visionquest soon. I had signed up two years earlier, but cancelled out a year ago because I'd hurt my back and was unable to travel. Now I was reminded, just in time. I read the letter, got out of bed and packed. I said goodbye to my wife and children, and then set off to the site. Once there I went off to the sacred mountain to cry for help.

I knew a little about the visionquest from my readings. It is a native American ritual wherein an individual goes off to the wilderness to pray for help. The Lakota call it 'crying for a vision'.

And cry I did. It was my first experience of this sort, though not the last. Now that I have some understanding of the process, I see that a critical part of the visionquest experience is the emptying which it allows. Whatever feelings I have are inevitably brought up for exposure, and there is no place to hide from them when I am all alone in the desert of my life. When fear comes I am afraid, almost to the point of panic, and then the monsters come. The shadows coalesce, and they come onto me without anything but my own psychic protection to shield me. And I am afraid, and full of fear, and it no longer whispers, but shouts. I listen, and talk back. And then I am not afraid. And when I am lonely, I am lonely until I cannot bear it any more, and it is gone. Then I am happy, and it goes. And angry, and depressed, and silly, and serious. Until after days of this nothing is left except me and God's messengers. And the shadows coalesce, and the voice shouts at me, and I can see clearly.

At that time I received only the start of what I needed, but it was enough. I met a helper. She was an ebon colored tree woman, and she pointed me towards a great mountain in the distance. I travelled to it, encountering many strange beings on the way. I came to a grave and leapt over it. At the mountain I climbed to the top, and looked out over towards a vast horizon. I heard a voice that said I should get a drum, and beat upon it, and sing.

Joseph Campbell has made it clear that the Quest is not complete until the Hero returns home with the elixir and heals his world. I returned home from that first visionquest feeling intact and whole because I had experienced the irrational in its full force, and accepted it as an inescapable, and beneficial, part of myself. I vowed to study the shamanic process more, if only to keep me a bit sane. I learned some songs, because I was told the spirit liked them. I bought a cheap drum to beat on when I had some time. For the time being, the shamanic work was my elixir, and everyone benefited from it since I was moving towards balance. One person who certainly benefited was my father, who had worked so hard to make me a rational person.

One day, we learned that my father had cancer. We knew before he did, because he had to have the doctors tell him. I had worked in hospitals and can read lab reports, and my wife, an experienced intensive care nurse, could actually tell what they meant.

After a brief exploratory surgery he was diagnosed as having cancer of the liver, metastasized throughout his body. He was given a few months to live. My wife and I discussed matters, and since we were both hospital employees we agreed that a hospital is absolutely the most terrible place in the world to die.

Furthermore, I knew quite clearly that tending to one's dying parents has been part of the natural human heritage for millennia, and I felt very strongly that I did not want to be robbed of the experience merely because I was living in the late 20th century American culture. I was scared, but summoned a courage which had let me do plenty of bad things, and now helped me to do a really good thing.

We told Dad that we wanted him to come to our house to die. We told him that we didn't think the hospital was a good place for people to die. He said he wasn't afraid of dying, but he *was* afraid of losing his mind first.

So he moved in with us. We made the living room into his bedroom, so that he could see the sun rise each remaining day. The kids crept into bed with him in the afternoon to watch the financial reports with him on TV. We talked about dying, and one time he said to me: 'I'm not afraid to die. I'm going a bit sooner than I expected, but I have had a full and satisfactory life.'

I was panicked, but determined not to hate my father to his grave. I admitted to him that I had intentionally tried to hurt him a long time ago, but I had changed. I said I had always loved him, but never figured out how to say it. And he understood.

Then his cancer went into remission. Everyone was astonished, but the doctor said he was OK for now. He went in for regular tests, and got stronger and stronger. He got an apartment nearby, and came over every evening to have dinner with us, except on Wednesdays when he made dinner and babysat so that I could play games while my wife worked.

During that period we had plenty of time to talk. One of the important things that I told him was how I envied the stability of his youth. I had moved seven times while I lived with him. Now I see that the semi-nomadic way of life helped me move into the state of mind necessary for understanding shamanism, but it had been very hard on me when it was happening.

So the time spent with my father was not wasted, and rather than having to cram everything into three months we got a chance to talk things over a lot. For the only time, I got to know my father man to man. And we both admitted, sometimes he was a crappy father and I was a lousy son, but we were both pretty good guys anyway. He even accepted my self-made career as a game designer. One day he said to me, 'You remember that time, over at the other house, when I asked you about getting a real job? I'm sorry about that. I was wrong. I still don't know what the hell you do, but you got a good job. But you sure do need a better business manager.'

He got ill again and went to the hospital. He declined rapidly and was the victim of hundreds of tests and treatments. After a couple of weeks the nurses complained to us (off the charts) about how Dad was acting. The doctors noted it in their charts, and (with cracked lips and glazed eyes) Dad said he felt like he was losing his mind. Knowing what fear and madness does to a man, I ran around the hospital to find the doctor, determined to stop this stupidity and try to fulfil my Dad's wishes.

'What are we doing here?' I asked, 'What's the chances?' The doctor said (off the record) that it was really only a matter of waiting.

'I want him out of here,' I said. We could supply the nursing and medical care at home. The doctor agreed, although at that point I would have taken him out even without the agreement.

68

I went back and told my father. 'We're getting you out of here.'
'When?'

'Now. We're packing. They're gonna bring some papers for you
to sign.' He sighed an absolutely huge sigh and smiled. And we
got him out, and back home to his bed in the living room. He
stopped going crazy. He was, I saw, happy now.

He stayed there, getting quieter and quieter all the time. The
kids still crawled into bed to watch his beloved financial reports
on TV. Every night we watched the news together, and we said
whatever needed to be said. I just wanted to atone for all the misery which I had inflicted on him. It was mutual.

One time he said: 'I've made a mistake. I left everything to your
mother in the will. I can't change it. You won't get anything for
all this.'

And I said: 'I don't want anything, Dad. I just want to do it
because I love you.' And, at last, he heard me.

As he got sicker we moved out of our own bedroom to the old
dining room so we could be close enough to hear him. He got
smaller and smaller, and quieter and quieter, sleeping more often,
eating less.

One of the last things he told me was: 'Stay away from violent
people. We Irish are that way, you know.'

One morning, before light, I woke and heard him choking, and
I rushed in as he toppled from the bed. I caught him before he
hit the floor and I cleared his mouth out, and he began breathing
again. We got him back into bed. He only nodded weakly when
I spoke to him. I went to bed and cried.

On the next day, after my wife went to work, I took out my drum
to beat on it to steady my nerves. It was something that I did regularly by that time. And, most unusually, I faced the West this time.
And as I drummed I felt an earthquake, the whole floor quiver-
ing beneath me, and I could see through the walls of the house,
through the whole neighbourhood, to the Western horizon where
the sky meets the sea. A tiny hole appeared there, and grew larger
until it became the Gates of the West. I felt my father walk through
the wall behind me, pass right through my body, then I watched
him walk into the Gates where a crowd greeted him warmly. He
did not look back.

We buried my Dad at sea. We held a feast afterwards, and an
hour after that was finished my family and I rushed off to our
best friends' house to participate in the home birth of their first
child. I guess the spirits did not want to waste an opportunity
to illustrate the circle of life for us.

Amid my grief my newfound spirituality provided me with great comfort. When trouble threatened to overwhelm everything, I could share it with the spirit world. It didn't make any logical sense, but the comfort that it gave to me in that difficult time encouraged me to pursue shamanism further.

I won a raffle and got a trip to visit the Huichol Indians, a Mexican tribe. There, in an isolated village in the Sierra jungles, I viewed a 106-year-old shaman lead his people in a ceremony in which he magically brought the children to their original ancestral homeland. Our instructor, a man named Prem Das who lived with the Huichols, told us: 'You can view it intellectually if you want, or just let go and let it take you where you will.' I did the latter, and I don't remember what I did for half the time, except that the butterflies were beautiful.

We had planned to go on a pilgrimage, but a day later we were told that we could not. We held a circle to discuss what to do, and in it I was shocked by the anger and bitterness which some of the people expressed. As I listened, I saw a figure moving around the circle: a man-deer, dancing. And when it was my turn I said what I felt: that the journey to this place was pilgrimage enough. We had come here, as if to the place of our ancestors, and there was more than enough to learn from this. It provided comfort for some of them. It was enough for me. It was after I returned home that I recognized the deer-guy as the childhood friend of mine, able at last to say something which I could understand.

Shortly afterwards I began to work with a student of Prem Das near my home. He offered a year-long programme to learn shamanic practices. I dove in with full intensity, feeling compelled rather than volunteering.

I had always had a problem believing what others have told me. Especially in matters of the spirit, since I had been ruined by the nuns in my youth. In shamanism this skepticism was a virtue, because it is a personal practice, not an institutional one. Nothing counts except a person's own experience. No one, for instance, can make someone else into a sweat lodge leader. A person becomes a leader when the Great Spirit assures him that he can do it, and he can lead the ceremony. I found that the isolation and loneliness of my previous experience were a help to me.

We participated in many forms of shamanism, with many instructors. Sweat lodges were monthly or more frequent, and visionquests were regular. Sitting alone in the desert time after time, starving for food and full of the spirit, I checked out the troubles of my life and slowly began to cast out the worst parts.

I grew, and became empowered, and made contact with the deep forces of Life and the Earth. The fearful shadowy forces which had haunted me since childhood came clearer, and I learned to understand the things which they had whispered for so many years. I learned how to communicate with these things which had haunted me for all my life. For instance, I learned, or admitted, that I loved the darkness, if only for the familiarity which it brought me. And there, in the darkness, I stopped denying the parts of myself which had been rejected. Again, balance entered into my soul, and some order entered my life of chaos. I learned of the medicine wheel, and as I communicated with the spirits they took their places around it. I decided that I was not mad after all. I found comfort and strength in practices. I discovered that these things *do* work. I am glad that I had some shamanic experience when everything fell apart.

As I grew more centred and powerful, my external life grew more and more stressed. I began to look more closely into my company, and abruptly my business partner who had been charged with administration quit. He left us bankrupt. And my family life disintegrated, too. One day I woke up unhappy and hung-over. I realized that I had not been sober for some time, and that it was wrong. I looked in the mirror, and I was horrified. I had to change.

Unlike every other dangerous time, I did not seek to be alone for this. Instead I called friends and asked for help and shelter. I moved out of my house, and immediately stopped drinking. Sober once again, I began to reassemble my priorities. I felt good, centred and powerful — my own man.

My wife was unable to cope with a husband who was sober, and decided to divorce me. Everything fell apart again. We had been joyously cohabiting in a classic co-dependency relationship which could not last under the strain of health. Of course, I had not yet learned what co-dependency was, and all of the things which I had projected on to her were, abruptly, gone. I felt rendered and torn and lost. I felt part of me was slowly dying.

Not again not again not again, I thought. Not again. What must I do to end this? And my spirit said, 'Let it die.'

I looked for help anyplace, and this time did not find it in chemicals but in friends. Unconsciously, I broke the old habit of being alone. I went to the spirits and friends I had made in my spiritual practices and asked for help.

My teacher said: 'I know that if you can scalp your enemy, you can win this.' I was confused. He said, 'I asked Spirit what I can do for you, and he said you should scalp your enemy, and put his scalp on something round, and you will know what to do next.' It was gibberish to me. He gave me a piece of flint. 'Use this ancient knife for it. Ask your allies for help.'

And a week later I woke, feeling quite mad. Within me my guts fought a war between crushing, incapacitating despair and a violent, battling rage. I leapt from bed, half dressed, and ran off in the dawn to a river. I tore at branches and clubbed trees and the earth senseless. Heedless, I raced up the path until I dropped, exhausted, to the muddy bank. There I met one of my nightmares, the Bad Guy. I knew what to do.

We fought and I killed him. I knocked him down into the mud and knelt upon his chest. Without mercy, I grabbed his hair and with one ripping cut, tore it off. Quickly I took from my pocket a small wooden sphere and tied the hair around it, then shoved it deep into the mud, up to my wrists, and asked the Earth Mother to take it and change it. To recycle the pain and rage and despair, and to turn it into fertilizer for my life. And I wept and I sobbed, and I let it all go. It was the best fight of my life. The fight I did not run from. The fight that I had trained all those years for. And when I was done, I went back and changed my clothes.

Shortly afterwards I joined a men's group, and in the safety of the group one day I asked God and all his invisible companions to help me. 'Let it go,' they said, 'Let it go.' And I did. In a ceaseless roaring and raging like a volcano I let all the pain and fear and loneliness go out of me. At last I felt a moment of quiet, and looked down a long tunnel at a great golden being. It moved towards me, and to my absolute horror I saw it was another monster. A golden monster!

Monsters monsters monsters, I thought, there is no end to the monsters, and fled that place. But the next day, as I was cleaning the house where I was staying, I was filled with new courage. I thought: 'I asked for help. Maybe it was not best to run away. I bet I could see that monster again.' It seemed different. And so I set up a safe place, a magical circle, and with my drum beat called it out again. And the tunnel was there, and up it came the golden monster. As it came closer, I saw it was a great lion. The same lion, I realized, which had pursued me through my nightmares all my life. 'Hey, pay attention,' it said.

'Ah, monster thing,' I said, 'What do you want?'

And it said, 'What do you want?'

'I don't want to be crazy,' I said.

'But you are,' it said. 'You had to be crazy to take in your father like you did. You have to be crazy to keep trying so hard to do something which everyone else has forgotten. You are good crazy.'

'Why is it so hard, then?'

'You're fighting the wrong things,' it said.

And for the first time I realized how I had been fighting all my life. Fighting against things which I had not known, which I had not admitted, and which (sometimes) had been imposed upon me. So I stopped, and I allowed that great golden monster into me. Yea, I thought, yea, I have a monster in me, but it isn't an evil one. I am not the evil creature which the Black Lady said I was going to be, I am not the corrupt son of a bitch my ex-wife said I was, and I was not devoid of love and compassion which was in my life. I was filled, instead, with a flood of comfort and love. With a pleasant peace.

I had to look then at the things I feared, and I was given a choice. I could live with my denial, and stay in the Hell where I had been falsely condemned, or admit who I was and what I could do. I chose, and I realized that I was not evil after all, and that the darkness was a healing place, and that the great eight-legged monster which pursued me was a healer. I embraced it, accepted the changes required, and began healing.

After that things got calmer. I began to think that maybe I had changed. After all, it would be meaningless if I did not bring the elixir home. I felt I had reached a place where I could change my life, and maybe even improve it. I wondered if it had worked. How would I know if I had brought it home?

I proved it, brought it home, on my 40th birthday. A great moment of manhood.

I was just getting over my devastating divorce. I was starting to feel whole again, even more whole than before, and to think that things were getting back together, and maybe things would go my way for a while. I was in a new apartment, and I had a birthday coming up. My three children were staying with me, and I expected to have a fine, quiet dinner with them.

All I wanted to do was go have a Chinese dinner for my birthday. Not much to ask. I knew I wasn't getting any presents from them, and didn't care. Their simple presence was enough. At 40 birthdays aren't a matter of getting presents. I just wanted to share a quiet dinner.

So when it was time to go the two young ones cheered and dashed out to the car. Noah, 18 years old, balked. Balked Big.

'I'm just tired of Chinese food, Dad,' he said. 'I don't want to go.'

'Well, gee, son, it's my 40th. Surely you can tolerate one more meal for my birthday.'

'No, Dad, not this time. Just go without me.'

'No, I can't do that. It wouldn't be special without you. Please come.'

'No, Dad, not today.'

'Please? Come on, Noah, it would be special to me.'

'Uh uh, not today, I just don't want to go.'

'Come on, Noah, you have to. It's my birthday.'

'Nope.'

'Yes. You have to. I say so. Now come.'

'Not tonight. I just don't want to.'

'Get in the car.'

'No.'

And so it went on. I asked politely, I pleaded, I bargained, I threatened, I cajoled, I insisted, I bribed, I threatened again. How could this be? Such a simple thing to want and my son is giving me this shit! It was intolerable! How DARE he! I was disappointed, then angry, then damn mad. I demanded, I begged. Then I got furious.

'You come now,' I roared, 'Or else.'

'Nope.'

And so I began to carry out the 'or else'. I knew what it was, and how to do it. My father had 'or elsed' me in a similar spot when I was about Noah's age. I knew the routine well. Or else.

And in that moment of absolute RAGE the voice, my spirit voice, whispered something to me. It said, 'You're wrong.' And I didn't care. I just knew that I wanted to push my son's face through the wall for hurting me (today of all days!). I knew that I could do it, too. I'm not a big guy, not a powerhouse, but I'm bigger than him! I can. I want to. I had permission from my father, after all, and training too! I wanted to: my monster raged.

'Pay attention!' roared a lion.

I had a choice. And I didn't. I didn't.

I stood there for a minute, breathing so hard, watching the room spin around me. It was wrong. I left the room and sat down, sweating and trembling a moment.

It would be wrong. It wasn't what I wanted. It was the FARTHEST thing from what I wanted. Beat up my son on my 40th birthday? Jesus, fuck, how could I ever live with that? Great memory for him, too... I went back into his room.

'Okay,' I said. 'Okay. We won't go. Will you help me prepare dinner here? It's more important that we eat together than eating at a Chinese restaurant.'

'Yea, sure Dad. I'd like that.'

So I went outside where the other two children waited, somewhat impatient and frightened at once. 'Come in,' I said. 'We're eating here, as a family.'

And we had a great dinner, and they even washed the dishes.

That night I felt something moving around inside of me. I felt that something had permanently changed. I had broken a chain. I had brought something important home. Something which would last.

When Noah graduated from high school he prepared for college. I wanted to do something special for him. What? I could buy him things, and did. I could give him advice, and tried to. But it wasn't enough. I wanted him to have something which would stick with him. Something important.

I called all my men friends together, and the fathers of Noah's best friends, and invited their boys to attend too. I asked my closest friend if he would lead a ceremony of manhood for Noah. We held it late one night, and we all explained what we thought it meant to be a man. An adult man, with responsibilities. We explained what the hard and bad parts were, and what the easy and good parts were. Our leader for the night incorporated some simple ceremony which proved to be incredibly powerful for everyone. Then we welcomed my son to be among us, as a man, and offered our friendship. It was an incredible, though simple, event.

I spoke with my son this week. He explained how he felt good about himself, and confident, and sure that even if he wasn't sure what he was doing, he knew he was doing OK. It was the greatest gift I have gotten from him.

Now, thanks to a balance of ecstasy and reality, I live a healthy life in both worlds. Now I help to publish a magazine about shamanism, to bring word of this to others. Now I am a leader of the sweat lodge ceremony, to bring the healing place to others who need it. Now I can hear the voice, and know what it is saying, and do what it asks without hesitation or embarrassment. I can see the darkness in other people, and when they ask I can sometimes show them what is there, and explain what I did to find my way out to provide a path for them.

I know I have made it. When despair comes, as it still does, or rage envelops me, I have experience in dealing with it, and it does not run me. I am whole. Now I know what I am doing. I am no longer embarrassed by religion, ecstasy, mischievousness or anger.

I live in a world of mythology and love, and invite you to it too. Ask your monsters for help.

FOUR HILLS OF VISION

By

JOHN ROWAN

The experience of working with male groups seems to be always a salutary one, one indeed which most men who do it — either as leaders or participants — find deeply disturbing and shocking. This is in part because men in groups are used to behaving in a certain way, to keeping a certain distance between themselves and their fellows, presenting themselves in a way that agrees with the basic structure of the male ego. In the kind of group run by John Rowan (or indeed by Robert Bly and Greg Stafford), this ego-based behaviour is rapidly broken down. The participants are made to recognise different aspects of themselves — their inner feminine, their power-politics, their deeply embedded desire to destroy what they cannot or will not understand. John Rowan has had some 15 years' experience of leading such groups, and in the chapter which follows he gives a powerful account of the realisations which have arisen from this work. It is not always comfortable reading — but no man who stops to consider his true place in society, or his relationships to women, can do so without feeling at least a degree of unease.

=== 4 ===

FOUR HILLS OF VISION: WORKING WITH MEN IN GROUPS

INTRODUCTION

For some 15 years now I have been working with men in groups, specifically on issues of male consciousness in a patriarchal society, or what Eisler is now calling, perhaps more helpfully, a dominator model of society. If humanity is to survive, we have to move away from a dominator society towards a partnership society, such as has existed at various times in the past, but now with a much better chance of being understood and being successful.

This is difficult work, because it involves encouraging men to face the oppressor in themselves, as well as the hurt child, the inner person with feelings, the inner female, and so forth. So it is rather like working on racism and other uncomfortable topics of that kind.

The type of work I have been doing is group work, specifically experiential group work. In this kind of work, I set an exercise for a group of men, and when they have completed it, we work through the feelings aroused by it in a spontaneous and unstructured way, trying to do justice to the feelings which emerge.

For example, I might say: 'Please find a partner, and when you have done so, look into your partner's eye for one minute, without saying anything.' Some men will find this quite easy, others will be unable to do it at all, others again will find various feelings arising, which may be stronger or weaker. For a few men, this is a very threatening exercise, which makes them feel weak, and which they then avoid in various ways. For example, one man might say, 'I couldn't look directly into the eyes, so I looked instead at the eyebrows, and I found that easier.' We will then explore the implications of this.

As I have gone through the years, and have worked with different types of men in different contexts, I have come to believe that this work can be done in terms of four different positions. These are, as it were, four hills, standpoints from where we can survey the scene before us. Some of us may find it helpful to think of each hill as higher than the last, while others may find it better to think of each as simply separate and distinct from the last, without the idea of higher or lower. For that reason I have referred to them as positions, rather than as levels or stages.

The first is the conscious position, where we are going into matters like how men treat women, how men relate to other men, how men talk about women with other men, and so on.

The second is the unconscious position, where we discover possibly surprising things about how men relate to their mothers or fathers, how internal conflicts arise and how they function, how the dominance model gets into the bones, so to speak.

The third is the transpersonal position, where we go into the question of the anima, the shadow and other archetypes, and also such things as rituals of death, rebirth and initiation. What is our myth, our legend, our fairy story about men and women? The discoveries here are again often surprising or disturbing.

The fourth is the position of god-forms, where we meet the Horned God and the Great Goddess, and try to do justice to what we may discover there. Actual experiences of wells, of standing stones, of tree circles and so forth can come in. Here the surprise and the disturbance are likely to be greater, because these things are even more hidden from our daily lives.

Let us look at each of these in turn, and see if we can come to terms with the phenomena which arise in each of these positions.

POSITION 1: CONSCIOUS

There is a useful distinction, which Daniel Cohen made in a newsletter article many years ago, between *male chauvinism* (a type of behaviour which is usually fairly easy to change once the awareness of it is made conscious); *sexism* (a more fixed attitude which is much more resistant to change, but can certainly move if tackled in the right ways); and *patriarchy* (an underlying pattern affecting people on many different levels and extremely hard to shift).

Male Chauvinism In the kind of groups which I most often organise, it is quite common to work successfully on male chauvinism. This is a point of view from which one simply takes it for granted that everything masculine is better than everything feminine, without ever examining it very closely.

One of the best people to discuss this is Bob Connell who has talked about 'masculine hegemony' in a way which I think must be convincing to anyone willing to consider a political analysis of gender and power. He argues the case for feminism with great attention to the way in which men actually think and believe. He challenges successfully the notion that males are, and should be, on top. This is thorough sociological work.

Once the male chauvinist assumptions are challenged, they quite quickly give way in the group setting, and change can come about reasonably fast. One of the exercises I do to explore this is called *The Disappearance*. Here I tell the group of men: 'Two hours ago all the women in the world disappeared. There are no women any more. And this includes girl children and babies, foetuses and embryos and ova kept for research purposes, and so on.' And I just leave them to discuss the scenario for one hour, an hour and a half, or two hours, depending on the length of the workshop. This is a powerful exercise, because the men can see for themselves how they talk and behave: it is not a question of telling them.

Usually what happens is that they talk a great deal about sex — how can they possibly get on without it; will marauding bands of men from other countries have to be dealt with; how can women be replaced somehow by biological research? Sometimes the men form themselves into a committee and have definite offices. This can all be discussed in the light of the idea of male chauvinism. (In my book *The Horned God* I tell the story of the Minzies and the Frongs, which casts some light on this.)

Sexism is more deeply ingrained, and harder to get at. It often requires a real change in the whole attitude structure of the person before it can shift. So this is more long-term work. Sexism is often based on low self-esteem, so that the man in question is only able to boost himself up by putting women down, or so it seems to him. So the whole pattern of low self-esteem has to change before sexism can go, and this is a long-term therapeutic operation.

However, all these things are kept in place by social assumptions about the male ego and how it should be. It is often stated in articles and books that the male ego needs a lot of support and boosting (and this job is, of course, mainly done by women) in order to keep it functioning at all. This seems a bit suspect. One of the most striking statements I came across in the early days

79

of the men's movement was a quote from Keith Paton (later Mothersson) in a newsletter which said, 'The healthy male ego is oppressive and wrong.'

In a group, one way to explore this is to ask two men to share one sheet of paper and to make a picture. The way in which they do this is very revealing about the male ego and how it works. Usually there is competition rather than cooperation, the two men each seeing how much of the paper they can dominate. This simple demonstration is more convincing than any amount of instruction or research evidence.

And so we have to work on this level quite consistently to achieve any real change, because the social reinforcement of sexism is always there. There is also the reason why group work is much more effective than individual psychotherapy in this sort of area — the real presence of other men working on the same issues makes it clear that this is a social, not just an individual problem. I shall be coming back to the male ego later.

Patriarchy When we come to the patriarchal level, we find a much more difficult pattern to deal with, because it is reinforced from so many different angles. Someone who has spelt this out very well is Elizabeth Dodson Gray in her spirited and readable account of patriarchy and what it is all about.

Eisler speaks of the dominator model of society as another way of talking about patriarchy, because the word 'patriarchy' can be taken so literally by some people. She emphasises how the dominator model is deeply embedded within each one of us, and hard to reach because of the continual social reinforcement which it receives.

So to deal with this is very difficult, and here we may need even more to go into the unconscious and into the transpersonal, if we are to deal with it successfully and bring about real change.

POSITION 2: UNCONSCIOUS

One can only go so far by simply working on the conscious level. Ultimately it is necessary, in any real attempt at change of dominance patterns, to go to the unconscious level. One of the key things here, of course, is the original family pattern from which the man emerged.

How the man related to his father as a child is crucial. What kind of a model of masculinity did the father represent? All kinds of positive and negative messages come from this early relationship.

Feelings about the father may often be closely related to sexuality. Perhaps the father was too sexual, or not sexual enough. Often the father's sexuality is quite mysterious, because of the absence (physical or mental) of the father from the family. Coming to terms with this may be a very important step in discovering one's own sexuality.

Similarly, a man's relationships with women are very strongly influenced, at an unconscious level, by how he related to his mother as a child. Did he love her? Did she love him? These are surprisingly often very loaded questions. They may carry a big charge, and be quite salient in the man's development.

One of the key exercises in this area is to ask the man to get in touch with his inner female. This is almost invariably a revealing and opening-up experience, which can bring some very important insights. This can be done through a guided fantasy, but I usually prefer to do it like this:

A CONTRASEX EXERCISE

Breathing, grounding and centering.

Now find a space where you can have a cushion or a chair in front of you; cushion facing another cushion or chair facing another chair.

Sit on one and face the other. Close your eyes if you find that helpful. Now find in yourself the opposite sex. See if you can concentrate on finding a woman inside yourself, a woman in every physical sense, and in every psychological sense. See if you can allow yourself to be this woman. Really experience what it is like to be a woman. But it must not be a woman you know in the outside world. It has to be a woman from inside you. Really be that women.

And then put that woman on the other seat — imagine her as completely as you can. Get as full an image or impression as you can. How is she dressed? What age is she? What expression does she have on her face? What is her hair like? How is she breathing? And then start to speak to that woman. What would you like to ask her? What would you like to tell her? What would you like to demand from her? Perhaps think of times in the past when you have been aware of her.

And when you have done that, and got some sense of how it goes, switch over and be that woman. And start to speak as that woman. What does that woman say? What do you say as that woman? Let her talk to you, respond to what you said to her. Have a dialogue with that woman. Get to know her, relate to her, find out how things go with her. Visualise her, concretise her, be with her. Go back and forth as you may need to. You have ten minutes for that.

This can be done in a very shallow way, or in a very deep way: it depends on all sorts of factors which it will be. But such an exercise should not be offered by anyone who is not a therapist or counsellor, or has a great deal of that kind of experience in groups, because of the depth of feeling which can sometimes come up with this exercise.

This is of course not the only exercise which can be done at the unconscious level — we also work on dreams, use guided fantasy, encourage regression to earlier ages, use certain kinds of massage to stimulate early memories, bring in art work and so forth.

POSITION 3: TRANSPERSONAL

Another way of seeing the deeper relationship with women comes from the collective unconscious. An archetype such as the anima is highly relevant to the whole way in which the man perceives women. The anima is the woman inside the man. Very often the details of her appearance or character are derived from the mother, but this is not a mother complex, it is a deep archetype.

Also found in this area are the rituals of initiation. All real changes in the personality take the form of initiation into a different state. And very often this initiation takes the form of death and rebirth.

Group work lends itself to ritual, and new rituals seem to arise quite spontaneously in many groups. But they can also be devised consciously, as in the following example of a ritual which was used by Sue Mickleburgh and me in a workshop we did for a big conference on Sexuality and Spirituality on the island of Lanzarote in May 1987.

As people arrived, there was music playing, earthy and simple. We divided the participants into two groups, 20 men and 30 women. Sue took the female group, and I the male group. The female group occupied the main space with Sue, and the male group went outside with me.

The women were told that we were going to create a powerful space, full of energy — female, goddess-type energy — and hold on to it, even when the men re-entered the group. The first thing they did was to form a circle and introduce themselves by saying their names and, at the same time, performing a movement or gesture which expressed how they were feeling, or wanted to feel.

Then came a series of breathing exercises. Breathing unites body, feelings, thought and spirit by operating on all four of those levels.

Then Sue asked the women to hold their arms in front of them, with the palms of their hands about two inches apart, and gave instructions for a ball of energy to appear and grow between them. Then they slowly lowered their hands down to their sides and joined hands. They stayed silent and still for a while, holding hands and feeling the energy being transmitted around the circle. Sue then explained that they were going to use this energy, in a joyful way, to remind themselves where it had come from and to give thanks for it.

They danced around in a circle, still holding hands, singing 'The earth is our Mother, we must take care of her, the earth is our Mother, we must take care of her.' As they went round and round, the singing got louder and louder and there was a feeling of energy and joy.

The Joining

They stopped, and the men quietly entered the circle, stooping low to get underneath their linked hands. As they entered in this way their bent bodies and hunched shoulders seemed symbolic of the saddened and chastened men of the world realising how much pain and suffering they had caused women and feeling humbly grateful that they were still, after all the bad things they had done, accepted and welcomed into a joyful place where the strength and power of the women was quite different from anything they had ever experienced.

As they did so, the women faced into the centre of the circle, and extended their arms and hands into the centre, raising them as they breathed in and lowering them as they breathed out. They breathed in unison, making a constant wave of female energy directed toward the centre of the circle.

The important thing now was for the women to keep the atmosphere as it had been before the men entered the circle, and not to seek to comfort them and give away everything they had spent time raising. The men were in the circle, lying on the floor, seeming very miserable, and the women were standing tall and proud giving them attention in a strong and loving way. Slowly the men started to make contact with each other, and after a while the women linked hands again and danced around in the circle. Some of the men joined in the dancing and soon everyone was dancing.

The Male Group

When the men were outside I told them about the whole question of initiation, and explained that it was like death and rebirth.

'There will be three steps in this initiation. The first step is to give up everything that makes us male — to divest ourselves, one by one, of each thing. The second step is to go into the Goddess space and feel what it is like to be surrounded by female energy, not keeping it out and not defending ourselves against it, but accepting it and relating to it. And the third thing is to go deeply into ourselves and find the deeper masculinity within the Goddess space.' There was then some explanation of the Orphic Mysteries, and some discussion of this. I went on to explain the ritual itself.

'You are going to pass through ten gateways, and at each one you will give up something masculine. See if you can allow yourself to experience what life would be like without this thing. And remember that this is cumulative — once you lose something it is gone, and so you lose first one thing, and then two things, and then three things, and so on, until they are all gone.'

'Now. Take one step forward, through the first gateway. Here you lose the male attitude to emotions and feelings. This is the attitude which says that emotions and feelings are rather a nuisance, they only get in the way of what is really important, they are irrational and time-wasting.' [Here there is a pause of two minutes. This does not sound very long, but in fact it does seem a very long time. This two-minute pause is kept throughout the ritual, between each of the gateways.]

'Now take one step forward, through the second gateway. Here you lose the male attitude to children. This is the attitude which says that children are not very interesting unless they can talk sensibly about things and enter into proper conversations. Before they are messy and inconvenient, or perhaps sometimes cute and adorable, but not really to be taken seriously.' [Pause]

'Take one step forward, through the third gateway. Here you lose the male attitude to work. This is the one which says that work is the most important thing in life, and that it must take precedence over everything else. If anything else conflicts with work, the work comes first. Be aware of what it is like not to have any more the male attitude to feelings and emotions, or the male attitude to children, or the male attitude to work — try to make it real for yourself.' [Pause]

'Then take one step forward, through the fourth gateway. Here you give up the male attitude to relationships. This is the one which says that relationships should take of themselves; I do my part, the other person does their part. It is something like a contract; each person carries out what they have agreed to do. And that is really all there is to it.' [Pause]

'One step forward again, through the fifth gateway. Here you surrender the male attitude to women. This says that women are there to be used. They may be used to cook or keep house, they may be used to look up to or have sex with, they may be used to look good on one's arm or play hostess to one's friends and contacts, but the key is to use them well, and never to be used by them. One must be in charge at all times, or run the risk of looking weak and foolish. Be aware of what it feels like not to have this any more.' [Pause]

'Now another step forward, through the sixth gateway. Here you lose the male attitude to science and technology. This is the one which says that science and technology are the answer to everything. Everything that is now unknown and uncontrolled can one day be known and controlled through science and technology, and that would be a very good thing. These things have been successful in the past and will only be more and more successful in the future.' [Pause]

'One step forward, now going through the seventh gateway. Here you give up the male ego. The male ego continually needs to be stroked and looked after and protected; it inflates and deflates very easily, and it is important to keep this under control. It continually thinks of itself as being very important and very worthwhile. It very easily becomes impatient. It is very keen on appearing masculine and desperately afraid of being seen as feminine. It likes showing off, but it hates and can't bear being criticised. Now is the time to let go of this, and really allow yourself to feel what this is like.' [Pause]

'One step forward, through the eighth gateway now. This is where you have to give up your male body hair and beard. All those types of body hair which are typically masculine, including bald heads too. Imagine having nothing to declare you masculine in the way of hair. When we get to these last three, there is sometimes a tendency to laugh or giggle. See if you can do it without laughing, just feeling it directly, and breathing through it if necessary.' [Pause]

'One step forward, now going through the ninth gateway. Here you have to give up your testicles. This is the act of castration, which the priest of Attis always used to do as a sacrifice to the Great Goddess. No testicles, no testes, no balls now. Feel what that is like.' [Pause]

'One last step forward, and now this is the tenth and last gateway. Here you lose your penis, your phallus is gone now. The last masculine possession goes too. See if you can stay with that experience, of having nothing left at all.'

Now here we had to pause until the Goddess space is fully prepared. It was only a matter of three or four minutes before we could go in, waiting for the cue which I knew was going to come. But the men did not know how long it was going to be, and the sun had now set, and the wind was beginning to get cold, so that the weather echoed very well the feeling of loss and deprivation.

The Joining

Now the men were asked to blindfold themselves or shut their eyes, and hold hands in line. I led the way, and bent down to go under the arms of the women in the circle. All the men bent down as they came in, and we circled in around the inside of the women's circle until all the men were in. They lay on the ground at first, taking in the fact of being in a circle of female energy. I encouraged them to take it in, not to resist it or compete with it. I reminded them that their task now was to get in touch with their deeper and truer masculinity, as we had discussed earlier, along the lines of my book *The Horned God*.

Then I encouraged them nonverbally to make contact with other men, just stroking their hands and joining hands. Some of them made closer contact, in twos and threes, others just stayed in contact as they were. This felt much better.

Then I encouraged them, nonverbally again, to stand up together. When they were all standing up, I started the music. This was South American music, rather folky and unfamiliar. They began to move in response to the music, and so did the women.

The Final Phase

The next phase started spontaneously; we gave no lead at all as to what should happen, apart from starting the music. The women started to dance round in their circle, and the men danced their way into an inner circle. Then all at once the men began to turn outwards, so that the two circles were facing one another. As the music became louder, the circles became more irregular and eventually broke apart, and peope were dancing on their own or forming and reforming small groups of dancers all over the room. This dancing went on for quite a while.

We had thought that people might like to talk in small groups about the experience at this point to digest it, but the energy was much too high for that.

We asked people to sit in a circle, and brought out the bread and wine we had ready. We got people to pass it from one to another: as they passed on the wine they said, 'May your spirit be strong', and as they passed on the bread they said 'May you have sustenance.' (These phrases come, of course, from the Wicca tradition.) Someone had found a candle and put it in the centre of the seated circle. It was just getting dark and the little light shone brightly for us. We grounded the energy we had raised. We parted with many expressions of feeling. The workshop came to an end.

Next day several people came up to us and said how much they had enjoyed it and got out of it. One man shaved off his beard, which was an unintended side effect! The organiser told us later that he had had some glowing reports about our workshop. We certainly felt that we had learned a great deal.

Some Questions

But of course this raises a great many questions. A woman who had read an account of the workshop said she felt uneasy about the negativity of the approach to men. And one or two men have said the same thing — couldn't I be more positive, more celebratory?

I have experienced a number of efforts for men to discover themselves on their own, in men's groups of various kinds — consciousness-raising groups, therapy groups and spiritual groups. I have not been impressed with the results. So often the group, no matter how it started and with what intentions the men got together, slides into some kind of warm self-congratulation of some kind of cold break-up. I referred to some of the reasons why that might be in *The Horned God*. Reports of the Bly groups in the States reveal much the same picture. Such groups can be very moving experiences for men, but they don't seem to help much in changing the patriarchal set-up between men and women, and that is what interests me. The best clues I have got about the latter, have been from disciplines like paganism and Tantra, where the relationship between the male and the female is directly referred to. Here is a quote from Arthur Avalon's *Shakti and Shakta* (p172):

A glorious feature of the Śākta faith is the *honour which it pays to women.* And this is natural for those who worship the Great Mother, whose representative (Vigraha) all earthly women are... 'Women are Devas; women are life itself' as an old Hymn in the *Sarvollasa* has it. It is because Woman is a Vigraha of the Ambā Devī, Her likeness in flesh and blood, that the Śākta Tantras enjoin the honour and worship of women and girls (Kumārīs), and forbid all harm to them such as the Sati rite, enjoining that not even a female animal is to be sacrificed. With the same solicitude for women, the *Mahānirvāna* prescribes that even if a man speaks rudely (Durvācyam kathayan) to his wife, he must fast for a whole day, and enjoins the education of daughters before their marriage. The Moslem author of the Dabistan (ii. 154, ed. 1843) says 'The Āgama favours both sexes equally. Men and women equally compose mankind. This sect hold women in great esteem and call them Śaktis, and to ill-treat a Śakti, that is, a woman, is a crime.' The Śākta Tantras again *allow of women being Guru*, or Spiritual Director, a reverence which the West has not (with rare exceptions) yet given them. Initiation by a Mother bears eightfold fruit... A high worship therefore which can be offered to the Mother today consists in getting rid of abuses which have neither the authority of ancient Śāstra, nor of modern social science and to honour, cherish, educate and advance women (Śakti).

There is a lot more, but you can see the drift. This seems to me very compatible with Western paganism, as promulgated for example by Starhawk or Sjöö and Mor.

Coming now to the question of how this applies to the psychology of masculinity as worked out in men's groups, it is as if there are at least three models of maleness and how to work with it. First of all, there is the standard phony social model, where the male has to be a 'proper man', and not effeminate or cowardly. Here it is OK to be male as long as one stays within the bounds of socially stereotyped masculinity. If one strays outside it in the macho direction, that may be a cause for punishment or treatment, but basically it is acceptable or winked at. If one strays outside it in the feminine direction, however, that is much more suspect and condemnable. We need not say too much about this model — it is too familiar. It is well worked out and defended in Baumli's book *Men Freeing Men* about the so-called 'Free Men' in America.

Secondly, there is what one might call the monistic model, which is usual in personal growth and the kind of psychotherapy I normally do. This is where we say that the man has to go down into his depths, finding perhaps first a bad layer of self-putdowns, and then a layer of pain, and then a layer of deeper truth which is OK — or whatever model of layers is being used. It is OK to be male, and it is just a question of finding the deeper, truer version of it.

Then thirdly, there is what one might call a dialectical model, which is much more rarely used by group leaders, where we say that the first 'bad' layer is found to be bad or harmful only because it is separated from female energy and female power. Connected up again in a proper relationship with that energy and that power, the 'bad' transforms into a deeper truth which is OK. One familiar symbol for this is the Yin-Yang diagram, where the white area has a black spot at its centre, and the black area has a white spot at the centre, indicating that opposites interpenetrate each other.

Now, there are one or two ways of talking about masculinity which are quite compatible with this dialectical model. I heard it said in one workshop that the male was like an electron circling the female nucleus, and that this was the healthy state; to split the atom could be destructive. This is a very similar point to the one I have been trying to make. I have also heard it said that what was most vulnerable and precious in the person could actually be seen as the vital centre of the person. Again this seems quite compatible with what I am saying here. But very often in groups the leader seems to be adhering to the monistic model, asking men simply to own and to rejoice in their own masculinity.

Now it seems to me that these three approaches are not necessarily contradictory. I think they correspond to three different types of work in this area.

Three Types of Work

The first type, which uses the model of adjustment to social reality, is the positon of most of the psychotherapy which is generally available. The highest aim is to be able to play one's role in society properly.

The second type, which takes the monistic approach, is the position of personal growth. Chart 1 shows how this relates to the adjustment model, which is detailed in the first column. Looking at the second column now, it can be seen that here one is interested in the personal unconscious, in the healing of the splits (such as mind/body, left/right, intellect/emotion, topdog/underdog, but in particular here the split between the male and the female), and generally in the integration of the person as a social and psychological being. This is what Ken Wilber calls the Centaur position, and what he and others have called the position of the existential self or the real self.

Chart 1

A COMPARISON OF METHODS OF PERSONAL CHANGE

(from Banet, A G (1976), 'The goals of psychotherapy' in A G Banet (ed) *Creative Psychotherapy: A source book*, University Associates, La Jolla)

	Psychotherapy	Personal Growth	Transformation
(Wilber Level)	(Ego/Persona)	(Centaur)	(Subtle Self)
(Rowan Level)	(Mental Ego)	(Real Self)	(Transpersonal)
Self	I am defined by others	I define who I am	I am defined by the Other
Motivation	Need	Choice	Surrender
Pesonal Goal	Adjustment	Self-Actualization	Union
Social Goal	Socialization	Liberation	Salvation
Process	Healing — Ego-Building	Development — Ego-Enhancement	Enlightenment — Ego-Reduction
Traditional role of Helper	Physician (Analyst)	Teacher (Facilitator)	Priest(ess) (Guide)
Representative Method	Hospitalization Chemotherapy Psychoanalysis Directive therapies Transactional Analysis (Cognitive therapy) (Rational-Emotive Therapy)	T-Group Gestalt therapy Encounter Sensory Awareness (Body therapies) (Psychodrama) (Co-counselling) (Regression)	Zen Yoga Arica Altered States Mysticism Monasticism (Psychosynthesis) (Jungian therapy)
Focus	Individual (Group)	Group (Individual)	Supportive Community

NB Items in brackets added by John Rowan.

The other type, which uses the dialectical approach, is the position of spirituality and the transpersonal (the third column on Chart 1), seen through the eyes of paganism. It says that the male and the female must be related through the *hieros gamos* (second marriage) if the male is not to be destructive. This is not about healing the split between the male and the female, but about enabling them to relate together in an appropriate way — a way that actually works in today's world.

So one way of putting this point would be to say that we have three positions from which we may work: in the first position we stick to adjustment, helping the person to make changes at the conscious level to make life more bearable and successful; in the second position we are concerned with the unconscious and with deeper changes which involve real self-discovery and owning up to one's inner reality; and in the third position we are concerned with the spiritual and the transpersonal. Thus we have here three layers — on top the conscious, under that the unconscious, and under that again the transpersonal.

Another way of viewing this, which I now think is more useful for some purposes, is to see the three layers as circular, thus:

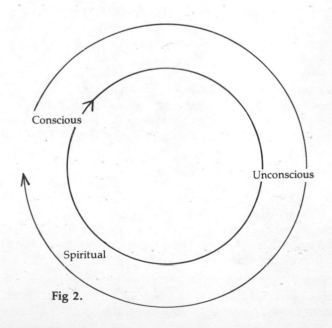

Fig 2.

In this way of seeing it, we go from the conscious to the unconscious, from the unconscious to the transpersonal, and from the transpersonal back to the conscious, and so on round and round in a spiral of growth. (Perhaps you have seen Jill Purce's book on the spiral, which I think is excellent.) The advantage of seeing it in this way is to underline the point which Starhawk makes, that it is only the pagan view of the transpersonal which has a political significance in making the male safe for the world. Because it is only in paganism that the male is in the right relationship with the female. And this entails using what I have just been calling the dialectical model of the male.

This would be to take male-in-relation as safe and to be the focus of attention, and male-out-of-relation to be dangerous or suspect. I feel that the monistic can all too easily become the autistic, and that the autonomous can all too easily become the overweening — as in the story of Inanna and Dumuzi, as told by Perera.

I hope that this discussion will clarify the reasons for envisioning the ritual in this way. It very firmly grasps the third position, and works entirely from there.

POSITION 4: GOD-FORMS

But if we really want to understand death and rebirth, we have to be prepared to go into an even more difficult area, the realm of the god-forms. The Horned God is the consort of the Great Goddess, and can form an ideal image of how the male can relate to the female.

This goes beyond the archetype into an area of religion proper. It is only here, I believe, that men can realise that the question of female power is crucial to their own development. And this takes us back to politics. Politics is about power, and we have to understand about female power before we can shift male power from its present dangerous position.

Men are really afraid of female power, I have discovered, and find it very hard to come to terms with. But the way to come to terms with female power is to worship it.

It was an exciting day for me when I came across the seven-page entry for Kali-Ma in Barbara Walker's book and found that it said things like this:

Kali was the basic archetypal image of the birth-and-death Mother, simultaneously womb and tomb, giver of life and devourer of her children: the same image portrayed in a thousand ancient religions...

Kali stood for Existence, which meant Becoming because all her world was an eternal living flux from which all things rose and disappeared again, in endless cycles.

The Nirvana Tantra treated the claims of male gods with contempt:

> From a part only of Kalika, the primordial Shakti, arises Brahma, from a part only arises Vishnu, and from a part only arises Shiva. O fair-eyed Devi, just as rivers and lakes are unable to traverse a vast sea, so Brahma and other gods lose their separate existence on entering the uncrossable and infinite being of Great Kali. Compared with the vast sea of the being of Kali, the existence of Brahma and the other gods is nothing but such a little water as is contained in the hollow made by a cow's hoof. Just as it is impossible for a hollow made by a cow's hoof to form a notion of the unfathomable depths of a sea, so it is impossible for Brahma and other gods to have a knowledge of the nature of Kali.

The Yogini Tantra said of Kali, 'Whatever power anything possesses, that is the Goddess.' Shakti, 'Power', was one of her important names. Without her, neither man nor god could act at all...

As a Mother, Kali was called Treasure-House of Compassion (*karuna*, Giver of Life to the world, the Life of all lives). Contrary to the West's idea of her as a purely destructive Goddess, she was the fount of every kind of love, which flowed into the world only through her agents on earth, women. Thus it was said a male worshipper of Kali 'bows down at the feet of women', regarding them as his rightful teachers.

This was extraordinary stuff for me to read, because it overturned all the ideas I had had up to that time about Kali, who I had thought about, if at all, as a thoroughly destructive and nasty entity. Our modern consciousness has split apart the benevolent and the destructive aspects of Kali: as Sjöö and Mor succinctly put it, 'Paradox is split into dualism, an act characteristic of patriarchal consciousness.' Soon after reading this I saw a film called *Indiana Jones and the Temple of Doom*, which underlined all the old errors about Kali, and even added some new ones: for example, the threat to the heroine of being sacrificed to Kali. Kali never had female sacrifices of any kind, not even female animals.

Now, the consort to Kali is Shiva, and I read on avidly to find out what Barbara Walker said about him. Here is some of it:

> Shiva was called Lord of Yoga, i.e. of the 'yoke' that bound him to the Goddess... Among Shiva's many other titles were Great Lord, Lord of the Dance, Lord of Cattle (Pasupati), Beneficent One (Sankara), Lord who is Half Woman (Ardhanarisvara), God with the Moon in His Hair (Candrasekhara), He Who Belongs to the Triple Goddess, He Who Gives and Takes Away, Consort of the Goddess Uma, Condemned One, Destroyer, Howler...
>
> Tantric yogis insisted that their supreme Shiva was the only god and all other gods were only inferior imitations of him. He was certainly older than the Vedic heaven-gods...
>
> As Lord of the Dance, Shiva represented one of Hinduism's most subtle concepts... Shiva performed this dance in a place called Chidambaram, the 'Centre of the Universe'; but the location of this place is within the human heart...therefore the god is located within the core of man's own self...
>
> Shiva was seldom depicted alone, for his power depended on his union with Kali, his feminine energy, without whom he could not act. The puzzling vision of Shiva as Shava the corpse, under the Goddess's feet, illustrated the 'doctrine that Shiva without his Shakti can do and is, so far as the manifested is concerned, nothing.' Yet joined to the Goddess, he became the Bindu or spark of creation. Every human orgasm was believed to share in this creative experience as 'an infinitesimally small fragment and faint reflection of the creative act in which Shiva and Shakti join to produce the Bindu which is the seed of the universe.'

Again I found this was exciting stuff. It seemed to offer a mythological account which made perfect sense of the dialectical relationship which I had found to be so important. And when I came to investigate, I found that the relationship between Shiva and Kali in the Eastern religion was paralleled in the relationship between the Great Goddess and the Horned God in the Western traditions.

This is now spelled out in a masterly work which has only recently become available from the Farrars. Here we can see how the Horned God Cernunnos, or Herne in the pagan traditions of our own area, has all the characteristics we have found in the East.

> He is usually portrayed with horns and accompanied by animals. He usually either wears or has looped on his horns the torc (circular necklet) of Celtic nobility. Often, as on the Gundestrup Cauldron, he holds a serpent with a ram's head or horns. (p97).

This is exactly how he is also portrayed in the Mohenjo-Daro representation of Shiva Pasupati, Lord of Animals. The serpent is, of course, the representative of female underworld wisdom in myth and legend worldwide. But the ram's head indicates that this is a specifically masculine version of serpent wisdom. It is a way of saying that the relationship between the male and female is particularly close and particularly important for the Horned God.

The Farrars note that the Ulster hero Conall Cernach, whose name has cognate roots with the other names of the Horned God, goes to relieve a castle which has been invaded by a terrible serpent, where the serpent submits to him without resistance, 'jumping into his girdle, where Cernunnos's attendant serpent is often found'. Such familiarity with the Underworld, the space of the Goddess, is very characteristic for the Horned God. He is not afraid of the Underworld, but connects with it in a lively way which does it honour and respect.

The Horned God, like the Great Goddess, has many names: they include Dionysos, Pan, Dumuzi, Tammuz, Osiris, Orpheus, Adonis, Attis, Mithra, Quetzalcoatl, Hu, Dis, Hades and Hermes, among others. All these can be studied with advantage. And the Farrars suggest a useful ritual for getting in touch with him in his guise of the stag.

CONCLUSION

At the end of this examination, we have come up with some disturbing news for men. They have to re-evaluate their assumptions radically if they are to come to terms with a more adequate vision of how males and females can relate. And it is not easy for men to do this. One very sophisticated and knowledgeable man wrote to me, after reading some of this material, and said that it looked to him as if I were saying that women should be given precedence in all matters. This felt to him as if I were saying that he should agree to be hurt or wounded by women, and 'to lie down and be prepared to be run over by every passing steamroller'.

I replied by saying that unless men agree to be wounded nothing much is going to change. Any man who says, 'I refuse to be wounded — this thing can be tackled by intelligence and good will and positive thinking', is highly suspect to me. Suspect because feminism is in a way all about hurt, and unless men actually feel some kind of hurt, rather than sympathising with it in a patronising way, they are not going to experience the message of feminism on any real kind of human level. Many men seem to get the message of feminism only as far as their heads, which means that they get the words but not the music, not the real dance. If we are going to get the response anywhere near adequate, we have to accept that we are hurt too, we do actually feel something ourselves. The refusal to lie down under every passing steamroller is the refusal to be broken. The 'healthy male ego' has to learn how to be *broken* by feminism. This is not an easy lesson or an easy option — it is hard and has to be hard, because of the resistance which gets in the way. But unless this lesson is learned, men are going to continue to play the 60/40 game.

The 60/40 game was first identified in the early days of the anti-sexist men's movement by Keith Paton (later Keith Mothersson). This is where a man living with a feminist admits that she is most often right about feminist issues, particularly when she confronts him on his own actions. He sees that she has more insight, more feeling, more motive in such things. But in his head this gets translated into a kind of proportion or percentage. She can't be right all the time — no one can be right all the time. So maybe she's right 90% of the time, or 80%, or 70%, or 60%. Of course, this means that every issue still has to be argued and fought out, because this might be one of the — admittedly few — cases where he is right.

> And all the other cases the same (funnily enough) so you don't give an inch. The 60/40 game is a heap of *shit*. You know it but you won't *break*. You insist on fragmenting your POWER, your BLOODYMINDEDNESS, into a hundred little issues — on each of which (once safely parcelled out) *you* are prepared to argue rationally, it's just that she gets so worked up.

I think this rings as true today as it did then.

And this goes with my belief that the male as such is suspect. Men are continually coming up with apparently reasonable notions, such as that they are not there to be run over by every passing steamroller, and then using them to avoid even the most obvious changes in their behaviour. Men can be incredibly awful — I haven't told even the half of it in this chapter. Whenever I hear men talking about sexual politics, I cringe, because what they are saying is generally so dreadful. If it is not dreadful in the direction of making the challenge of feminism so bad and so demanding that no one can live up to such a challenge, and so we all retreat into guilt and inaction. This is one of the points which Lynne Segal has made so powerfully in her new and excellent book.

The precise point of all my work — and of course I may not have succeeded in my aim, but anyway this is the aim — is to go fully into the guilt and despair, but not to rest there. In this, it is rather like the Joanna Macy approach to nuclear war. Being a man is like being the pilot who dropped the bomb on Hiroshima. Perhaps more for me, who cheered the dropping of the bomb on the two grounds that it was a marvellous step forward in the mastery of Nature and would also get me back home from India that much quicker, than for those readers who are too young to have had such an experience. Believing something so terrible is important, but equally important is not being paralysed by that belief. These are the two steps. I think the only real, genuinely well based and grounded kind of hope is the hope which comes on the other side of despair, and which actually grows out of despair. I spit on the phoney hope which believes that all is basically OK, and that all we have to do is to celebrate the excellence of men and the marvellousness of women.

If any man says to me that 'We do *sometimes* need to protect ourselves', my answer is that obviously we need to protect ourselves from being killed or having our houses burned down, or something irreparable like that — I am not urging some absurd abandonment of all our interests. But what we do not need to protect, and what is very important not to protect, is our ego. It is the ego which we are protecting whenever we indulge in the 60/40 game. The male ego has to be broken. It can then come into existence again on a deeper level, where it is in right relationship with the female, and does not need the self-protection which was so important before. A man can be strong and vulnerable at the same time: they are not opposites, they are all part of the same thing. It is the openness, the non-defensiveness, which is so important and so hard to learn.

If any man says to me that 'Men have to come to their *own* understanding', of course I agree. Some of women's formulations, while excellent for them, just cannot be used in the same form by men. For example, women can totally exclude any contact with men, for short or long periods, and this may be a useful stage in their own development; but men do not have this option — we have to remain in contact with at least one man!

If any man says to me 'We can't prescribe for other men', of course I have to agree. I hold to the general ethical belief that 'you can't lay your trip on someone else', which I learned in the LSD culture of the '60s. But I have also become very impatient with the avoidance practised by so many men in relation to feminism. So I prefer to say things in a rather challenging way that sounds rather pushy and prescriptive, just to arouse some response. Then when I get the response, I can come back with some more detailed examination of the answers.

If any man says to me 'You sound very self-righteous', I am worried and think it deserves some examination. Self-righteousness is 'righteousness for which one gives oneself credit'. Righteousness is 'Justice, uprightness, rectitude; conformity of life to the requirements of the divine or moral law; virtue, integrity.' I don't know why stating the obvious about patriarchy should be self-righteous. For example, when Bob Geldof told some of the United Nations people that they were a bunch of hypocrites, he seemed to me righteous but not self-righteous. I really don't know how to say some of the things I want to say without taking the risk of seeming self-righteous to some people. I suppose Bob Geldof seemed self-righteous to some people.

It seems to me that in a million ways you, and I, and all of us, support and maintain the system that dropped the bomb. This is just a sober recognition of the way in which we all subscribe, in our daily purchases, in our taxpaying, in our media consumption, in our work, in our leisure, to the horror world. If I counted up, in the course of one day, the number of actions of mine which supported patriarchy and the number which opposed or questioned it, the first number would be larger than the second. And I suppose the same would be true of you. So that is one way we drop the bomb on Hiroshima. And to the extent that we perpetuate the linear thinking and competitive attitude that we were brought up with, that would be another way in which we drop the bomb all over again. I myself feel that I have dealt with quite a lot of that at a deep level, and I assume that some readers at least would feel the same, but I wonder, if push came to shove, whether we have quite eliminated it all?

So I leave you, the reader, with some unanswered questions and some painful issues. That is what happens sometimes in my workshops too. And this is because masculinity is such a difficult issue, now and in the immediate future. But it is an issue which we have to deal with successfully, or die.

REFERENCES

Avalon, A (1978) *Shakti and Shakta*. Dover, New York

Baumli, F (1985) *Men Freeing Men*. New Atlantis Press, Jersey City

Connell, B (1987) *Gender and Power*. Polity Press, Cambridge

Eisler, R (1990) *The Chalice and The Blade*. Mandala, London

Farrar, J and Farrar, S (1989) *The Witches' God*. Robert Hale, London

Gray, E Dodson (1982) *Patriarchy as a Conceptual Trap*. Roundtable Press, Wellesley

Macy, J (1983) *Despair and Personal Power in the Nuclear Age*. New Society Publishers, Philadelphia

Paton, K (1973), quoted in Rowan J (1987)

Perera, S B (1981) *Descent to the Goddess*. Inner City Books, Toronto

Purce, J (1974) *The Mystic Spiral*. Thames & Hudson, London

Rawson, P (1973) *The Art of Tantra*. New York Graphic Society, Greenwich

Rowan, J (1983) *The Reality Game*. Routledge, London

Rowan, J (1987) *The Horned God: Feminism and Men as Wounding and Healing*. Routledge, London

Segal, L (1990) *Slow Motion: Changing Masculinities, Changing Men*. Virago Press, London

Sjöö, M and Mor, B (1987) *The Great Cosmic Mother: Rediscovering the Religion of the Earth*. Harper & Row, San Francisco

Starhawk (1979) *The Spiral Dance: A Rebirth of the Ancient Religion of the Great Goddess*. Harper & Row, San Francisco

Walker, B G (1983) *The Women's Encyclopedia of Myths and Secrets*. Harper & Row, San Francisco

Wilber, K (1980) *The Atman Project*. Quest Books, Wheaton

THE GOD IN WESTERN MAGICAL ARTS

By

R J STEWART

The appearance of the God in Western magic has for long been a difficult subject — most especially for men. The tendency has been to relate to a Goddess, and where the God is evoked this invariably leads to the appearance of imbalances within the personality, as masculinity is emphasised over the balanced polarity of the male/female energies present in all men.

R J Stewart's chapter addresses this problem squarely and finds much in need of balance and re-alignment. Above all, the dangers of overwhelming masculinity — maleness out of control — are dealt with, as is the question of magic and sex. We may read of the historical results of both these subjects in Robert Lawlor's chapter; here we are presented with some very deeply considered practical ways in which to deal with the problems facing men who seek to follow the path of the Western magical arts.

In particular, the breaking down of the many aspects of male deity is of great value, since there is a tendency towards subsuming all of these vastly different figures under a single heading — usually that of a stereotyped image from partly digested mythology or psychological classifications of type. Here, R J Stewart gives equal weight to the many diffrent faces of the God, and shows how we can relate directly to them. All too often these deities are regarded as fragmented parts of the psyche — here we may recognise them as totally separate, as beings in their own right, from which we may learn, always providing we approach them in the correct way.

=== 5 ===

THE GOD IN WESTERN
MAGICAL ARTS

(This chapter is based in part upon material from *The Bright One Unmasked: Celebrating the Male Mysteries* by R J Stewart, Arcania Publishing, Bath 1991)

Although this chapter cites a number of historical and cultural sources and examples, such as those of ancient Greece, the Celts, early Christianity, and so forth, this is not a historical or sociological essay. The approach taken to this discussion of the God or gods in the Western Mysteries and magical arts is essentially practical; it is based upon experiential work within the traditions of Western magic, and always emphasises their inherent practical methods for psychic transformation and development, rather than an academic or theoretical approach based solely upon literary research.

In other words, this chapter contains many things that we can actually *do* in addition to simply reading or studying. The 'doing' is in the fields of consciousness, the imagination, meditation and relating to inner forces, but it is no less practical than working with stone or wood. To facilitate the practical aspects of encountering the God or gods in Western tradition, a short visualisation is included at the end of the chapter, with some guidelines and working notes.

Before we can begin to consider the God in Western magical arts, we need to dispose of a number of general misconceptions. The first is that such magical arts are confined to the well-known branches of occultism deriving from the 19th century, such as the Hermetic Order of the Golden Dawn, and the subsequent development of this stream of magic by Aleister Crowley. The second is that magical arts may (or even must) somehow be subsumed under an esoteric Christian heading: this is a more subtle problem, which is best demonstrated by the typical assertion that all 'god-forms' ultimately lead back to an orthodox deity or god. In magical practice there can be no doubt whatsoever that many do not, and we shall return to some examples of this important divergence. The emphasis here is, of course, on practice, and not upon theology, metaphysics, philosophy or abstract higher contemplation; all of these fields of human communication and consciousness present their own case for, or experience of, unification and the wholeness of universal Being. Magic usually works through specific limitations, which are used intentionally for inner transformation, rather than through spiritual generalisations or true spiritual realisations.

In this study we will consider the use of god-forms in Western magic and show, within the limited space available, just how varied the streams or traditions of the God in magic really are. When we begin to open out this area of magical work, we find that 19th century occultism and religious orthodoxy can and often do play a surprisingly small role. Before discussing typical manifestations of imaged divinity in Western magic, we should briefly define the magical arts and traditions themselves, as there is much confusion, ignorance and prejudice still widespread on this subject.

Essentially 'magic' is a collection of arts and primal sciences, reaching far back into ancestral beliefs and practices, but slowly updated and re-assessed within each century. It is based simply upon the use of the human imagination and associated vital energies to interact with other energies, entities and images. It permeates religion, art, music, folklore and tradition; in the ancient world magic was the source of sophisticated and powerful techniques of inner transformation, therapy, and a detailed understanding of human psychology in both mystic and metaphysical terms.

A great proportion of magic is holistic, concerned with the wholeness and interrelationship of living creatures and the land and planet. Due to 19th century intellectual occultism, this major aspect of magical tradition has been ignored until fairly recently; now it is undergoing a considerable revival of attention. Contemporary concern with interrelationship, holism of life forms and the environment, has helped to dispose of the rigid notion that all magical arts are essentially superstitious nonsense. No one will deny that there is much ignorance and superstition in the material, purporting to be magical, handed down through the centuries. Ignorance and superstition, however, abound in every aspect of human life, though often the superstition manifests as irrational prejudice and bigotry.

Practical magic is not limited to historical inheritance or slavish adherence to tradition. Each generation contributes certain organic changes to the overall structure of any spiritual or magical tradition, without necessarily moving away from or demolishing the tradition itself. This is because the magical arts are founded upon the collective sources of mythology and human consciousness in relationship to the land or planet. Nowadays we might say that magic is environmental. In our present context we should focus upon the use of images in the magical arts, upon the wide range of interrelated techniques in which the imagination is used in a relatively controlled manner, accordiing to traditional patterns and techniques. The aim of this aspect of magic is to define certain key images and interact with them; to exchange and amplify energy through such interaction. This technique nowadays comes under the general heading of 'visualisation' and is widely used in various schools of meditation and therapy. As the magical arts inherit and still work with material from a variety of religious, mythic and cultural sources, we frequently find images of gods and goddesses used for visualisation in magic.

Many people nowadays are familiar with the visualisation of deities or mythic beings through the development of the theory of archetypes in Jungian, post-Jungian and transpersonal psychology, and this helps, to a certain extent, in presenting magical art to a modern perception. While this therapeutic or modern psychological type of visualisation does indeed play a part in the magical arts, traditional magical techniques and practices go a lot further.[1]

One confused area of understanding for modern individuals, and indeed of practice in contemporary magical arts, is that of the reality or apparent reality of magical images such as goddess- or god-forms. This confusion is undoubtedly the result of modern materialist psychology, which has fastened upon mythic images, particularly in the case of Jungian or post-Jungian therapy and theory, and repeatedly asserted that they are mental constructs or inherent psychic forms with no entity, will or reality of their own.

Thus we frequently find modern magicians talking and even writing that one may 'use' a god-form to embody certain inherent psychic properties or energies, or to clarify one's own thinking through the psychological or psychotherapeutic effect of such images. Even the important word *archetype* (which has an ancient Greek origin) has been widely abused and misrepresented through the influence of modern psychology. Men now frequently consider the presence or power of a god, or the God, as a projection of an archetype, or as some fragment of the male psyche. In some modern books on magic, this psychic fragment is said to benefit males by being projected or extruded as an imaginative form, filled with energy by various esoteric methods, and then deflated and re-absorbed. We might be tempted to observe the Freudian phallic undertones to this post-Jungian theory of magic!

Magic is often regarded solely as an art or science by which such projections are made. At a recent conference a trained psychologist asserted that her own practice of modern revival witchcraft consisted of projecting the *animus* and *anima* (as defined in Jungian theory) as, or into, the ancient God and Goddess forms, and that by doing so her group of fellow 'witches', male and female, were greatly balanced, healed and liberated. This type of thinking is so far removed from actual magical practice through the ages that we might wonder how it has crept into revival paganism at all; it certainly has no connection with genuine witchcraft, in which the God and Goddess are real, independent entities with power and will (Cf: 'The God of Wicca', pp 169-81 (Ed).).

In all the magical arts, as in pagan religion, the god and goddess forms are understood as living entities, which act as vehicles or holistic aspects or harmonics of a universal God and Goddess; they are never regarded as projections of the human psyche. This might be flippantly considered as evidence of the ignorance of our ancestors, were it not for the fact that there is often a highly developed understanding of the human psyche in ancient religion, magic, metaphysics, and esoteric or magical practices. Indeed, complex and highly sophisticated discussions on this very subject permeated the philosophy and magical arts of the classical world, and are known from even earlier sources such as Assyrian or Babylonian texts and fragments.[2]

So our first assertion must be that the God (by which we mean any aspect of male-imaged divinity) in Western magical arts is a real entity. This divine entity takes a number of forms defined by various streams of myth and religion, and these forms or entities behave in quite distinct and characteristic ways when encountered in meditation, visualisation or ritual working. Our second assertion is that these god-forms, variations of expression of a universal God (just as goddesses are variations of the universal Goddess), are not always subsumed under any one orthodox religious heading. While it would be accurate to say that many god-forms or images lead progressively towards a central figure, often defined as the Son of Light and having centralising, harmonising solar powers, this god-form and related consciousness is not controlled or owned by any one orthodox religion. Furthermore, there are streams of consciousness and imagery, aspects of the God, which do not lead to this solar or central god-form. These can be of major importance in magical arts, and have been given far too little attention in modern research, publication and practice.

The question of polarity comes into all discussions and practices of this sort: in many sources the Light Son is often related to a Dark Mother. But we seldom encounter any suggestion that we should work with a Dark Son and a Light Mother. This is surely the result of patriarchal political religion and monosexual propagandised images of divinity. Nor is it sufficient to rely upon a psychological interpretation, however valid this may be in a modern culture or nuclear family social context.[3] The absence of the Dark God is a terrible weakness and indictment upon our culture, just as much as the absence of the Dark Goddess.

We need to be very clear at this point: we are not talking about images of 'evil' when we discuss dark god and goddess forms. There is a classic problem found among modern meditators, visualisers and magicians, one which runs more deeply than personal psychological manifestations or life-problems. A typical scenario, rather comical if it were not so serious, is the one in which the magician seeks to invoke the great God of the ancient world, known variously as Pan or Cernunnos (to whom we shall return in visualisation at the end of this chapter). Such invocations are always, without exception, successful, though the effect may vary from hidden and permeating results over a period of time to a full sense of contact and presence and considerable power. If anything like the second effect occurs, the poor religiously-conditioned magician often feels that he or she has conjured up something difficult, even evil, because of the level of raw power and the nature of the God himself. No sooner is the God present than he is hastily requested to depart! But the evil is in ourselves, not in the God; if we were to pass through our *panic* and emerge on the other side, we would find that the God cleanses us of our corruptions, and that we no longer reflect our own fears and imbalances on to exterior forms, whether they be human or divine.

In modern or New Age cults, 'masters' have tended to replace the ancient gods and heroes, performing similar functions but with an emphasis upon their super-humanity and non-divinity (as a result of centuries of patriarchal political monotheism).

The variety of male images, god-forms, in Western magic is large. How much of this variety derives from purely literary sources, and how much from practising magicians and living tradition, is often difficult to estabish in a strict historical sense. As I hope to demonstrate in the examples and discussion below, a historical pinpointing of the sources of these images is probably irrelevant to their authenticity or potential use in magical arts: more important is their general presence within an enduring tradition. This presence within the stream or flow of tradition is very important indeed, for it reveals the difference between a genuine god (or goddess) image, however masked or faint, and the product of modern fantasy or entertainment. God-forms do, of course, appear in modern fantasy and entertainment, but not all images or characters that are said to be 'magical' are truly so.

We will shortly examine some of the basic sources for god-forms, always bearing in mind that these are also the basic sources for goddess-forms, as taught within Western magical and mystical tradition. Before we do so, we should briefly discuss the important phenomenon of *mirroring* the god-forms, and its conscious manifestation in advanced magical arts, the art of *mediation* (not to be confused with *meditation*). A basic understanding of this type of magical process greatly assists our understanding of traditional teachings and their associated glyphs, symbols and published illustrations, such as the Tree of Life and the Wheel of Life, both of which we will return to in the context of god-forms.

ORIGINS AND MIRRORING OF GOD-FORMS IN WESTERN MAGIC

God-forms, in which we can include for the moment images of archangels, angels and spiritual entities (though these are not true god-forms in their right), come in a surprising number of guises. If we take, for example, an image such as an archangel found in both Jewish and Christian orthodox religions, we often find this same entity in mystical practices and ritual magic. While in an orthodox sense the archangel seems to be clearly defined, and in modern Christianity virtually defunct and ignored, in the magical arts a deeper resonance of the image often comes through. This deeper level may contain old god-forms, which the orthodox religion has suppressed. Thus we cannot strictly call archangels, angels, heroes, saints and so forth god-forms, but in certain circumstances and through alterations of consciousness, we may find god-forms attuned to them or awakening through their initial interface.

In Western magical tradition such forms are derived from classical, Middle Eastern, Celtic and, less frequently nowadays, Norse or Scandinavian tradition. The Middle Eastern variants are confined to those of Jewish religious origins, or of Christianity, though much of the Christianity in magical arts is inherited from Gnostic sources rather than Roman orthodoxy. There are some connections to ancient Egyptian religion, through the mirroring of god-forms within one another, but the majority of Egyptian symbolism in modern magical arts was assembled no earlier than the 19th century. Exceptions to this are genuine Egyptian magical papyri which appeared in Europe from time to time, but these were of a late period and not necessarily connected to the ancient religion, more to Renaissance magic, Gnosticism, Neo-Platonic tradition, and so forth.

The quality of mirroring is important when we consider images and the forces within the images of gods and goddesses in meditation, magic and spiritual traditions. Although I have used the term 'mirroring' (thinking of the visual aspect of an infinity-box where mirrors are arranged to reflect one another), the concept is also one of holism, for there is no 'true original' in god-forms. We consider an image, usually defined by collective mythic tradition: within that image are older forms, variant forms and, to the skilled visualiser or seer, future forms. They mirror one another to infinity, but for practical purposes we are usually aware only of a specific set or a limited number of images.

This is where a true magician and an intellectual occultist or theoretician differ considerably; both work with sets of images and patterns, but the theorist always tries to define originals into a rigid set. The working magician knows that images will change repeatedly, revealing inner aspects of themselves, yet always remain true to the original starting image. Much confusion arises for students who cannot initially grasp this, and who seek rigid, even dogmatic, forms, often at the expense of true magical experience. Men are particularly prone to this problem in Western society, and tend to seek rigid authoritarian and hierarchal god-forms and structures.

A more specific example of the mirroring of god-forms will help to explain this process clearly. We can begin with the rather mysterious and virtually ignored English St George, a mythic saint rather than a historical martyr. Indeed, the Roman Church has removed him from the modern approved list of saints, for such mythic figures as St George are generally set aside by orthodox religions in an inevitable process of ossification.

The magical image of St George is that of the hero versus the dragon, found also in the classical myth of Perseus. He links also to the Archangel Michael, often used as the model of (patriarchal) Light subduing Darkness. But is this sufficient? If we look within these images, a remarkable sequence unfolds. It leads us away from a patriotic English saint and dragon-slayer towards a primal god of light and liberty, who does not kill the dragon or serpent of the earth, but is in truth empowered and set free by its transformative forces.[4]

The earliest churches of St George, in Lydda, Palestine, are built upon ritual temple sites dedicated to Horus, the hawk god of Egypt. St George is sometimes shown with a hawk's head, symbol of flight into the eye of the sun. And, suddenly, this leads us westwards again, to an ancient youthful god of spring in Celtic tradition, the Hawk of May. This is only the merest summary of a series of connections supported by history, iconography, archaeology, and so forth. But in magical terms such mirrored gods are greatly empowering, while the rigid, firmly attributed images so frequently found in modern texts on magic are always in danger of becoming stereotypes, or of imbuing stereotypes into the individual psyche.

A second example of a complex god-form, harmonically mirrored, is that of Merlin. People are surprised at the proposal that Merlin is a god rather than a magician, but it seems likely that historically the name *Merlin* was a title assumed by certain prophets within a Welsh and Scottish line of tradition. This tradition links back both to the Goddess of the Land, dating from at least as early as the megalithic culture of the West, and to her divine son or consort.[5]

Today, of course, Merlin is seen as a stereotypical wise elder in modern fiction and popular belief, but we find that the earliest legend of Merlin show an entire life cycle, from prophetic youth to mad wildman of the woods, and only then to the elder. Merlin, particularly the young Merlin, is associated with the power of dragons within the Earth (resonance of St George), with prophetic vision and the knowledge of many worlds and orders of creation. He is similar in many ways to the young god Apollo in Greek tradition. As Caitlín Matthews has shown in her books *Mabon and the Mysteries of Britain* and *Arthur and the Sovereignty of Britain* and as Geoffrey Ashe has summarised in *The Book of Merlin*,[7] the Celtic Apollo was Mabon, the Child of Light, associated with the orders of creation, therapy, music and prophecy.[8] So within the stereotypically elder Merlin is a harmonic set of reflections leading to a divinity, the primal Child of Light. As many of these connections are shown in the pattern of the Tree of Life, let us now proceed to a summary of god-forms in Western magic, referring to Figures 3 and 4.

THE TREE OF LIFE

Most divine images are definable upon the Tree of Life, a pancultural symbol which shows relationships between various traditional orders of existence, such as gods and goddesses, spirits, angels, and so forth, the human psyche and spirit, and the solar system (see Figure 3). The Tree of Life is often described, in various publications, as deriving solely from Jewish mysticism and Kabbalah, but it has many Western variants plus, of course, further expressions worldwide. The form currently in use seems to be fusion of Neo-Platonic tradition with Renaissance Kabbalah and planetary and classical mythic patterns. It is a combination of classical Greek, Jewish and Western European lore such as that of Celtic bardic wisdom teachings and other poetic systems preserved in Europe for many centuries. Complex as all this seems on paper, the result is surprisingly simple and accessible.

My own theory, totally unproven, is that the Tree of Life is a pattern that reappears in each tradition, regardless of cultural or historical origins. It does so because of its inherent properties, by which our consciousness relates, even unwittingly, to the pattern of the solar system. Regardless of any such theories, it exists, and performs the remarkable task of linking and harmonising all inner or mythic patterns with those of the outer world, be it in the form of the human being or the solar system.

God-forms upon the Tree of Life

God-forms upon the Tree of Life are generally defined as follows, though there are a number of variants or alternatives, and no rigid or dogmatic formula. Each numbered section refers to a sphere, as shown in our illustration.

10 Gods of the land, of nature, of Earth. May include heroes, ancestral beings, fairies and spirits of nature

9 Lunar gods, ancestral deities, and certain older gods of Water.

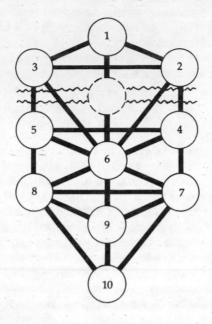

Fig 3. The Tree of Life

10 Earth: Kingdom/human body/material substance
9   Moon: Foundation/human blood and semen/mingled life-energies
8   Mercury: Glory/collective and individual human mind/relatively pure
    energies of intellect
7   Venus: Victory/collective and individual human soul/relatively pure
    energies of emotion
6   Sun: Beauty or harmony/collective and transpersonal human spirit/
    relatively harmonized and balanced energies from and to all other
    spheres or planets
5   Mars: Severity/solar and universal power of taking or breaking-
    down/destroyer of form at the ending of any cycle or phase of existence
4   Jupiter: Mercy/solar and universal power of giving or building/emitter
    of form at the inception of any cycle or phase of existence

The Abyss: experienced by humans as the measureless depths of space
and time. Experienced in altered states of consciousness as the threshold
between individual or solar and universal or supernal consciousness.

3   Saturn: Understanding/Great Mother/deep or universal matrix
2   Neptune: Wisdom/Star Father/Zodiac
1   Uranus: The crown/being/breath or spirit/ultimate source/seed and
    sum of being emerging from and returning to the void

May include heroes, and innerworld or otherworld male images that embody divine forces

8 The messenger god, Mercury, Hermes, the Hermetic tradition

7 Gods of the emotion and feelings, Orpheus, the Orphic tradition

6 Solar deities, Apollo, the Son or Child of Light, gods of harmony, therapy, balance, the Sacred Kings and redeeming figures of world religion, Christ

5 Mars, gods of taking, death, vigour, martial skills, and the transition between death and life; gods of hunting, culling, herding and animal breeding appear here in a higher octave or form than that of the earthly expressions (10)

4 Jupiter, gods of giving, creativity, outpouring energy, joy, mercy and compassion

3 The dark brooding gods, Saturn, lords of endless time, mediators of grief and suffering, deep cosmic tides of change

2 The Zodiac, deities or mythic images associated with the 12 signs of the patterns of heaven, stellar deities in groups or holisms. Also identified with Neptune, not simply as a sea god (9) but as a great god of the ocean of stars. Functions of ferrying, wisdom, transition and enlightenment, and awareness beyond death and beyond personality are found here

1 Ultimate Being, the primal God. Identified sometimes with Uranus, the father of all gods, and of course with the orthodox concept of God in formal religion.

THE WHEEL OF LIFE AND THE SEVEN DIRECTIONS

The Wheel of Life relates the Four Elements, the Seasons, the Directions, and various states of power. It also relates, through its ceaseless turning, the phases of a life cycle, both for gods and humans. Traditionally, certain images are located in certain Quarters of the Circle or Wheel. In Western magic this concept is fundamental, and in magical and spiritual training worldwide the concept of the Seven Directions occurs repeatedly. The Wheel, as we see in Figure 4, appears to have only four Quarters, those of East, South, West and North. But it is a flat glyph or map, completed by the presence of a human standing within it at the centre. It is, in fact, a definition of our standing position and zone of awareness; thus it represents the surface of the land or planet, and the sphere of awareness or being. This sphere ultimately embraces the universe, though most of us are content to settle for a sphere of awareness that is a little smaller!

The Seven Directions, then, are Above/Below, East/West, South/ North, and Within. God-forms and images are related to each Direction: more traditionally, we would say that the gods are found in these Directions, that they dwell there naturally.

The Circle or Wheel and the Tree of Life are part of one another; the Tree grows in the centre of the sphere, it is both the upright human with the stars above and the land below, and the Axis Mundi, or pivot of the worlds, through the centre of the solar system.

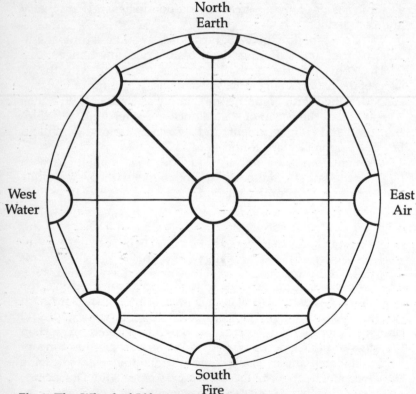

Fig 4. The Wheel of Life
Air/Dawn/Birth/Spring/EAST/Beginning
Fire/Noon/Adulthood/Summer/SOUTH/Increasing
Water/Evening/Maturity/Autumn/WEST/Fulfilling
Earth/Night/Age/Winter/NORTH/Ceasing
(Between North and East is the threshold of death and rebirth)

East In the East we find gods of spring, change, turbulence, swiftly moving force. The Element is Air, which is both Breath of Spirit and the howing hurricane of destruction. The gods of Air are frequently associated with warrior skills, and therefore have a further level of honour, protection of the weak, defence of the victim against the oppressor. Because Air is also the Element of communication, in terms of speech, music and, more subtly, consciousness or swiftly moving thoughts, we find messenger gods, teacher gods and communicator gods in the Eastern Quarter. The techniques and forces of arousal, be it sexual or intellectual, are taught and enabled by the gods of the Eastern Quarter. The magical implement is the Sword or Arrow.

South In the South we find gods of ascension, of summer, of light, of balanced power. The Element is Fire, in the form of burning flame, the midsummer sun, and the universal power of Light. The gods of this Quarter maintain a balance and harmony of the fiery powers, and are concerned with therapy, enlightenment, harmonising inner forces. The forces that are aroused in the East are elevated and balanced in the South. In this Quarter we find the gods of redemption, the great saviours and enlighteners of humanity. We also find the midsummer gods of the land, who bring the highest solar forces to bear upon the Earth within the turning of the wheel of the year. The implement of the South is the Rod or Staff.

West In the West we find gods of maturity, of autumn, fruitfulness, giving, generosity, plenty. The Element is Water, and the gods of transit, the ferry-men, the subtle changers and gentle teachers are found here. The potent water gods of the ancestral world are found here, both as deities of the rivers and oceans, and as local guardians of springs and wells. The cosmic tides of space and time are the higher octave of this Quarter, and so we also find gods of universal love and compassion, the transformative and enabling powers of the spirit in the ocean of Being. The implement of the West is the Cup.

North In the North we find gods of old age, of winter, of death. The Element is Earth, and the old gods are not weak or negative, but filled with the strength of the Earth. The higher octaves of this Quarter are that of wisdom, readiness and calm. It leads to the relationship of the night sky and stars. Paradoxically the earth-gods are also the star gods. Here also are the gods of sleep, peace, rest, forgetting, and final transition from one world to another.

Ancestral teachers and guides are found in the North, the gods that communicate wisdom and offer it to us as practical guidance.

In mythic circles, we often find that a hero or god travels around the Wheel, changing with the seasons. At spring he is newly born, filled with the rush and inspiration of life. At summer he becomes an adult, holding his peak of power in balance and harmony. By autumn he has become the mature man, the giver. At winter he is old and wise, often becoming a teacher. At the transition between North and East, he dies, to be reborn again upon a further turning of the Wheel.

Above is the realm of the stars, the eternal depths of the universe. There is a paradoxical relationship between Above and Below, which is adequately highlighted by modern theories of relativity. In a general sense, the Direction Above is that of Ultimate Divinity; this may be the Sky Father in a simple world model, or it may be a universal Being.

Below is the realm of the Underworld, which paradoxically holds the stars. The Direction Below is that of the Earth Mother, more universally of the Great Mother of all Being. Above and Below can be inverted or reversed at any time, and some very powerful magical techniques consist of exactly this process.

Within is the living spirit, the core or seed of Being. This may manifest to the imagination in innumerable ways: for men it is often the primal Child of Light, eternal, unchanging, radiant. At its deepest level, the Direction Within touches upon the Source, the utterance of Being out of Silence. All Directions, gods, goddesses, stars, planets and zones are Within, but to merely state this in words is insufficient, a set of phrases that leads us away from proper contemplation or experience.

GODS AND MEN IN WESTERN MAGICAL ARTS

Now that we have defined the general types of god-form or deity, and their mirroring through other images such as saints, teachers or inner-plane masters,[9] we should consider the relationship between male deities and male humans. This is both complex and simple, a paradoxical relationship which is, as in all magical arts, rapidly clarified by experience, but frequently confused by words and wishful thinking.

One of the standard teachings in magical and spiritual orders

114

or traditions is that power works through hierarchies. The ultimate Being is addressed, so to speak, through a chain of communication, leading from humans through spirits, angels and heroes, to archangels, masters, aeons, lesser divinities, and finally through the Great Father and Great Mother to the Source. This linear concept has unfortunate correlations with dogma, authoritarianism and militarism, hence its appeal to rigid power-hungry occultists such as those of the 19th century, who were working in a culture in which status and authority were given very high values. People of this type, particularly men, are still found in Western magical arts today, though there is an increasing move away from rigid authoritarian and elitist roles and practices among a new generation of dedicated magicians.

The linear suggestion of hierarchy is, of course, a delusion. When the early texts on magic and mysticism were printed during the Renaissance, and indeed in earlier alchemical documents, the linear order was inevitable due to the dimensions of the printed page or illustration. All such linear hierarchies are flat or two-dimensional maps of holisms; they were never intended to be taken literally, as this can lead to gross confusion, megalomania and coagulation of the spirit within.

The process of mirroring, briefly described above, works through all levels of existence. Magic is an art that begins by defining an area, a Sacred Space, and then through imagery and pattern-making specifically limits the mirroring that occurs within that space. This means that any man is, literally, able to reflect any god. This is not a vaguely mystical statement, such as that all humans are ultimately part of Divinity; in magical arts each and every human may mirror or mediate the power of any divinity, male or female.

In practical group work this mirroring is generally balanced by the Four Elements and specifically by polarised partners, making a stable pattern. In individual work, such balance is more difficult to find, but the problems of gaining such balance are tremendous sources of training, energy and empowerment.

Any man may mirror any god! What a seductive concept for the greedy, the imbalanced, the power-mad, the ruthless ego, the corrupt. We ought to say, more truthfully, that any man may mirror or mediate any god, if he is willing to pay the unknown price. Let us briefly consider some of the ways god-power manifests through modern men, and the price that they pay.

Perhaps the most obvious examples in our culture are those men in the rock and pop music business who seem to have a special

115

power, a force flowing from them which uses both music and man as a vehicle for form. Indeed, large rock concerts today are one of the few mass ritual events still occurring in the Western world. And we know also what price the stars may pay for such seemingly divine power; ruin of personal life and relationships, deep emotional and mental problems and, in many cases, death through drugs or drink.

The modern rock star is a stereotyped materialisation, indeed an imbalanced or warped manifestation of the mythic hero.

THE HERO

Heroes play a large part in the mythology and legendary history of our world. In recent years it has become fashionable to laugh at the hero, and in modern film and fiction to delight in the 'anti-hero'; this is because we have seen through the false hero, but have not yet recovered the true hero.

The false hero is the sexual all-male stereotype with bulging muscles, jutting jaw, all decision and action, and little or no emotion or introspection. These types appear frequently in early films: gentlemen detectives, war heroes, and so forth. They also dominated much of early 20th century popular fiction. We may rapidly set such images aside; they are a dead end.

Primal heroes, however, are a different matter. They embody certain strengths and weaknesses that are inherent in every male: many of their legends reveal much to us concerning initiation, spiritual growth, emotional maturity, and humankind's relationship to both environmental and apparently supernatural forces. Many heroes are the sons of divine beings, often of a union between one human parent and one divine: such unions reveal a great deal of information on ancient methods of initiation and transformation, they are not mere allegories or superstitions.

In modern terms, we may look at the inherent character of the hero through the ages. Certain persistent fundamental qualities and actions define a hero, even down to our modern stereotypes who pale into insignificance beside their ancestral counterparts.

What makes a Hero?

A hero is, inevitably, a warrior of some sort, usually but not exclusively a trained fighter, a bearer of arms. There are, of course, heroes who never lift a capon or fight a physical battle: their heroic deeds are, nevertheless, still definable and recognisable. The hero has certain strengths, be they of muscle or will, brain or body. But he is also unfailingly motivated by gentleness and compassion, without which he is merely an unfeeling thing or a solider pawn in the hands of unscrupulous manipulators. He protects the weak, assists them and will, if necessary, sacrifices his own interests, even his life, to protect, defend and benefit others.

These qualities are all essentially nurturing, they are those of the mother — feminine qualities. The hero is not a superman, he is a highly empowered, active, dynamic male whose maleness is balanced by feminine qualities, feelings and abilities.

In some legends we find this truth exemplified by the relationship between a hero and a goddess. The Irish hero Cuchulainn,[10] for example, has astonishing powers, skills, strength, energy, sexual prowess, beauty, and so forth. But he fails to recognise that a major part of his potential is realised through the blessing and protection of the Morrigan, the primal goddess of sexuality and death. Because he fails to recognise her, both literally during several meetings and of course inwardly, she eventually withdraws her blessing and protection. Through his failure to identify the goddess, Cuchulainn loses much of his supernatural strength and skill, and so may be killed by his enemies.

This theme recurs frequently in the Arthurian and Grail legends of later medieval literature: the feminine qualities, the mysterious powers of the goddess, are essential for the king, the knight, the hero. Without them he is incomplete, a one-sided stereotype. The sword Excalibur is nothing without the Scabbard: Arthur is weakened and destroyed without Guinevere, and so forth.

But can a male mirror a divine force in a balanced way, in which the counter-force (the price paid) is balanced and willingly given?

THE SACRED KINGSHIP

The ancient Mystery of the Sacred Kingship was, and still is, one of the ways of spiritual service at the very heart of Western magical arts, reaching back thousands of years into the roots of primal culture. Within this Mystery, a male willingly sacrifices himself for the benefit of others. The act may be small and simple, or it may be explosive and devastating, or it may permeate slowly through an entire lifetime. When the process is undertaken consciously, through formal initiation into the Mystery, the response from the inner kings and the related god-forms is clear and powerful. Certain men can and do embody this type of god-form, both consciously and unconsciously. The conscious path, worked through mediation (or mirroring), visualisation and ritual, is one which eventually leads to full ability to mediate or mirror any god-form, for they all relate to the central image of the Son of Light or Divine King.

Without some balance, centrality, harmony and conscious work, mirroring or mediation of god-forms often leads to madness. Think of the power and charisma of a dictator, mediating the imbalances of powerful forces concerned with ruling and control. Think of the corrupt charisma of the popular cult or religious leader (be it Western or Eastern), shedding light and loving kindness while collecting dollars and indulging in every secret vice. Think of the power inherent in world leaders, military lords and masters, or the hidden all-encompassing power of the financiers, ruling the planet by devious and hidden ways at the expense and suffering of millions of fellow humans. These are all imbalanced reflections of god-forms, coming to our outer world in ways that lead to evil. The inner power itself is neutral; it is a force that can take its path through the human male for good or evil.

MEN AND THE GOD

So many confused, contradictory and interrelated assumptions are made concerning the relationship of men (by which we mean males rather than a collective term for humankind) to the gods, the God, or God, that is almost impossible to untangle the resulting complex mess. Nor should we need to do so, as much of it is already rotting away and, thankfully, being discarded. In our present context, we do not need to delve too deeply into the dogmatic assertions of formal religion; we are working instead upon a subtle or esoteric level that both transcends and underpins many aspects of religion, psychology and inner or transpersonal development without necessarily confirming or rejecting any particular dogma or faith.

There is no suggestion here of elitism, merely that it is possible to learn directly from perennial educational initiatory traditions. The wisdom traditions reveal the essentials behind magic, religion and mythology. Such essentials are simple, but they are often obscured by an accumulation of formal arts, sciences and religions in each century.

Modern developments of magic do not demand or require religious faith, but neither do they deny it. Of more concern, however, than any fruitless argument over dogma or faith are the long-term psychic and social effects of dogma and spiritual suppression. These long-term effects have worked deeply upon both men and women, and on this collective and individual level clearly the relationship between males and the God is in a very sorry state indeed.

Nor has modern psychology been helpful to us, especially those branches of Jungian and post-Jungian psychology which seem or claim to take a great interest in mythology and perennial imagery. Such psychology is all too frequently limited to those segments of ancient wisdom, magic and mythology which fit a psychological theory, while blandly discarding or ignoring those (comprising by far the greater part of the perennial body or lore) which do not.[11]

Much emphasis has been placed by such schools of psychology and psychotherapy upon masculine and feminine qualities of the psyche, which are reputed to make themselves known through archetypes or god-forms as defined in ancient myth. These so-called archetypes (for the word is regularly misused in psychology) are assumed to be fragments or resonances of either a collective or an individual psychic state, as aspects of consciousness. But they are not considered to be aspects of any ubiquitous transcendent, universal or, for want of a better word, divine Being. In other words, when psychology deals with the gods, they do not exist in their own right, they have no relationship to any universal holism or existence beyond the human psyche.

There are many subtle implications of this type of psychological theory, not the least of which is that of empowering concept or potential experience of either god or goddess is constantly undermined by suggestions that it is nothing more than the projection of a simple psychic construct, psychological archetype or sub-personality. Nothing could be further from the ancient magical concept of the goddesses and gods.

THE GOD WITHIN AND WITHOUT

Let us begin by considering the *God within*. What is this notion of a divinity inherent in humanity? Why do we feel, through all ages and cultures, that there is something inherent in every man that pertains to a god or gods, and in every woman that pertains to a goddess or goddesses?

In the magical tradition one of the major empowering techniques and experiences is to realise the presence of the God within, and of the God without. There is an unfortunate tendency for the concept of the God without to be used for religious suppression of individual freedom, and for the concept of the God within to lead to egotistic inflation and, in some cases, to the extreme evils of scientific materialism and the abuse of life and the land.

As we discovered in the late 20th century, the egomania of materialistic science, striving ever onwards and seeking to wrest secrets from nature, linked to the profit-motive in which anything is allowable to turn a dollar, seem to be leading to destruction of the planet.

We are not, however, solely concerned here with these negative manifestations of concepts, but rather to seek a balanced insight into the most simple roots and energies that comprise the relationship between a male human and the empowering entity or energy of a god. At this stage it is irrelevant what name or origin the god may or may not have.

If we were to strip the entire subject of both religious and psychological jargon, we would find a very simple set of concepts, a situation which can be accepted or rejected. If we accept these concepts or, more importantly, if our intuition and meditations confirm that there is truth in them, they act not only as a foundation for establishing parameters of consciousness and energy but as initiatory thresholds towards inner change. This is what the magical arts, and indeed any Mystery or structured system of self-revelation and inner change, are all about.

Gender and Polarity

The male entity, defined very generally but not exclusively by gender, is the human biological equivalent of a universal relatively male or positive polarity. The female entity is relatively negative in polarity.

By the terms 'positive' and 'negative' we emphatically must not imply good and bad, or any illusory fixed value whatsoever, but should simply define relative polarities of energy. These polarities cause movements of energy and form, which arise, cycle and transform, through an infinite number of states or conditions in our universe. The relative divisions or interactions are simply a property of consciousness in time, our way of filtering the universal holism into smaller archetypes or subsets that we can relate to. In altered consciousness, different from our habitual or conditioned state, resonances or octaves of the universal holism are perceived.[12]

In the human physical organism our sexual definition is that of the penis and vagina (the first being physically outreaching, the second being physically receptive), but upon inner levels of energy we find that the male is sexually negative or receptive, while the female is sexually positive or outreaching: the polarity cycle is ever-spiralling. This teaching has been known for thousands of years in magical arts, yet has been heavily suppressed by orthodox religion and related social and political expressions in our culture. It lies at the very heart of sexual or polarity magic in which energies are exchanged, transformed and greatly amplified through the flow between the alternative polarities of the humans working the magic, visualising or ceremonial pattern.

Esoteric tradition uses a number of simple but profound conceptual models to show this subject of cyclic polarity, and to relate them within a holism that ultimately resonates through all Being. Typical examples of such models are shown in our Figures 3 and 4; the Tree of Life and the Wheel of Life.

The basic condition of being male, which is defined by but not limited to physical gender, means that when various life-energies manifest upon the physical level, they tend towards a positive or male polarity. Upon inner levels, which are reached through imagination, visualisation, meditation and (less frequent but very effective) through ritual or ceremonial patterns, the polarity or energy flow will change many times. Each threshold or change reflects an inverse: that which was immediately male upon the physical level becomes female inwardly: cross another inner threshold and it becomes male again.

Energy works through a universal 'law' or tendency of octaves, by which the same pattern reiterates itself upon levels or rates that are octaves of one another.[13] Thus a male body has a powerful octave of male polarity, and this is what we might justifiably call the God within. Between the outer habitual male form and the inner power are various harmonic levels of energy and polarity.

The Three Aspects

For the moment, let us consider only the situation in which a man seeks to realise the God within. In other words, a male meditates, invokes, visualises, seeking to build a bridge between his outer mask, or personality, and his inner octave of universal male

121

energy. This type of exercise has been undertaken by men for millennia though the methods and forms vary according to religious, cultural and environmental factors. However, certain constants or archetypes permeate all systems and examples, and we may consider these before progressing to any actual visualisations or bridge-building exercises for the modern man.

In psychology, as we have mentioned, classical god-forms are often borrowed either as working archetypes or as analogous examples for temporary identification 'explanation' in therapy. Thus we have the obvious patterns of a god of war, a god of wisdom, god of healing, and so forth, which are supposed to represent archetypes or to be present as sub-personalities in the human psyche. This is all reasonable as far as it goes, which is not, in terms of esoteric psychology, very far at all. The initiatory traditions certainly recognised the god-forms and related to them extensively in practical work, but in a quite different way to their use in modern psychological and alternative or New Age methods of therapy or inner development.

One of the major differences is that the family relationships inherent in the pantheons, much discussed in modern publications, were relatively unimportant. Modern researchers spend an inordinate amount of time and energy defining pantheons and sets of gods and goddesses, comparing them wit' one another and showing how their relationships and mythic adventures are reflected in the modern psyche in interpersonal situations. When such deities were actually worshipped, they were of a far more complex nature than is evidence in modern interpretation and reductions; the ancients knew perfectly well that each god or goddess has within his or her image many levels and aspects; there is no fixed, unchanging god or goddess in the pantheon of any culture. Upon a deeply mystical or philosophical level, we always find the ultimate concept of the One Being, but not as any kind of deity with a fixed and permanent image. Such images were for public ritual or specialised meditation and visualisation, acting as archetypes between humans and the forces of the land, planet, solar system and stars.

In the ancient mysteries initiates were taught that the deities themselves went through the cycle of the Wheel of Life, and that they had changing aspects or relations with one another which were not always publicly declared in state worship. In the case of a god, the roles of warrior, lover, father, healer and so forth, were of less importance than the aspects. The Three Aspects or Faces are as follows: Youth/Man/Ancient.

This might seem to be merely a matter of chronology, and it certainly has its parallel in the human life cycle, but the Three Faces of a god (any god) tend to relate harmonically or holistically to certain properties and energies of consciousness: Bright Prophetic Child or Youth/Wild or Mad Adult Man/Wise and Experienced Ancient.

We may take Apollo as a typical example of these three phrases: but the stereotypically classical Apollo, god of mental discipline, music and intellect, is very likely a relatively modern (Victorian or post-Victorian) reduction. If we look at the myths and geomantic locations of Apollo, and of Celtic manifestation Mabon or the prophet Merlin, we find a quite different and fluid pattern, relating to the Three Aspects described above.[14]

FINDING THE GOD WITHOUT

The God may be found within or without. The God without has, for about 1500 years, been somewhat severely limited to a mono-sexual and imbalanced image, the 'demon Jehovah', the wrathful father, the creator of pain, suffering, inequality, restriction, elitism, misery, and so forth. This terrible image has been mitigated slightly by that of Jesus, but suffering and pain are also features of this divine son in most orthodox Christian cults or religious branches. The problem of rivalry and pain between father and son, or older and younger male, seems epitomised in the formal religions, particularly those of near-Eastern origin such as Christianity.

This unfortunate and destructive historical pattern, in which the corruption of a mythic father–son divine pattern has heavily influenced human historical development, undermining the collective psyche and creating conditions of imbalance and effective evil, cannot be simply undone, even today, after the virtual collapse of orthodox Christianity as a force in our world.

A man seeking the God without, outside himself, can still take the orthodox religious route, but it is fraught with terrible barriers and suppressive imagery. To reach the true level of divine love and compassion that was originally embodied within Jesus, a man may have to work his way through the entire ambience, collective imagery and forces of orthodox religion: he may well lose sight of his original goal en route or, as is more likely nowadays, simply realise that corrupt and defunct religion is not worth his life energy. The magical arts, however, offer a way of images — each leading or mirroring into another. This way can lead to powerful realisations of the God without.

THE GOD WITHIN

What are the ways in which a man finds the essential Being, the power, the divinity within himself? The entire issue of finding the God within, or the essence of our being, is related to sexuality. For most men the usual route is to work with a generally male self-image; that image is then modified and rapidly abandoned as the temporary mask that it truly is. But what does it mask? Energy, life-force and, beyond or within that, an entity or Being that is more than ourselves. In terms of our own consciousness, even when it is beyond the delusion of a rigid 'self', this higher or transpersonal entity is still male.

At the most profound levels of meditation, this sexual identification vanishes, and the essence of Being is known to be bisexual, transcending yet totally present within all sexuality, all polarity, all time, space and energy.

The further we reach within, inside ourselves through meditation, the less defined the sexual polarity becomes. In other words we do not intentionally pass within in meditation to be confronted by some male fragment of ourselves: we pass beyond any such relatively surface levels, and seek directly for the deeper roots of our being. This seeking will often, in itself, rebalance fragmented and habitual tendencies to exaggerated stereotypical habits and behaviour.

Many men are afraid, even terrified, of any type of inward-looking meditation. They tend to confuse it, initially, with self-examination or moody introspection. We may set aside, for the moment, obsessive self-examination or ego-mirroring, self-reassuring reveries and daydreams; these are not meditation, not true visualisation, and they do not reach beyond the more superficial levels of the psyche. In some individuals we find a highly energised loop of self-mirroring fantasies, such as perpetual self-examination, dwelling upon one's own thoughts, emotions, motives, decisions, and so forth. Modern psychology tends to reinforce this type of polluted self-examination by giving it an intellectual system.

Another typical and widespread self-mirroring fantasy that rules the lives of many men is the delusion of the 'man's man', the praiseworthy, phallic, achieving male. The God within is not a type of phallic super-male, nor is it the function of the God within to release energies to enable us to behave in a manner that amplifies and encourages our current habits and delusions. One typical problem is that when men encounter the power within, either through an early meditational experience (for early experiences can be very potent indeed), or through involuntary realisations (which come to all of us at least once in a lifetime), or through unusual, highlighted or tragic circumstances which lead to a sudden change of consciousness, they tend to re-route the experience. By this we mean that men may channel temporarily increased energy through habitual traps and filters of the false personality.

A true experience of divinity or Being, therefore, becomes a source of temporary energy or buttressing for the deluded personality, for the stereotypical male, for all our weaknesses and poisons. Many of the glowing, charismatic, wonderful teachers and gurus of male-dominated new spirituality are likely to be individuals who have access to a source of energy which is used (consciously or unconsciously) to reinforce the self-delusion of male-wonderfulness. To often, the guru or New Age teacher is a type of psychically amplified Medallion Man.

We must remember that magical power is merely energy. If we do not have appropriate channels for it to flow through, it can only take what channels we have; in some cases a sudden access of true life-energy will destroy us, drive us mad. Traditionally those who underwent the initiatory process became poets, madmen, or were found dead at dawn. These three conditions apply to us today — there are many dead men in all walks of life. We only need to think to realise how many we have met, and how many madmen, but how few seers or poets.

The magical arts teach us the perennial methods of obviating this problem, or realising the divine power within, by techniques which also break down and re-align the rigid stereotypes of personality. The forces of breaking, of change, are usually embedded within a certain type of goddess, the dark destroying figure whom many men, and many women, fear most of all. This experience may come through bitter situations in outer life or, more rarely, can be consciously faced and undertaken in inner work, through visualisation or ritual.

In modern use, we find that a visualisation which employs traditional archetypes, god or goddess forms, scenarios, and patterns of narrative or events may be repeated many times. Contrary to what we might expect from endless repeats of a popular entertainment, which is that in most cases it would rapidly become tedious, repeated visualisation develops an increased level of energy, and many new realisations come through it. Additionally we should say that many visualisers report that no two experiences of the same visualisation are ever identical.

Let us now proceed to a typical modern magical visualisation, seeking the primal Horned God, known as Pan in the classical tradition or Cernunnos in the Celtic tradition.

VISUALISING THE GUARDIAN
(modern contact with an ancient god-form)

In this visualisation we seek to establish contact with one of the great primal god-forms, central to the perennial Male Mysteries, and widely found in ancient Mystery-teaching, magical arts and religion. We should always be aware that the presence of a working image or method within an apparently outmoded ancient religion or formal tradition does not preclude its modern use. When we use images of this type to regenerate our inner energies, we are tapping into the mythic roots rather than any specific cult or historical or religious flowering of those roots. We are, in fact, slowly building a new branch of the Mysteries for the coming century.

The image of the Guardian is known worldwide in many variants, each variant having a fundamental identity and similar appearance to an archetypal Guardian. Local and historical expressions can and do take on specific forms and functions, and we need to be aware of the differences; indeed, the differences between expressions of an archetypal god or goddess form, ranging from universal to purely local, are important in direct work with images and energies. There is a constant emphasis in modern spiritual or meditative teaching that we must realise the unity and uniformity of all such images and traditions, that they are all ultimately one. This may be true, but for us as humans the way begins with a clear understanding of one or two specific paths: these ultimately lead to unity, but we must travel the path first, and cannot reach unity by merely acknowledging it intellectually.

When we talk of the Guardian it should be emphasised that this is not simply an outmoded or redundant ancient god-form, but an enduring image inherent within human consciousness. For practical purposes it gives shape and entity as a living being to certain 'male' forces or energies which we all, male and female, have within us. These energies, however, are not confined to any male human or imaginative or transpersonal entity or transformation of the psyche; they are also found in the environment, the land, the planet, the universe.

The forces embodied by the Guardian are also embodied by certain goddesses, but the gender of the image unquestionably alters and defines the manner in which it works and its deep effect upon human beings. (In *The Merlin Tarot*,[5] a pattern of polarity and octaves of power is found, broadly based upon the pan-cultural wisdom symbol of the Tree of Life. Tarot is often a good indicator of the inner and outer polarity of images, with male and female images alternating with every change of level or increasingly powerful card.)

In the classical world, the Guardian god was known as Pan, the lord of nature, of the wild forces of growth, the creative energies that flow through all forms within the land. The wild energies of this god were said to be impossible to resist: his presence brought the fit of *panic* that is felt when potent energies are at work.

Modern fiction, based upon religious propaganda, has tended to brand this image as evil, licentious, savage and degenerate. The early Church fathers identified Pan as a false god, *deo falsus*, and eventually with Satan, the Devil. This was simply because the sanctity of nature was regarded with suspicion by the Church; nature was seen as a delusion or as a source of evil, for the elect were supposed to find their way to heaven as rapidly as possible, leaving the damned to burn in hell, and ignoring an abandoned Earth far behind. This type of dualistic, escapist elitism re-appears, in subtle variants, in much of the current fashionable New Age literature and in related teachings.

To emphasise light against or over darkenss is one of the most corrupting and weakening concepts known to us. Light and darkness exist in a rhythm together, and humans, like plants and simpler life forms, require the cycle of light and darkness to grow and change. On inner level, the god Pan represents not only wild, vital forces but the herdsman or controller of such forces: it is through his power that we both grow and learn to give form to growth, to drive and tame our energies according to a set of natural simple laws. Thus he is also a god of taking, of limitation. The Mysteries of Pan, and of his Celtic counterpart Cernunnos, to whom we shall turn shortly, were particularly loathed by the orthodox Church, as they represented a way of spiritual liberation through natural energies, and were closely linked to the ancient all-pervasive worship of the Great Mother. The Herdsman, Guardian or Green Man is the wild son of the great Mother.

Worship of the Horned God, known to the Celts as Cernunnos, was widespread in the ancient world. Versions of his image are found in prehistoric cave paintings, and as far West as America among the gods of the native people. He was Guardian of the Mysteries of the Underworld, sometimes shown (as in Romano-Celtic images from the 1st century BC) sitting upon or close to a hoard of coins, gold or precious metal work. He held serpents in either hand, and was often identified with the fruits of the Earth, both in the form of animals and growing plants.[7]

Thus we might summarise this deity, embodying for us a set or pattern of energies, as the Keeper, the Protector, and the refiner of forces into beneficial form. No beneficial growth or form can occur without limitation, purification and selection. So he is also a god of taking, of challenge. In human terms he is one of the Guardians of thresholds of consciousness and energy: he prevents us from accessing more energy than we may truly cope with. Yet if we are able to pass through his strict test controls and therapeutic inner transformations, he gives us free entry to the realms of power, symbolised by the mysterious Underworld, but manifesting as form in nature.

Other guardians arise within consciousness due to individual circumstances, and yet other guardians are known upon collective levels, and in specific locations. But as far as humanity is concerned, the pervasive image of the Guardian is generally that of a horned man. While awareness of this image and its potential has been suppressed in our culture for several centuries, it returns now, inevitably, as we awaken to the destruction and pollution of nature, in which we include ourselves as simultaneous aggressors and victims of such madness. The Guardian was, and is, one of the major controls of such madness, leading our wild energies into proper paths.

Meeting the Guardian[15]

The individual or group spends a preparatory period in silence, using the meditation of Stillness[1] or a similar calming and clearing technique. As always with such preparatory stages, the emphasis must be upon stillness and silence, and not on any specific image, divine or meditative form, or religious meditational technique. The aim of this period of stillness is to calm all energies/

thoughts/emotions and so become ready for a clear and uncorrupted or undistracted image to be built and to work within the imagination.

First we visualise a forest: tall trees and primal, untouched woodland growth. The great trees rise up to the sunlit sky above, filtering the light through their huge canopy of branches, until it falls in green and golden shafts and pools upon the rich carpet of deep loam and mosses below. This is an ancient oak forest, and many of the trees have wide, gnarled trunks showing great age.

Gradually we enter into this forest, and feel the presence of the trees, emanating an intense, radiant force like warmth all round us. We hear birds calling, and the wind constantly stirs the leaves and higher branches, making a flowing ceaseless sound like the rippling of water, or the tides of the sea. As we walk deeper into the forest, we find a narrow deer trail, and follow this through the trees to a clearing. The clearing is small, with a huge, ancient, wide-trunked oak tree in the centre, growing out of a pile of jumbled rocks. From a cleft in the rocks, a tiny spring flows, making a damp pool of lush green growth. We see that the rocks are red, and that there are tracks of many animals coming to this central spring, to drink the water and lick the salt. In this clearing we pause and wait in silence, knowing that we seek the presence of the Guardian.

(Here a silent pause is made in the narrative or guided visualisation. The length of time depends upon the individual or group; for individual work this is usually a brief period, but for guided work with groups it may be lengthened.)

As we meditate we realise that we have been joined by someone: from behind the tree a man has emerged, who looks steadily upon us as if in calm, unhurried judgement. He is a teacher and guide in the ancient Mysteries, and is willing to take us into the presence of the Guardian if we truly seek to do so. With this man there is an animal, keeping him close company. Look upon the animal and remember it.

Our guide beckons us towards the spring rising from the rocks, and shows us a small, scarred, rough stone bowl by the side of the water. He fills this with water and splashes some into our faces, as if in lustration and preparation. The water is ice-cold and shocks us wide-awake. Even as we wipe the water from our eyes, we see that our guide has moved behind the tree, and we hurry to follow him.

As we pass to the other side of the tree, we seem to step from light to darkness, day to night. Ahead of us we see the guide and his animal passing swiftly over a bare star-lit plain; the trees of the forest have disappeared, and the ground is hard and cold. We realise that we are run-

ning now, and that we must breathe deeply to keep up with our guide and his companion animal. The cold air fills our lungs and we breathe in and out deeply, seeming to gain speed with every breath. The effort is hard at first, but gradually brings with it a deep rhythm that gives us increasing strength and speed.

Far ahead of us we see a glimmer of light, as if the sun is beginning to rise. As we settle into the rhythm of running and breathing, we realise that the plain is not empty, as we had first thought. Occasionally on either side, we see the dim shapes of other creatures moving in the starlight. Sometimes they approach, as if curious, while others flee at our coming. Some of the shapes are vast, and we uneasily recognise creatures from other times and places, creatures which we fear. Yet the speed and rhythm of our running sets us moving ahead, following our guide and his animal; their presence seems to deter anything from being too curious or coming too close.

Now we find that it is growing light, and we come to the end of the bare plain. Our guide slows his pace, and pauses to wait for us to approach. We find that we are once again on the edge of a forest, and as the sun rises a dawn chorus of many birds rises to the light. But this forest is of trees and plants that we have never seen: the trees have smooth, glossy green and red bark, rising to a vast height, and the leaves far above shed a deep blue and purple light, filtering the sun as it rises. The crying birds lift a vast chorus of calls and whistles, which is joined by the roaring of great beasts, and the screaming of small animals in the huge branches above. As we ran across the plain we felt like warriors at the chase, but now we feel small, like children, dwarfed by the tall trees and the presence of such seething, roaring life.

Our guide briefly touches the animal that accompanies him, and they step aside to reveal an entrance leading into the earth at the foot of two huge trees. The thick, smooth roots of these trees tangle together, forming a low arch, and our guide indicates that we must pass within. We feel the growing heat and light of the day, and the air is moist and filled with powerful scents. Within those shadowy roots seems to be a resting place, a shelter from the primal forest, and we slowly stoop to pass within.

We find ourselves in a low earthern passageway, which leads gently downwards. It is of hard compacted soil, and bears the marks of many passing hooves and claws; suddenly we are less certain about this place. Our guide and his companion animal have remained above, and we move slowly downwards alone. The tunnel widens out into a large chamber, which has a strong animal smell as if many beasts have sheltered here. The far end of this chamber is lit by tiny lamps burning with a dim yellow flame: a raised platform of fresh green branches is laid there, and we smell strong resins and sharp bitter herbs, cutting through the animal *odour. As we look upon this platform, we feel a deep uncontrollable fear rise within us, making our hair stand upon end and our skin shiver. We realise that we are in the presence of the Guardian, and his power brings us to the edge of panic.*

Set far back in the shadows, where the light of the lamps barely touches, we realise that a figure is sitting cross-legged upon the green branches. His face is hidden from us, but we see strong sinewy arms and legs, covered in deep spiralling tattoos. The flickering lamplight first reveals and then conceals these patterns, which seem to writhe like snakes upon his dark skin. We realise that he has long hair and beard, and that a tall crown of spreading antlers is upon his head. His eyes are in shadow and we are, for the moment, relieved that he does not look fully upon us in the light. Slowly, uncertainly we sit and gradually calm ourselves, waiting in the presence of the Guardian.

(Here a silent period is spent: this should be as long as possible. As a general rule this level of the visualisation can be brief, but with practice it may be lengthened.)

As we sit, we gain many realisations concerning the Guardian: what he conceals, what he reveals, how he may keep us from passing where we might destroy ourselves, and how he may prevent us from destroying that which we do not understand. In the lamplight his face is slowly revealed to those that dare to look upon him. He sits still, unmoving, unmoved by our presence, yet we feel a huge vigour and power flowing out from him; it encompasses us, enters into us and triggers energies within ourselves which we have never known before.

(A brief silence here.)

As we sit in that underground chamber, we slowly realise that the scent in the warm air is changing. At first it was the odour of many animals, seeming to come from the earth itself; then the resinous and sharp smell of herbs and healing plants arose from the leafy platform at the end of the chamber. Now this astringent smell is replaced by that of flowers. Faint at first, then with increasing presence, we smell the perfume of many different flowers, as if the blooms from a rich wild garden have been scattered all around us.

As this complex and delicate sequence of perfume grows stronger, we realise that a figure is standing at the edge of the raised platform. In the lamplight we see that this is a beautiful young woman with long flowing hair; she wears a simple robe woven with a pattern of plants and flowers. The figures of the Guardian has receded into deepest shadow, though we know that he remains seated on the platform. The lamplight reflects from the brilliant colour of the young woman's dress, revealing first one plant, then another, then scenes and images, woven in and out of the flowers, hidden deep within the pattern of the fabric.

We look upon her long golden hair and cornflower blue eyes, and feel that her presence lifts many shadows from our hearts, our personal shadows that the Guardian had drawn up from deep within us. The young woman steps across the chamber, and as she moves the perfume of flowers grows intense; the sound of her robe is like the rustling of a great garden in early morning wind. At the entrance way, she lifts her hand and we see that she holds a small living branch with fresh green leaves, buds and opening flowers. We pause to look upon her standing at the doorway.

(Here a short silent pause is made.)

Now the young woman beckons to us, and we follow her through the tunnel and up the sloping way towards the surface. We emerge into red sunlight, shining directly into our eyes, making them water. Even as we recover our sight, we realise that the woman has vanished and that we stand back at the original clearing in the first oak forest, in the light of sunset. We have emerged where we began, coming from a passageway concealed within the roots of the oak tree, out through the rocks which also release the tiny spring into the glade.

In the trees we can see the movement of many animals making their way through the woods, and we hear the evening song of birds. The forest is filled with a sense of restfulness and peace.

(Here a brief pause is made.)

We realise that our guide and his companion animal wait at the edge of the glade, and know that we must travel with them down the narrow deer trail through the trees. As they lead us out of the forest, the sun truly sets, casting long shadows through the trees. At the very edge of the forest our guide bids us sit and rest. Once again the great sense of peace that fills the land at sunset washes through us, and we close our eyes to sit in silence at the threshold of day and night.

(Pause here.)

Gradually the sounds of the oak forest fade away, and we quietly return to our outer world. In our inner vision the trees dissolve, and we feel the springy grass beneath us become the surface of a chair. We slowly open our eyes, and return to a familiar room. Our meeting with the Guardian and with the Maiden is over.

Notes may be made at this point, or a discussion if required. It is important that people are not forced in any way to share their experience, and no demands should be made upon anyone unwilling to describe what occurred during the visualisation.

REFERENCES

1 Stewart, R J (1987) *Living Magical Arts*. Blandford Press, Poole, and *Advanced Magical Arts*. Element Books, Shaftesbury
2 Stewart, R J (1989) *Elements of the Creation Myth*, and (1990) *Elements of Prophecy*. Element Books, Shaftesbury
3 Stewart, R J (Ed) (1990) *Psychology and Spiritual Traditions*. Element Books, Shaftesbury
4 Stewart, R J (1989) *Where is St George?* Blandford Press, London (May also be obtained from Sulis Music, see note 15)
5 Stewart, R J (1986) *The Prophetic Life of Merlin* and *The Mystic Life of Merlin*. Arkana, London. Also (1988) *The Merlin Tarot*. Aquarian Press, Wellingborough
6 Matthews, C (1987) *Mabon and the Mysteries of Britain* and (1989) *Arthur and the Sovereignity of Britain*. Arkana, London
7 Stewart, R J (Ed) (1987) *The Book of Merlin*. Blandford Press, Poole
8 Stewart, R J (1990) *Celtic Gods and Goddesses*. Blandford Press, London
9 See notes 1 and 3 above for discussions of such beings
10 Stewart, R J (1987) *Cuchulainn*. Firebird Books, Poole (Extracts from the ancient Cuchulainn Saga are available on cassette from Sulis Music, see note 15)
11 See note 3
12 See notes 1 and 5
13 Stewart, R J (1990) *Music, Power, Harmony*. Blandford Press, London
14 See notes 1, 5 and 8
15 This visualisation and others by R J Stewart, John and Caitlín Matthews and a wide range of other authors are available on stereo cassette from Sulis Music, BCM 3721, London WC1N 3XX

THE GOD WITHIN

By

JOHN MATTHEWS

One of the most difficult and limiting factors in the development of masculinity is the inability of most men to relate to their own inner selves — or, even more profoundly, to the great masculine images of deity which lie outside themselves. Bob Stewart's chapter in this book deals admirably with this subject; in what follows I have turned to one of the more neglected gods — the Persian Mithras — in an attempt to provide one answer at least to the problem.

6

THE GOD WITHIN: A RITUAL OF SELF-EMPOWERMENT FOR MEN

Mithras, God of the Sunset, low on the Western main,
Thou descending immortal, immortal to rise again!
Now when the watch is ended, now when the wine is drawn,
Mithras, also a soldier, keep us pure till the dawn!

Rudyard Kipling: Hymn of the XX Legion

INTRODUCTION

We hear much today about men finding or coming into their power — a curious dichotomy considering the degree to which masculine energy is directed towards and channelled through strength and power of a physical and intellectual kind. What is therefore needed, it seems, is a way for men to open themselves to their own inner strength — spiritual and magical. In the past this was never a problem: men had a part in the Mysteries equal to that of women. In more recent times the emphasis has been so much oriented towards Goddess spirituality that the God has tended to take a back seat. In the same way, men who sought empowerment have tended to approach it by way of a priestess or through a Goddess-oriented group. Only in the last few years have men begun to found their own groups, and to work magically together towards the realisation of their own personal power. Even so, rituals which help to focus these latent energies are few and far between — whilst those who work alone, either from choice or circumstance, have to make do as best they can.

It is at these solitary workers that the present ritual is aimed, though it can be done by a larger group with the minimum of re-arrangement. Essentially it is intended to give the solitary man a chance to focus and dedicate his power in a ritual setting, in a sufficiently non-specific form to enable those of most persuasions to operate within it. What follows is based, loosely, on an ancient Mithraic ritual, which has survived in a somewhat altered form in an Egyptian version dating from the 4th century AD. It was first edited and translated by G R S Mead in 1907, and has not appeared elsewhere since that time. I have adapted it freely to suit the present requirement and have made additions in accordance with the intention of the ritual, which is to establish the inner god within the individual. This concept is itself of great antiquity, and refers to the Divine Spark which is seen as dwelling within each individual. In working to establish contact with this inner strength the Candidate is in fact opening himself to a source of tremendous energy which can become an extremely valuable step towards self-realisation. Those who wish to examine the original text may do so in Mead's *Echoes from the Gnosis*, Vol VI (The Theosophical Publishing Society, 1907).

MITHRAS: THE FELLOW IN THE CAP

A few words about Mithras and Mithraism in general are probably appropriate as this point, since it is hardly a well-known religion today and has received far less attention than several other forms of ancient Mystery teachings such as Hermeticism and Orphism — both of which are connected to the same strand of mystical realisation from which Mithraism derives.

Essentially, the cult of Mithras originated in Persia several centuries before the birth of Christianity. It absorbed many of the beliefs and teachings of Iranian Zoroastrianism and even older Vedic traditions which originated in India. It had a large following among the peoples of the Eastern world, and was taken up and propagated by the Romans in the 2nd century AD. During the next 200 years it became almost the official religion of the Roman Legions and, for a time, the most powerful adversary to Christianity — to which it bears many striking similarities. Indeed, the Western world very narrowly missed having Mithraism as its main religion, a thought which bears out the popularity and strength of the Mysteries.

Much has been done by way of reconstruction by scholars like Mead, Cumont, Vermaseren, Tyson and Ulansey, and readers who wish to follow up on this contact will find a brief reading list at the end of the chapter. Mithras was the God of the Risen Sun, and his initiates received the names of beasts and birds, such as

Lion, Raven, Bull and Bear. The cult thus betrays its shamanic origins, though these are lost in the later formalisation of the Mysteries.

The central myth of the God describes him as born from living rock within a cave, watched over by shepherds, and coming forth armed with a knife and a torch. He then endures a trial of strength against the sun, with whom he establishes a truce; then he pursues and catches the primal bull, riding on its back until it is exhausted and taking it back to his cave. Later the bull escapes and Mithras sends a raven to find it. He then captures it again, wrestles with it and finally slaughters it. From its blood spring corn and animal life. His cloak, filled with stars, billows out behind him and becomes the vault of the heavens. On another occasion, the dark god Ahriman attempts to destroy life on earth by flood from which Mithras rescues mankind by shooting an arrow at a rock, which causes it to burst forth in a perpetual fountain. Finally, he takes leave of the sun in a ritual banquet and ascends to heaven where he sits at the side of the father-god Ahura-Mazda.

The parallels with Christianity are numerous. Mithras is, like Christ, a saviour god whose birth was celebrated on December 25th, and who stands between the might of the Creator and his creation, acting as a mediator. His followers practised baptism for the remission of sins, held a symbolic meal of communion with consecrated wine, and believed in sacramental grace, the rebirth of the spirit and the promise of eternal life. Mithras is associated with truth, and with the fires which burn away the dross of the spirit. His name, in Sanskrit, means simply 'friend'.

There were seven levels of initiation into the Mithraic mysteries, which were a closely guarded secret. The interpretation of symbolic carvings in the surviving Mithraic temples has enabled these to be restored, and we can be fairly certain what they were. The initiate who undertook all of these grades underwent severe tests and trials until he was totally at one with the God. *Corax*, the Raven, symbolised the air and the rituals attending this degree must have been to do with this element. *Nymphus*, the Bride, seems to have represented the element of water, and part of the ceremony almost certainly included a symbolic 'wedding' to the god. *Miles*, the Soldier, symbolised Mithras as the undying soldier God, and explains why he was so readily accepted by the Roman Legions. Part of the ceremony of this grade included the presentation, on a sword-point, of a wreath, which the candidate then pushed off his head saying that Mithras was his only wreath. *Leo*, the Lion, represented the element of fire, and his emblem was the fire-shovel. Initiates of this grade were apparently anointed with honey as a symbol of purification. *Perses*, the Persian, was a guardian of the fruits of the Earth, and therefore of the element of earth. He too was anointed with honey, which seems here to have stood for the seminal fluid which was spilled upon the Earth when the Cosmic Bull was slain. *Heliodromus*, the Sun-Courier, received a whip, a torch and a radiant halo on initiation. He seems to have stood in the position of the sun itself, crossing the heavens in his fiery chariot. He was second only to the supreme figure of Mithras, represented by the final grade, *Pater*, the Father. Here the initiate stood in for the God himself, and was clothed in the cloak of the God. His is the wisdom of total realisation, and his symbols are the ring, the staff and the Phrygian cap of the God.

All of this is by way of introducing the reader to the figure of Mithras himself, who is at the epicentre of the ritual. However, it must be emphasised again that, unless he specifically desires to do so, the Candidate is not in fact invoking Mithras in person, but rather the principle of fiery inner strength which he represents.

NOTES ON PERFORMANCE AND PREPARATION

The text which follows, adapted from the ancient Mithraic ritual, is printed as it is to be performed. Notes on the performance, together with a glossary of unusual words or concepts, will be found after the text. They are indicated by an *.

Before your performance of the ritual you should fast for at least 12 hours, drinking only water as and when required. (This may be dispensed with in cases of medical need, such as diabetes.) If possible a ritual bath, containing cleansing or purifying salts, is recommended. A period of 30 minutes quiet meditation and breathing should be performed before beginning, in order to clear the mind of worldly concerns or worries.

You are now ready to set up your ritual space. Begin by making sure that you have sufficient space and time and that you will not be interrupted. (You need approximately one hour.) If you share accommodation it should be possible to arrange some time alone, and a 'do not disturb' notice can always be hung on the door. Disconnect phones or any other electrical devices likely to be distracting; remove your watch. You are now ready to begin.

Clear a space in the middle of the room and set up a small table to serve as an altar. On this, place a candle or night-light which you can leave burning unattended without it starting a fire. (This is a ritual which invokes the fire of the spirit, and all common-sense measures to prevent *actual* fire should be taken beforehand!)

If you wish, you may burn a little incense, of either the stick variety or the granular kind used with charcoal. If you already have a devotion to any deity place a statue or picture of this on the altar as well. A picture or statuette of Mithras would also be appropriate, though it is not essential (see Fig. 5). Museum shops which sell replicas of ancient artefacts are good hunting grounds for such items.

The ritual requires quite a high degree of concentration, which may result in a mild headache. If you find that you are not able to sustain the required level, do not worry. Simply stop, study the ritual some more, until you feel ready to begin again on another occasion. Read through the text as often as possible so that you know what you are doing. Make a photocopy if you need to and annotate it as much as you require. All these points of preparation make for a smoother and therefore more powerfully realised experience.

The ritual takes two distinct forms, one verbal and the other interior. Italicised sections are meant to be spoken aloud. The parts in ordinary type are meditational images which may be read beforehand on to a tape-recorder or simply read and then visual-

Fig 5. Mithras approaching Sol. After Cumont: *The mysteries of Mithra*

139

ised at the appropriate moment. Alternatively, if you have a friend whom you do not mind admitting into your rite, you can get him to read aloud the passages in question.

THE RITUAL

The Father's Prayer*

O Providence, O Fortuna, bestow on me your grace — imparting those Mysteries which only a Father may pass on, and that to a Son alone — his immortality — making him an initiate of his own power, worthy of the sacrament which Mithras, the Great God, bestows through the power of his Archangel — and so that I, an Eagle by my own power, may soar to heaven, and contemplate all things.

The First Invocation

O Primal source of my origin, primal substance of my substance; First breath of breath, the breath that is in me; First fire, God given, for the blending of blendings within me; First fire of fire in me; First water of my water; Primal Earth essence of the earthly essence in me; Thou perfect body within me (name) son of (mother's name)* — fashioned by the Honoured Arm and Incorruptible Right Hand of the God in a World that is lightless, yet radiant with light; in a world that is soulless, yet filled with Soul.*

If it may seem good to you, translate me, now held by my lower nature, into the Generation that is free from Death; in order that, beyond the insistent need which presses upon me, I may have vision of the Deathless Source, by virtue of the Deathless Spirit, by virtue of the Deathless Water, by virtue of the Deathless Earth, by virtue of the Deathless Air; in order that I may become reborn in Mind; in order that I may become initiate; and that the Holy Breath may breathe in me; in order that I may adore the Holy Fire; that I may see the Deep of the New Dawn, the Water that purifies the Soul; and that the Life-bestowing Aether which surrounds all things may give me hearing.*

For I am to behold today, with deathless eyes — I, mortal, born of mortal womb, but now made over by the might of Mighty Power, by the Incorruptible Right Hand of the God — I am to see today, by virtue of the Deathless Aeon, the Master of the Diadems of Fire* — I with pure purities now purified — the human soul-power of me subsisting for a little while in purity; which power I shall again receive transmitted unto me beyond the insistent needs of the world which press upon me, I (name), son of (mother's name), according to the ordinance of the Great God* *which can never change.*

For even that is not beyond my reach — who, born beneath the sway of death, will, unaided, soar into the height, together with the golden, sparkling brilliance of the God who knows no death.

Stay still, O nature doomed to perish, nature of men subject to death! And straightway let me pass beyond the need implacable that presses on me; for that I am His Son — I breathe! I am!

THE FIRST INSTRUCTION

Close your eyes and visualise the Risen Sun before you as a bright Disc of Light. Draw in your breath three times as deeply as possible, pulling the light of the Sun into your body until you are filled with it. Feel yourself raised aloft on a cushion of bright air until you are in the midst of heaven.

There, you shall hear nothing, neither man nor beast; nor shall you see anything of the sights of the earth — all that you see shall be immortal. For you shall see, in that same hour, the disposition of the gods, ascending and descending from heaven.

Then, as you see before you the bright Disc of the God, wondrous rays of light come forth from it. One of these touches you, and draws you inward into the Light. There, in brightness and dissolving gold, you feel a great wind blowing upon you, and from within the Wind comes the face of the God himself, looking upon you. Then, laying your first finger to your lips in a gesture of silence, make the First Utterance.

The First Utterance

O Silence! Silence! Silence!*

Make the sign of the God (see Fig. 6, p.142):

Protect me, Silence!

Next 'hiss' forth the breath: *S! S!*
Then 'puff' forth the breath.

Then shall you see before you the face of the God smiling benignly upon you, and filling you with the light of His countenance.

The Second Instruction

Slowly become aware of the mighty cosmos opening before you: great stars and suns, planets and other celestial bodies encircle

Fig 6. Sigil for the God within

you, and are part of you. You are joined to the Greater World, which is part of you as you are part of it.

When you see, with your inner eyes, the realm of the Cosmos clearly, then you shall hear a mighty thunder-clap, which startles you. Now say again:

The Second Utterance

O Silence! Silence!

I am a Star, whose course is as your course, shining anew from out of the depths.

As you say this, visualise the Disc of the God expanding. After you have said the Second Utterance, 'hiss' twice more with the breath, and 'puff' twice more also. As you do so, be aware of a host of stars emerging from the heart of the Disc and filling all the firmament. Then say again:

O Silence! Silence!

And, when the Disc is opened fully before you, behold on all sides an infinite number of fiery doors, which are shut fast. Prepare then to speak again:

The Third Utterance

Hear, and give ear to me (name), son of (mother's name), O Great God, who with thy breath has closed the Fiery Bars of Heaven. Twin-bodied One; Ruler of the Fire; Creator of the Light; Holder of the Keys; Inbreather of Fire; Beauteous in Light; Fire-hearted One, whose breath gives light; Thou who finds joy in Fire; O Lord of Light, whose body is of Fire; Light-Giver and Fire-Sower; Fire-loosener, whose life is in the Light; Fire-whirler, who sets light in motion; Thunder-rouser; O Glory of Light; Light Increaser; Controller of Light Empyrean; O thou Star-tamer!

Oh! Open to me! For on account of this, the bitter and implacable Necessity that presses on me, I do invoke Thy deathless names, innate with life, most worshipful, that has not yet descended into mortal nature, nor been articulate by human tongue.

*Eeo/oeeo/ioo/oe/eeo/oeeo/ioo
oeee/oee/ooe/ie/eo/ieo/oe
ooe/ieooe/ieeo/ee/io/oe/ioe
oeo/eoe/oeo/oie/oieeo/oi/iii
eoe/oue/eo/oee/eoeia/aeaeea/eeee
eee/eee/ieo/eeo/oeeeoe/eeo/euo
oe/eio/eo/oe/oe/oe/ee
ooouioe!

The Third Instruction

Utter this chant with fire and spirit unto the end, In this way you are calling upon the Immortal Dwellers of the Cosmos. And when you have uttered this, you will hear the crash of thunder all around, which will seem to shake you to your foundations. You feel yourself almost shaken apart by this, but ever you keep in your regard the Great Disc of the Sun in the heavens. Then, once more utter:

Silence!

Then you shall perceive the doors thrown open, and the inner Cosmos that is within shall be revealed to you, so that joy and rapture fill you, and your spirit rises up to meet the joy of the Cosmos.

Then, hold yourself steady and, gazing steadily into yourself, draw in the Breath of the Divine Other. And, when this is done, you shall say:

The Fourth Utterance

Draw nigh, O Great God!

As you speak these words, be aware of the rays of the Disc turned upon you, until they are upon all sides. Then behold the God, in the flower of age, fairest in beauty and with locks of flame, in a white tunic and a scarlet mantle, wearing a crown of fire.
Salute him with the Salutation of Fire:

The Fifth Utterance

Hail Lord! O Thou of mighty power; O King of mighty sway; Greatest of Gods; O Sun; Thou Lord of Heaven and Earth; O God of Gods! Strong is Thy Might!

O Lord, if it seem good to Thee, make announcement of me unto the Great God, who has begotten and created Thee!

For that a man (name), son of (mother's name), born of the mortal womb, and of spermic ichor — indeed of this ichor which at Thy hands today has undergone the transmutation of rebirth — one who, from so many tens of thousands, is transformed to immortality in this same hour, by the God's good pleasure, a man who presumes to address Thee, and supplicates with whatever power he has.

Upon this utterance the God stands before you revealed, and then begins to circle around you, leaving tracks of fire in the midmost of the air. Gazing intently, send forth your voice in a prolonged 'bellowing',* like unto a horn call, expelling the whole breath, with pressure on the ribs. Then say:

The Sixth Utterance

Protect me, Mithras!

When you have said this, you shall behold more doors thrown open, and issuing from the depth seven virgins in silken robes, with serpent faces and golden sceptres in their hands. These are they who are called Heaven's Fortunes.*
When you have seen these things, make salutation thus:

The Seventh Utterance

Hail, Heaven's Seven Fortunes, virgins august and good; you sacred ones who live and eat with the Great God! You holiest protectors, Hail!

Hail thou, the first! (name)
Hail thou, the second! (name)
Hail thou, the third! (name)
Hail thou, the fourth! (name)
Hail thou, the fifth! (name)
Hail thou, the sixth! (name)
Hail thou, the seventh! (name)

There come forth others, too; seven gods with faces of black bulls, in linen loincloths, with golden fillets on their heads. These are the Seven Uplifters of the Heavens. Unto each of these you make salutation by his correct name, thus:*

The Eighth Utterance*

Hail, Guardians of the Pivot, you sacred sturdy youths, who together revolve the spinning axis of Heaven's Circle; you who let loose the thunder and earthquake-shocks and thunderbolts, but who bestow upon me good health, soundness of body in every part, proper function of hearing, sight and touch, and calmness of Spirit in the presence of the Mighty Gods. O mighty ruling Lords and Gods of my inner Self!

Hail thou, the first! Luna
Hail thou, the second! Mercurius
Hail thou, the third! Venus
Hail thou, the fourth! Sol
Hail thou, the fifth! Mars
Hail thou, the sixth! Jupiter
Hail thou, the seventh! Saturn

When all these figures are present, in order, gaze upward into the air intently, and you will see lightning down-flashing and lights a-quiver and the earth a-shake. Then a God descends, a God of mighty and transcendent form, with golden locks, in the flower of age, clad in a robe of brightness, with a crown of gold upon His head. This is He who moves the Dome of the Heavens and changes its direction, now up, now down, according to the hour.

Then shall you see lightnings leap from His body, and stars also, that fill the firmament. Straightway, send forth a 'bellowing', prolonged, with belly-pressure, and concentrate all your senses towards working in harmony, saying:

The Ninth Utterance

Lord of my Self! I ask that you abide with me, within my very Soul! Leave me not! For the Great God bids you remain.

Gazing reverently and solemnly upon the Great God, with 'bellowing' prolonged, thus salute Him:

The Tenth Utterance

Hail, Lord! Thou Master of Water! Hail, Founder of the Earth! Hail, Prince of Breath! Hail, Lord of Fire!

O Lord, being born again, I pass away through being made great and, having been made great, I die unto myself and wake unto myself.

Being born from out of the state of birth-and-death that gives birth to mortal lives, I now, set free, pass to the state transcending birth, as Thou have established it, according to Thy ordination in this Mystery, which is now ended, as it is begun, in peace and harmony.

Having said this, slowly allow the image of the God to be absorbed into yourself, where you perceive that it will remain for as long as you need it. Then, sing the chant of the Dwellers in the Cosmos once again, beginning at the top and descending through the scale.

Eeo/oeeo/ioo/oe/eeo/oeeo/ioo
oeee/oee/ooe/ie/eo/ieo/oe
ooe/ieooe/ieeo/ee/io/oe/ioe
oeo/eoe/oeo/oie/oieeo/oi/iii
eoe/oue/eo/oee/eoeia/aeaeea/eeee
eee/eee/ieo/eeo/oeeeoe/eeo/euo
oe/eio/eo/oe/oe/oe/ee
ooouioe!

Now open your eyes and extinguish the central light and the incense. You should then make a general prayer to give thanks to the powers which have attended on you throughout the ritual. This can be either very general or very specific. A suggested formula might be:

I give thanks to Mithras for the light with which he has blessed me throughout this time, and I acknowledge that the fire I bear forth into the world is the fire of inspiration and not destruction. I give thanks also to the Seven Powers who have been with me and who have guarded and guided me through this ritual.

You may find that you get somewhat overheated during the performance of the ritual, which is, after all, derived from the fiery presence of Mithras. Therefore you might wish to drink some water at this point. Also, spend a little time in quiet contemplation before you depart, and write down any realisations which came to you during the ritual. If you feel that you derived nothing from the performance of this ritual, do it again after a space of about two to three weeks, and thereafter as necessary until you make contact with your inner God.

COMMENTARY AND NOTES

General Note   Throughout, the various aspects of the God which appear in the ritual may be seen as aspects of the Inner God of the Candidate, the deeper and more powerful Self which lifes hidden beneath the surface, but may be readily evoked. It should be understood that this, and other concepts of a similar kind, are not to be confused with psychological archetypes. The idea of the Inner God is an integral part of Western Mystery teaching; by performing this ritual you are, in fact, contacting the eternal, undying spark of the Divine within you — a concept wholly in line with Mithraism as well as a powerful means towards self-realisation and getting in touch with your inner power centres.

The Father's Prayer   There were seven grades in Mithraism, of which the Seventh, Pater, was the highest. Thus at the very outset of the ritual, the Candidate is calling upon the most powerful aspect of his own inner potential, the Father, and requesting it to initiate his lesser Self, the Son, into the mysteries of his own god-head. It is this inner, more powerful Self, which the ritual invokes throughout, and later in this same opening prayer, as 'an Eagle by my own power.' In this form, you rise above your own nature and are enabled to see, from on high, your true potential.

The First Invocation   Here you are invoking your perfect, cosmic body from within the depths of your own substance. The body when perfect is a microcosm which reflects the greater macrocosm; its substance is of an elemental nature: air of earth, water of earth, fire of earth, earth of earth, and so on through the four primary constitutents of creation. Fire, the essence of Mithras himself, is that which blends all of these.

Naming the Mother   The naming of the Candidate's mother is specific and important in the ritual. It is unusual in such a very masculine-oriented setting, but helps to balance this by acknowledging the derivation of all life from the Great Mother. If the candidate is uncomfortable with this, or is adopted, he may substitute the name of any Mother Goddess to which he feels an affiliation.

Aether The substance which, in the ancient Mystery teachings, was considered as more than air, as ensouling the very essence of gods and men, in which these could intermingle.

The Deathless Aeon A term borrowed from Orphic sources, which refers to the ruling God of the age and of Time. Mithras was certainly a God of Time himself, as is well attested in the various studies of his cult.

Master of the Diadem of Fire Another term for Mithras. He was not, in effect, the Sun itself, but something more powerful and cosmic. The Sun is his archangel, or projection, so that in all the symbology of the Solar Disc and the Rays of Light, we may see this as *filtering* the power of the God in such a way that it is perceivable by men.

The First Utterance I have retained the translation 'Silence' throughout. However, the actual word is Greek *Sige*, which represents the Supernatural Mother of all things, the Bride of the Divine Principle. Thus, by invoking her in this way, the Candidate is allowing the presence of the Divine Feminine to enter the ritual as a foundation upon which to build. The 'masculine' speech is thus framed by 'feminine' silences.

The Sign of the God The original text contains no instruction for this, and I have therefore supplied a sigil which represents the God in his form as a lion-headed deity with a serpent coiling around him. As such, he represents a central pillar of force, with the serpentine wisdom coiling around it.

The 'Hiss' and the 'Puff' The breathing in of air, the taking in of the divine essence into the lungs and expelling the non-divine, human air from them is described by various Classic writers. Here the action is represented by the sibilant sounds of the breath escaping between the teeth, and by puffing out the breath in short bursts. Even Mead in his commentary admitted himself somewhat baffled by the precise purpose of this. I have chosen to retain it as an integral part of the original ritual. Mead mentions a passage from the Egyptian *Book of the Coming Forth By Day* which describes the 'hissing' and 'clucking' of the 'Great Cackler' — the Great Bird or Mother who hatches the eggs of men. Further analogies would also seem to exist between this breathing and the cleansing breath of Yogic practice, and perhaps also refers to the 'Dragon's Breath', a drawing in and expelling of the fiery breath of Creation itself.

*Chanting This looks more difficult than it is. If you read through it a few times then practise chanting it aloud it soon develops an extremely powerful momentum. For chanting use a singing voice rather than a speaking voice, allowing the vowels to be carried by the breath. Sound each letter fully, pausing for breath where the / sign occurs. It will be noticed that the chant consists of seven groups of seven plus one. The purpose of this is to raise power, and originally invoked the seven levels of the Mithraic initiation (see Introduction). In the case of this ritual, it invokes the energy levels of the Candidate. Each one of the seven sections of the chant should, if possible, be vocalised on a rising scale of seven notes. While chanting, visualise in order the seven levels of the subtle body. These power centres of the body can be visualised at the base of the spine, the root of the belly, the solar plexus, the heart, the throat, the brow and the crown of the head, in turn. The repetition, on a descending scale, at the end of the ritual is to help in the process of 'winding down'. The pronunciation of the vowel sounds is as follows: E or EE = AY; O or OO = OH; I or II = EE; U = OO; A = AH.

*Bellowing This curious injunction sounds strange to our modern ears. In practice, however, if a sound not unlike a long-drawn 'Moo' is produced, in base tone, the effect is more than impressive. Mead notes: 'This is in some sort an inversion of the sacred syllable *om*.' This breath and sound should be visualised as coming from the root of the belly — thus producing a very deep, vibrant sound.

*The Seven Virgins, Seven Gods/Youths In Mystery teachings these figures, also called the *Tychai*, represent many things; the cardinal virtues, the colour spectrum, the planets, the seven levels of initiation or the seven liberal arts. I have therefore left them unnamed, to allow the Candidate to supply his own references, according to personal preference. They may, for example, represent certain qualities which the Candidate wishes to activate within himself, such as Truth, Strength, Honesty, Kindliness, Love, Joy, Bravery. The fact that the virgins have serpent faces and the gods bull faces betrays the Egyptian influence on the Ritual. They are also appropriate to the use of Mithraism.

The Guardians of the Pivot/The Seven Youths — These are, in most versions, the planetary rulers, the inner representatives of the Zodiac. In many representations of the God, Mithras is shown surrounded by an arch of Zodiacal symbols. I have left the names in the form that we are most familiar with in the West.

The Pivot or Axis of the Universe is the centre around which the Cosmos moves. By invoking it, the Candidate is in effect centring himself in himself, and allowing the lesser aspects of his nature to circle around him. Mead admirably refers to this as 'The Celestial biosphere of his (man's) own nature.'

REFERENCES

Cumont, F (1953) *The Mysteries of Mithra*. Dover Books, New York

Ferguson, J (1970) *The Religions of the Roman Empire*. Thames & Hudson, London

Godwin, J (1981) *Mystery Religions*. Thames & Hudson, London

Ulansey, D (1990) *The Origins of the Mithraic Mysteries*. Oxford University Press, Oxford

Vermaseren, M J T (1963) *Mithras: the Secret God*. Chatto & Windus, London

Wynne-Tyson, E (1972) *Mithras: The Fellow in the Cap*. Centaur Press, Congleton

ANIMUS: THE UNMENTIONABLE ARCHETYPE

By

EAN BEGG

Ean Begg's chapter brings us face to face with a difficult and sometimes controversial subject — the masculine element within women. We are used to hearing — often at great length but with less sympathy — of the feminine element within the male. The animus, as Ean Begg makes clear, is still something of a no-go area, particularly among women themselves, who are perhaps as unwilling to acknowledge this aspect of themselves as are men their femininity. Yet the animus, if it is properly acknowledged and understood, seems to offer a way towards reconciliation of the sexual and contrasexual problems facing people of both genders. To face the inner, fragmented self is never easy; yet just as the anima can help men to re-establish contact with a part of themselves long held in abeyance, so the active principle of masculinity present in women preserves what Ean Begg calls their 'heroically questioning quality, that wants to understand, reach to the heart of the matter, enter the forbidden room and persevere to the end of the road.' For men experiencing problems coming to terms with their own femininity, as well, perhaps, as with the masculine in women, this chapter holds out hope.

7

ANIMUS: THE UNMENTIONABLE ARCHETYPE

Though winning few medals for nappy-changing along the way, I have spent much of the last 20 years preaching in season and out of season on the theme of the return of the Goddess and the re-emergence of her underground stream. Black Virgins, moving Madonnas, Marian apparitions, the whore wisdom, Lilith, all aspects of the repressed feminine principle have found in me an enthusiastic champion. This self-appointed mission was not entirely altruistic, but grew out of my growing awareness of the need to realise the energy of Eros and anima, stagnant and coagulating within the souls of men — especially middle-class, middle-aged British males like myself. No matter how mixed my motivations, clutching my self-awarded credentials, I shall now venture into the Passchendaele of male psychologists, the realm of animus in women.

Jung's theory that all human beings have a contrasexual element within them — anima in man, animus in woman — which must be acknowledged, engaged and conjoined with if psychic totality, the purpose of life, is to be achieved, is now gaining some acceptance in the literate West. Whether one agrees with this idea or not, it is luminously clear and has venerable antecedents. We were, taught Plato, spherical monads until the gods kippered us, since when we have been condemned to seek, sorrowing, our lost other halves. Since the marriage at Cana, Christian mystics have described what is now called self-realisation in terms of the inner nuptials of Christ and the soul. For Jung this *mysterium coniunctionis* is the alchemical great work that sets the seal on the individuation process.

Radical revisioning and revisionism is transforming and destabilising the fixed structures of thinking that have dominated the last half century. Jung's model of the psyche and what gives it meaning has not been immune to a palace of revolution and a *trahison des clercs*. Creeping standardisation and the ideal of ecumenism are eroding much of what makes Jung's psychology so distinctive and original among the more ego-orientated schools. Many analytical psychologists are almost as embarrassed to use the traditional vocabulary of their craft — shadow, anima, animus, persona, archetype, collective unconscious, individuation, Self, psychological types — as they are by Jung's interest in alchemy, the *I Ching*, astrology, mediumism, gnosis and UFOs.

The word that has suffered most from prevailing attitudes, to the extent that we are almost on the point of losing the whole rich experimental teaching that informs it, is *animus*. My chief aim in this essay is to examine the causes of this decline and to show what I believe to be the importance of preserving both the word and the idea, as well as how this might be achieved. In presenting my case, I do not intend to brandish statistics or invoke opinion polls, for the soul slips through their satanic mills. I shall not be ashamed to be anecdotal, while avoiding case reports, and rely on my memory and impressions of 20 years working analytically with many hundreds of men and women, as well as on my own experience that of my friends, and common sense.

Most men are quite receptive to the idea of anima. She is glamorous, fascinating, often appears as a beautiful unknown woman in dreams; she is Diotima, Beatrice, the eternal feminine who leads us on, up and in; the Holy Grail who is the object of the quest. To have her, writes Jung, is 'the whole adventure of life'. She has, of course, her destructive side: as Lorelei and siren she lures men on to the rocks of life and down to the watery graves of unconsciousness; as the unregenerate Lilith she rapes men and withers them away; as Belle Dame Sans Merci she enslaves those who follow her path and leads them to despair, sickness and death. The anima-possessed man is a pathetic victim of his moods, unable to sustain a relationship or an erection, a second-class, hysterical woman, impotent in thought and deed. The negative anima is Maya and she makes men believe impossible things, especially about women, causing much surprise, anguish and rage to real women who become entangled with her through men's projections. Nevertheless, with all her feelings, she animates in an interesting and romantic way.

When, however, we come to consider the animus in Jung's writings, it is a different story. Although his function, just like that of the anima, is to relate women to their individuation process and act as guide of souls on their journey, somehow he fails to come across to women today as a desirable or interesting inner companion. Jung's statement (*Collected Works of C G Jung 9*, pt 2, p15) that: 'Man has the feeling — and he is not altogether wrong — that only seduction or a beating or a rape would have the necessary power of persuasion' when confronted with animus-possessed women has not been fogotten or forgiven. 'Why', women may say, 'should his thing be more important than my thing?' If Freud gave women penis-envy, is Jung not guilty of making them compare odiously their masculinity to men's femininity?

A perusal of the relevant references in the *Collected Works 7* shows that Jung says much about the animus that is both just and convincing. This, however, is not the impression that has prevailed. To begin with, he wrote very much less on the subject that he did about the anima, and clearly found it a hard nut to crack: 'If it was no easy task to describe what is meant by the anima, the difficulties become almost insuperable when we set out to describe the psychology of the animus' (*Collected Works 7*, p205). His way of expressing himself is sometimes unfortunate enough to make even the mildest of scolds bridle: 'An inferior consciousness cannot *eo ipso* be ascribed to women; it is merely different from masculine consciousness' (ibid, p 206).

Jung encountered and encouraged many gifted and educated women, from Sabina Spielrein in 1908 until the end of his life, and was in his turn influenced and impressed by them but, as well as being a radical genius, well ahead of his time, he was also the child of his age — the Victorian era — and its prejudices. The Basle University of the 1890s was an all-male world and intellectual preserve. He was closer in spirit to Dr Johnson's scoffing attitude towards women preachers than to the remarkable new breed of woman scholars like Jane Harrison and Jessie L Weston, who were to enhance academia and arouse its admiration at the turn of the century. Since their time — and Jung's — the world has undergone more and greater changes than at any other period in recorded history, and nowhere more so than in the position of women and the relations between the sexes. Much of what Jung, a true pioneer, in his way, of women's liberation, has to say about animus, and therefore about women, now sounds dated and sometimes patronising. Emma Jung's excellent essay on animus is 60 years old and needs to be seen and valued as a period piece, as well as a statement of timeless principles, and the same is true of most first generation Jungians writing up to the 1960s.

It is difficult not to sympathise with the current suspicion of all labelling and any too-clear definition of pairs of opposites. The disadvantage of such a tendency, however, if carried to extremes, is that all certainties become blurred and mushy, until we are no longer sure what it means to talk of masculine and feminine. To reconnect with what once seemed clear, in the mist of perplexity, however fruitful, we have to re-assert the crude differentials of anatomy and biology and ponder on their consequences while hesitating to equate masculine and feminine totally with male and female. To begin with, male and female genitals are designed to do very distinct things and correspond to a contrasting genetic programming. 'Eggs are expensive, sperm is cheap', says a biologist of Cornell University, Thomas Eisner. A man gets something out of his system whereas a woman takes someting into hers, something that may alter her life inexorably and radically for at least 20 years. Both men and women are instructed by their genes to reproduce but, while the male order is to go out and fertilise the world, picking women who are young enough to bear and bring up his children and attractive enough to arouse him sexually, nature's programming of the female is more discriminating. For the good of the race, women, as the agents of natural selection, need to be very choosy about who fecundates their precious ova. Such inbuilt characteristics may well be subject to the manipulations of conditioning, but they cannot be eradicated, and each male or female baby embodies its own specific archetypal patterning anew.

Here, it seems to me, is where some feminist thinking becomes one-sided, insufficiently based on common sense and objective reality — in fact, animus-y (belonging to the animus) in the old perjorative sense. The failings and failures of men and the world they have largely created are manifest and cry out for the re-evaluation and development of the feminine principle, as well as the active collaboration of women illumined by the creative intelligence and spirit that is animus. Undoubtedly our ideas of gender roles and the appropriate way to rear and educate boys and girls need to be questioned, but only within the framework of the real differences between the sexes that have been observed to exist at all times among all peoples. Experimentation seems to demonstrate, for example, that little girls are more advanced in verbal skills, while little boys are better at hitting a moving target with a missile. Little girls are more interested in sharing and communicating; little boys are more directly competitive. I take this to mean that at an early age girls are rehearsing the feeling skills that will enable them to raise children and teach them to talk, communicate with other women of the tribe about matters of interest and importance relating to its well-being and, if they have time, to domesticate and teach men the arts of love. Boys, on the other hand, are practising to be hunters and warriors, communicating no more than is necessary for the fulfilment of these functions.

Feminists, insofar as they have not completely given men up as a bad job, seem to be saying: 'Why can't a man be more like a woman?' If only one could catch the little monsters early enough, perhaps one might condition them to be more gentle, related, intimate and nurturing. Surely there is something drastically wrong here unless conditioning of the human being as *tabula rasa* is all there is, and innate, inherent tendencies are totally discounted. Women, it is true, can be great warriors: the Amazons may be no more than a vestigial folk-memory, but the Romans' amazement at Celtic women's fighting qualities is part of history, and in Celtic myths the great heroes are taught the arts of war — and love — by women like the fabulous and eponymous Scathach of Skye, who taught the hero Cuchulainn the arts of war. Nevertheless, it is difficult to believe that nature designed breasts to be cut off, Amazon-style, to further the practice of archery. In her arrangements for the human species, the woman must hold her baby to her breast to nourish it, and as a reward for this enforced bonding she can know a sweet pleasure that a man holding a bottle to the infant's mouth will never experience.

We are, however, not just our biological lowest common denominator — nature and survival may require us to adapt to our environment in many and varied ways and there may be many factors that make up human individuality of which nothing is known. It is, for example, impossible to tell whether a horoscope is that of a man or woman. Furthermore, the so-called male signs and planets may predominate in a female chart and vice versa. Thus, at least astrologically, the spectrum between the 'ultra-masculine' man and the 'ultra-feminine' woman is a wide one and encompasses an enormous range of possible variations. But, already, we have begged the main question, as the quotation marks indicate. How can we be sure what are feminine qualities and what masculine, beyond the physical differences and those widely agreed, though not by some feminists, to be innate and discernible in early childhood, whatever the conditioning?

If we invoke instinct we are once again treading on dangerous and contested ground. Take the mutual attraction between the sexes. In theory, supported to some extent by surveys, women are attracted to men who are taller than they are; are slim, with small, tight buttocks, show themselves to be strong yet sensitive; possess a good sense of humour and a nice voice and withal are mad, bad and dangerous to know. Men fancy women who have long, shapely legs, well-formed upward tilting breasts, long blonde hair, big blue eyes, who are gentle, tender, entirely interested in them and their welfare, softly spoken and not too talkative or assertive. Unfortunately, dating agencies have few such paragons on their books. Fortunately, in reality, people know that these are collective ideals and are content with sexual partners and spouses who fail to live up to them. Beauty and love are in the eye of the beholder and what lies behind the eye of the beholder will probably be the imprinting of certain images in early childhood.

What may lie further behind is the pure male or female archetype — the animus or anima as *Ding-an-sich* (the-thing-in-itself). Inner images of the opposite sex are partly influenced by mother, father, elder brothers and sisters, other relatives, nannies and various members of the household. Their origin may also be more mysterious. I was about eight years old, sitting with my family in a beautiful restaurant high in the Savoy Alps, when a vision of beauty in the form of a woman entered the room, and I was struck with the force of a mystical experience by the reality of Aphrodite, though I could not have expressed it thus. My mouth fell open and I gazed in amazement and worship at this goddess, and something of my rapt state must have touched her, for she came right up to our table and acknowledged me with a smile and curtsey. 'Oh brave new world', I could have cried with Miranda, and indeed the world was not the same again, for I now knew, in the Gnostic sense, the wholly other, numinous and fascinating archetype that woman embodies. I no longer recall in detail the appearance of the one with whom I fell instantly in love. Was she blonde or brunette, junoesque or petite, peaches and cream or bronzed? I can't tell; but I am convinced that she bore little or no resemblance to my mother, sister, nanny and godmother who were sitting there with me, or to any other woman I had clapped eyes on till that time. Could we have been lovers in a previous incarnation; was she an angel sent to awaken me; did she correspond to my nascent ego as a compensatory soul-image, glamorously seducing me from a fate of all too prevalent conformist good-boyism? I shall never know, but that summer on the Lake of Annecy my young life was disturbed for a spell by the hints of sexual delights and torments.

Behind all the personal matter, might there be further layers, what Szondi called the familial unconscious, in addition to the needs and presuppositions of the clan, tribe, nation and species? Contrary influences seem to apply their tensions to the soul, pulling the individual away from the familiar and collectively approved to the unknown and exotic. All my ancestors for centuries have been Scottish, and urge me to keep the race pure and continue the tradition, but neither my brothers nor I have obeyed their injunction and, to our children, being English or Scottish does not seem to be an issue. Thus has Aquarius cleansed the Augean stables of clannishness and nationalism with a new commandment, first given by Simon Bolivar at Angostura in 1811: *Mézclanse!* (miscegenate). In traditional societies, operating as small groupings, exogamy has generally been favoured, though clannishness is strong. Now this deviant principle operates autonomously on a grand scale without the need for organisation. Sensible and traditional marriages pair like with like to preserve and enhance the family fortunes: romance is the quest for the new and exciting in the trans-class, trans-national and trans-racial world of today. Models of animus and anima are thereby greatly diversified, with the assistance of mass travel and television.

On the other hand, to return to the general principles involved in boy meets girl, 'the fundamental things', to quote the old song, 'apply, as time goes by'. Some of the new images have not yet clicked with instinct. The sad truth is that women do not find most new model, new age men particularly exciting or attractive. They may be wonderful helpmates and househusbands, but somehow they fail to fit the inbuilt picture of man in the feminine psyche. Men know this and avoid the kitchen, depriving themselves of much possible pleasure. I somehow doubt whether re-writing all children's books and television programmes to present such models as prime objects of desire is going to change things much. Consciously women want men to contribute more to family life, but their unconscious fascination with the traditional, dominant male often keeps them from valuing the new ideal in practice.

French men used to have two unflattering terms for feminine characteristics they disliked in the days before English women developed a rather different reputation. '*Institutrice anglaisé*, English school-mistress, denoted a prissy, spinsterish, opinionated, unswitched-on woman, who shunned the company of men: the victim of her conditioning, no doubt, but also recognisably, in Jungian terms, the victim of the punitive animus who jealously guarded her against falling into a relationship with another man. The other phrase was '*elle est anglaise*', a euphemism for 'she is having a period'. It meant more than that, including the excuses that some animus-dominated women employ to avoid the possibility of making contact with a man.

Let us pursue this subject on to some very dangerous ground indeed, women and menstruation. I wish to leave on one side the related issues of men's attitudes towards menstruation and of the interesting possibility of analogue observable cycles in men, to bring together two unmentionables — menstruation and animus. It is clear that many women suffer little from their monthly periods and experience little or no pre-menstrual tension, but for the majority of women — and the men in their lives — menstruation and the effect it has on their emotional state does play a major part in their world of relationships. This is not just a by-product of so-called civilisation and its discontents; in some traditional societies it is — or was — the custom for women to be segregated during their periods, to rest and introvert on their hammocks in the women's house, where they were looked after by their tribal sisters. Does not this example point to the natural monthly emergence of an altered state of consciousness that should be taken into account? The developed world, incidentally, is far less tolerant and understanding of women's real needs in this respect.

Jung's statement, quoted above, about beating, rape and seduction as methods of treating the animus, may be relevant here. If you are a man, put your hand on your heart and say truthfully whether you have never felt like this when the woman in your life is expecting her period. We men may be very bad at dealing with these monthly crises, but so often we have the feeling that whatever we do is wrong, and this may be simply because nature has ordained this time when women should be free of the burden of burdens, the magnum opus of relationship to men. I am not suggesting that women are only under the influence of the negative animus during their menses, but there is a clearly established pattern here which men are well aware of, whatever they may call it.

This curse that God laid on Eve, which her daughters still experience with every moon, has also been called the *wise wound*. Through it the primal woundedness of our nature is re-opened and touched, the fallenness from the unity and integrity of Eden. Each individual recapitulates the fall in successive stages: conception; sexual differentiation; quickening; birth, with its farewell to womb and placenta; the cutting of the umbilicus; every separation from the mother, culminating with weaning; school; puberty; loss of virginity; marriage and children; children's home-leaving; death. Men have their cycles too, but since they are mainly invisible and unconscious they lack women's wisdom of the wound and resent its incursion into their routines. In Genesis, man's main curse is that he shall identify with work and its difficulties to the exclusion of love. Thus woman and Pscyhe are wounded for the loss of Eros. Women are more conscious than men in this realm, but their very consciousness and the desire to throw more light on the man they sleep with may scare him away.

Maybe the Age of Aquarius will reveal a true conscious androgyny that will allow the sexes to relate in a new way satisfying to each, but for the time being women are not finding what they seek in men. Fathers were not there for them, lovers shy away from intimacy, husbands have their work and their golf, sons leave them. If the man changes just because the woman tells him to, he becomes a tamed and shabby tiger or a crafty manipulator. Is there anything women can do other than give men up as a bad job?

Some women I know, not least the woman I share my life with, have found a solution — or it has found them — in the form of an inner masculine figure whom they have dreamed into being, whom they can invoke at will and who is always there for them, right behind them, to strengthen and support. My first spiritual teacher called him 'My shining one', and it is often as a being of light that other women have described him to me, even women whose experience of their father was thoroughly negative. Such figures often appear in dreams — a shepherd, a shoemaker, a gardener, a man with golden hair, a prince, a saint, a seigneur or one whose name gives a pointer to his essential nature. The whole art lies in keeping him *real*, keeping the connection alive. For the woman who can do this there are many blessings, not least the harmonising of her relations to men out there in the phenomenal world.

This practice of active imagination with an unseen figure, far from being an extravagant novelty, goes back at least 4000 years and has always been part of the prayer life of Christians. St Teresa of Avila would speak to God in a most uninhibited manner, and the Catholic tradition of visiting the Blessed Sacrament provided the opportunity for 15 minutes talk with a fatherly God about one's needs or whatever was of concern and interest. St Gregory Nazianzen called prayer a conference or conversation with God; St John Chrysostom saw it as a discoursing with the Divine Majesty; while St Francis of Sales described it as a conversation of the soul with God, by which we speak to him and he to us. In the devotion to Jesus, meditation on his bleeding gashes plays a major role — the ancient prayer known as the Anima Christi contains the words 'hide me within your wounds'. So, given the historical lack of satisfactory male figures on whom to base a relationship to the animus, women — and men — have long had recourse to the idealised and one-sided images of father/creator of the universe and his divine, perfect son. It is striking that it is to Christ's anima we must pray to be made drunk with his blood, cleansed with the water from his side and healed with his sweat before being hidden in the wounds. Women, in menstruation or parturition, could surely identify with such an image although, bizarrely, a male one. *The Treasury of the Sacred Heart* contains three pages of prayers to the most holy wounds with successive addresses to the wounds of the left and right foot, the left and right hand and the side.

This gorily surgical school of devotion finds little favour today, but it is based on sound psychological principles. Encounter with the archetypal world may be dangerous, but it is also healing. Generations of suffering women of simple faith have eased their wounds by raising them up to those of Christ. In the very flow of blood and water the supreme spiritual animus is at one with the way of all women. Five, the number of humanity, the senses, the fingers and toes, is also that of the wounds of Christ, which manifest the sorrows of incarnation. We are all sent painfully down here to the holy planet of purgatory, like angels on an assault course. But the spiritual animus has an anima, a sacred heart, that nourishes all creatures and radiates unconditional love. This is the Holy Grail that we have once more lost and this time, it seems, women, rather than Arthur's knights, must seek and achieve it if the Wasteland is to be redeemed. It is not only possible but salutary and essential that women, rather than abandoning the quest for the relationship to the positive masculine in favour of an increasingly exclusive sisterhood dedicated solely to the Goddess, should look for it first in the right place — the imagination that Blake called Jesus.

At this point in my first draft of this essay I was feeling stuck: there are so many of us today who lose the old and cannot gain the new, for whom the old words and images of Christianity no longer work and the planned schizophrenia of active imagination seems too difficult or alarming, for whom the wisdom of the East expresses itself in a mode alien to the Western heart. Then something happened. I went to collect my post, amongst which was a fat cardboard parcel containing the *Arthurian Tarot* by Caitlín and John Matthews, beautifully painted by Miranda Gray. Here were a score of masculine images specifically designed as meditation instruments, capable of speaking to the condition of women today. Each has his story harking back to the pre-Christian era, an archetypal story belonging to our Western tradition, perhaps forgotten but still latent within the soul, an image for each stage of the individuation process.

The most archaic is the Three of Stones, the phallic chalk giant incised in a green hillside, like Cerne or Wilmington, the ancient smith god with his hammer, anvil and tongs; Wayland or Govannon. He tempers the sword of the spirit, woman's logos-blade of power and eloquence. Number 20, the Sleeping Lord, resting in the natural landscape of Logres of which his barely discernible form is now a part, awaits the right time to return and unify the warring elements within us as the symbol of regeneration that will make all things new and redeem that which was lost. The Seeker, the Zero card, one foot on the rainbow bridge that leads to the adventure of incarnation and the quest that only a perfect fool would undertake, reminds us that we chose the right conditions in which to be born, however unpropitious they might seem, including, most importantly, whether we manifest in the body of a woman or a man, balancing out apparent inequalities through successive incarnations. There are many figures representing the varying moods of the quest. The Sun, a beautiful naked youth, trots optimistically along on his white mare whose blond mane matches his, on a fair path beside a clear stream (the perfect *puer aeternus* toyboy who invites woman to play). The Stone Knight is silhouetted against a sombre wintry lake where no birds sing, weaponless save for a chessboard in place of a shield, warning us that the journey has its moments of despair at the reversals of fate, inviting woman to introvert and play chess with him. The Grail Knight is a bard or troubadour whose well-tuned harp soothes the sadness of soul and plays the music of life to which we must dance. The Sword Knight stands dedicated and ready for the fray, attentive to the energy of two worlds that streams from Glastonbury Tor, while the Spear Knight gallops one-pointedly at full tilt to do battle, symbolising woman's need to trust in her intuitive powers. All are responsive to an invocation of any oppressed maiden or damsel in distress.

Of those great fathers, the kings, one, Amfortas the Fisher, lies, blood pouring from his wounded thigh. Until the right questions are asked and the Grail is achieved, the land will remain waste and the creative nature of both men and women will lie impotent. Among the lesser powers of the deck, the Grail King has the answer; he wears the antlers of the old herdsman of wild things and lord of the forest, Cernunnos. He is seated cross-legged, his back against a great oak in a clearing beside a stream, an earthenware cup in his right hand and a golden bowl hanging from a branch before his eyes, above a green flat stone. As guardian of the Goddess or her priestesses he is replaceable annually or with the seasons. This recalls the Celtic woman's privilege to bestow the friendship of her thighs on whom she chose as worthy, just as the sovereignty of the land demanded as consort none other than its greatest hero. Arthur is the archetypal king-emperor and it is on sovereignty's throne that he sits with drawn sword to survey and, if necessary, defend the land. He has been to the Underworld to redeem Guinevere and the hallows of Britain; as the great leader he has won his twelve great victories and driven the invader from the realm. He gazes in steadfast melancholy, without hope and without fear, at what he knows must be, since Merlin has foretold it; the unfolding of the Goddess's law of cause and effect and the inexorable cycles of success and failure, birth and death. He is attended only by a chough, *nigredo* and *rubedo* incarnate. All the works of men, he can see, are no more than children's sandcastles, lapped by the encroaching tide. Yet there remains hope in the Flowering of Logres once again with the return of the one we call Arthur, and the last of the Major Arcana illustrates something of what this might mean both for the land and the individual. Fatherhood was a curse to Arthur but here, rejuvenated, he dances in a round with a little girl and boy within a rainbow in a rich landscape while a butterfly and a bee pass by. It is this joyful companionship with fathers, brothers, lovers and husbands that so many women yearn for and despair of finding.

Six of the greater powers remain. Merlin must take precedence, the mediator of the Goddess's will to humankind and almost only wizard in literature to surrender to the greater power of love. He is women's magician animus, that in everyday life can help them to do four things at once and think nothing of it. At a more profound level he stands for feminine wisdom; the intuition, feared, respected and often persecuted by men, which knows things hidden from the rational mind. Above all, it is that rare blending of authority and relatedness that gives a woman power to face all things and overcome all difficulties. Merlin-women know when to use the Grail and when the Spear.

Taliesin, greatest of the bards, sings of the oneness of nature and the many transformations that he underwent in the long succession of lives that he recalls. Continuity through rebirth is one of the secrets of the Goddess that were repressed with the advent of Christianity: through the cord that encompasses him, he passes this knowledge on to the boy and girl who sit at his feet. In the end, he says, we experience all forms of existence through the totem animals, the different stages of life and the archetypal modes of being, specific to the two sexes. Gawain, Hawk of May, is, in the subtitle of John Matthews' book about him, the Knight of the Goddess. He is the active young warrior animus who empowers women to stand up for themselves, but he is an impersonal spirit who may not be projected on to a real man and possessed. He illustrates this truth in the great quest he undertakes to discover what it is that women really want. Through kissing the ugliest hag in the world he learns the secret — women wish to have their own way. When he kisses her she assumes her form of beauty and asks him whether he would rather have her thus by day or by night. He has understood the answer to the riddle, for he begs *her* to choose, after which she is beautiful all the time. Man might learn from Gawain, if they could remember to rub their women's backs, listen patiently to their complaints, spoil them a little and kiss them — or even leave them benevolently at peace — during the pre-menstrual, menstrual and menopausal periods.

The White Hart captures exquisitely the archetypal moment when a man sees a woman for the first time and falls captive to the Goddess in her. The knight kneels before the maiden who carries water in a blue vessel, symbolising, perhaps, a new Aquarian equality between the sexes, while she, avoiding his eyes, gazes at the great stag standing amid the bluebells, bathed in golden light at the end of the glade. Such a beast appeared to Lancelot and Guinevere by the Pont de Secret in Brocéliande to remind them of their responsibilities and the spiritual nature of their love. The Victorians idealised women while exploiting them, so women have grown wary of their vocation as the eternal, spiritual feminine which leads on and up, purifying and gentling the hearts of men in the process. The sixth sign of the Zodiac, like this sixth arcanum, reconciles the virgin and the whore and transcends the false dichotomy between them in the quest for that purity of heart that wills only one thing.

If it is to be women who now undertake the burden of the quest for the true and the good, then they must come to know the Grail Hermit, for they will meet him on the way, perhaps in many different guises. Here, he sits by a menhir carved with symbols both Christian and druidic, writing in his book, while his eyes connect with far-away things. The fire of consciousness blazes in the centre of the clearing and his simple beehive hut lies beyond. Simplicity, like that of Percival the fool or Alice in Wonderland, who surpasses him as a questioner, is the essential quality of the seeker. Martha, cumbered about with much serving, is careful and troubled about many things, while her sister Mary knows that but one thing is needful. Woman's, and above all, superwoman's work is never done, so how shall she find time and energy to undertake the quest? But women do, in ever greater battalions, and far outnumber men in the quest-groups and workshops of today, just as they were prominent in the early Church that marked the inauguration of the new Age of Pisces. But for women who are still too beset by business, while yearning for more space, the Grail Hermit demands time for reflection and an answer to the question *whom does the Grail serve*. . .what is all this for? It is *women* who are seeing the dirty uses of the world today and asking of materialism, success and unsatisfying relationships: 'Is that all?'

The Green Knight, clad in leaves, wielding a runic axe, who turns up on your doorstep in midwinter bringing a wren and all the snow into the hall with him, is very different from the Devil of other decks. He belongs to an older dispensation than the Judaeo-Christian Satan, proffers no curses or accusations, and has no chains to enslave men and women to their animal nature, though he himself is a nature spirit. He comes to invite any who dare to the game of life and death, and to a deeper understanding of the male-female relationship. To know him is to face and overcome every mortal's instinctive fear of death. Dealing with death has always been one of women's mysteries. They are reborn after a little death each month, and in war or peace risk extinction, their own or their baby's, with each pregnancy and labour. They know traditionally that there are fates worse than death, like loss of integrity, and may often choose to return their lives to the Goddess while their minds are far from disturbed. They are the most potent sensitives and channels who communicate between the two worlds for, like Morgan and Arianrhod, they hold sway in the beyond and link it to our lives in the here and now. A prophetess of our century, Alice Bailey, has predicted that before its end we will have transcended the last frontier and found proof of the survival of the soul after death.

I have seen and used many Tarots, and love especially the old Marseilles deck, but I know of none so rooted in the past of these islands and yet so adapted in terms of its human images for meditation by modern people. If they lead the user inward to study and become familiar with the ancient matter of Britain, a fund of healing myths will thereby wreak their magic on the soul, but to tell oneself one's own stories, to let the cards speak to one's own imagination, so that one's own individual sagas may emerge, may be even more salutary. I am talking, not of divination and the answers to specific questions, but of permitting a talisman to find its way to you, that can act as a companion for as long as needed. Women who have problems in relating to a positive image of the masculine might try picking at random one of the cards mentioned above and carrying it with them in their heart throughout the day. The Tarot is, however, but one aide-memoire to stimulate the store of lost or semi-effaced archetypal images of man that lie latent in the heart of woman. Women may seek for their own portrayals of animus in paintings and photographs or, better still, draw and paint them from their own imagination and watch and pray for them to appear in dreams, where all of us entertain angels unawares. A woman dreamed recently that she was a goddess crouching naked behind the head of a sleeping man, and while stroking his head she gave birth.

It will be obvious that I see women's quest for the right image of the right man at the right moment to be essential for their wholeness and psychic hygiene, which should on no account be given up in despair or anger. This is not mere theory or pious hope but a conviction that grows out of my work with many women who seem to be deprived of contact with a fitting masculine model in the psyche and thus leave themselves open to unsatisfactory relationships, partly elicited by their own complexes, and to possession by their own unconscious animus who degrades and torments them in a variety of ways.

This essay began with my fear that, owing to the hostility of many women and the pusillanimity of many men, the concept of animus was in danger of repression. What partly led me to this judgement was a recent book by a friend and colleague of mine, Heather Formaini, *Men: The Darker Continent*, which offers many interesting insights based on interviews about the impasse that men and women find themselves in today, but makes no allusion to the concept of animus. In an earlier work, *Sex and God*, however, she gives trenchant utterance to her rejection of the contrasexual principle: '...the concept of the animus...has kept women silent in Jungian circles. The practices of the theory (of anima and animus) reinforces and perpetuates all the old ways of enhancing the lives of men while diminishing not only the lives but the true power of women. The animus in women is in my view the voice of the patriarchs, of the Inspector of the World.' Admittedly, this is how things often work out in practice, but to abandon the work on the animus for this reason is surely defeatist and merely compounds the problem. Feminists fighting against sexism in the front line may lack the perspective to see how much has already been gained — are not the patriarchal walls of Jericho already crumbling, less dramatically but just as surely as those of Berlin? Overt sexism is now considered just as reprehensible as racism and just as illegal, which is far from implying that it no longer exists and that women are not still horribly abused by men. Woman presidents, prime ministers, entrepreneurs, clerics and even bishops no longer occasion much surprise, though in the world of high finance and heavy industry there are still few women bosses. If women still find themselves doing more than their fair share of the household chores, or more than they would wish to do, is this not perhaps because of their lack of an integrated animus to stand up for them so that they may firmly and fearlessly arrange matters in a way that suits them, daring to face the consequences in the interests of truth and integrity, as so many of them are doing today, necessitating a metanoia in their men.

A woman analyst of an older generation, Irene de Castillejo, sees utter sincerity and a sense of honour as essential in eliciting the positive animus. But first his various manifestations, as in the *Arthurian Tarot*, must be differentiated: '. . . if only we can succeed in splitting the animus into distinct and separate persons we can deal with him. Then I can kneel and ask the blessing of the priest, befriend the feeble-minded boy, face firmly, but with due respect, the devil and order the mealy-mouthed sycophant out of my house.' Her personal helpful animus manifests as a torchbearer who helps her to focus and concentrate on one thing (like Mary rather than distracted Martha). 'He throws light on the jumble of words hovering beneath the surface of her (women's) mind so that she can choose the one she wants, separates light into the colours of the rainbow for her selection, enables her to see the parts of which her whole is made, to discriminate between this and that.' De Castillejo also boldly solves the problem of Jung's alleged favouritism towards the anima by awarding this invaluable organ to women as well as men, without completely invalidating the principle of contrasexuality.

June Singer describes the positive animus in similar terms, as the clarifier and also as 'that masculine drive that enables her to break through the limitations that being a woman has imposed for centuries on end.' She is very aware of the hostility Jung's animus theory arouses in women but in a later book also points out how men have suffered from the repression of anima, a repression from which they are beginning to be freed by the work of the Women's Movement. While recognising the limitation of Jung's Victorian *Zeitgeist*, she claims that he was able to transcend it intuitively through his understanding of alchemy, his great life's work.

'It is true that Jung was bound by his times and his society with respect to his views about men and women and their sex-linked qualities. But his genius was such that he soared above these stereotypes in his search for the archetypal Masculine and Feminine.' The secret of this interplay is conscious androgyny. . . ' the rhythmic interplay of Masculine and Feminine within the psyche of one individual.'

I have not noticed, as Formaini claims, that women are cowed into silence in Jungian circles — certainly not in professional settings where they are often in a majority and position of power, which many of them wield with skill and tact that well exemplify the integrated animus. My own work with female analysts taught me to respect the authority of women without having to fear it. Experiencing the recognition of animus by my analysands and their attempts to co-operate with this fertilising and soul-guiding content of the soul, I have felt myself free to adopt the role of midwife and nourisher which is most proper to the craft of analysis. In our dance, it is the woman and her spiritual animus who should lead, and I who must learn to trace and follow their steps. The animus is the heroically questioning quality in women, that wants to understand, reach to the heart of the matter, enter the forbidden room and persevere to the end of the road. On one level it may lead a woman to find what she wants to do and enable her to do it. More profoundly, it is the unflagging quest to discover the purpose of her life and the means of realising her self in it.

REFERENCES

De Castillejo, I (1974) *Knowing Woman*. Harper & Row, New York

Formaini, H (1990) *Men: The Darker Continent*. Heinemann, London

Hurcombe, L (ed) (1987) *Sex and God*. Routledge, London

Jung, C G (1959) *The Archetypes and the Collective Unconscious*. Routledge, London

(1959) *Aion. Collected Works* vol 9, pt 2. Routledge, London

(1966) *Two Essays on Analytical Psychology. Collected Works* vol 7, 2nd ed. Routledge, London

Jung, E (1959) *Animus and Anima*. Spring, New York

Matthews, C and J (1990) *The Arthurian Tarot* and *Hallowquest* Aquarian, Wellingborough

Matthews, J (1990) *Gawain, Knight of the Goddess*. Aquarian, Wellingborough

Shuttle, P and Redgrove P (1986) *The Wise Wound*. Penguin, Harmondsworth

Singer, J (1973) *Boundaries of the Soul*. Gollancz, London

(1977) *Androgyny*. Routledge, London

THE GOD OF WICCA

By

RICHARD WYBOLD

In the modern religion of Wicca the God holds sway over a large proportion of the ritual life of the coven. Harking bark to ancient folk-lore, dying and rising gods, with their strong ties to the agricultural year and the harvesting of the corn, he is a powerful figure who has been far less written about than the more ubiquitous Goddess. In the chapter which follows, Richard Wybold, for a number of years a respected figure in Craft circles, gives his own poetic, allusive account of the God as experienced by his worshippers. He finds that the ancient patterns still exist, but more than this, sees the God as making an appearance in the modern world of computers. Truly a God 'for all seasons', the dark-light Lord of Wicca is offered here as a powerful re-assertion of an ancient, once-dominant strand of masculinity.

8

THE GOD OF WICCA

If any Wiccan male is asked to describe the Goddess of the Craft, he may well talk for an half an hour on his vision of her, her beauty, her wisdom, understanding and generosity. For to him, she holds the essence of all the outstanding women he has ever met or imagined, and more. But ask him the question, 'What is your God like?' and he is very likely to answer, 'Ask a woman.' Because if he has to be described in isolation, for exactly the same reasons, the woman's picture is likely to be deeper and more meaningful.

It really makes no sense to discuss him by himself at all. Probably the first essential of Craft belief is the perfect complementary balance of God and Goddess. While humankind rightly invests them with immense power, like humans they need and receive each other's support and love, and it is the endless dance of their love that is the power-spring that sustains their people.

A valid symbol of this may be seen in the familiar symbol of Yin and Yang, in its constant rotation and its unbreakable intermingling. But in this case it should not be seen in its usual presentation of white and black. For the relationship here is not what the symbol is often said to mean, the male element being the one-way source of light and energy, and the female the receiver, changer and reflector of that power. Though the moon is one of her symbols, the Lady is not to be thought of as visible only by the reflected light of her Lord. Nor the antithesis of light and darkness anything to do with it. To get the feeling of balance, try seeing the symbol in the gold of sunlight balanced by the vivid green of Earth's mantle of vegetation. Let it start to rotate; then see this become the clothing of the entwined figures of the divine pair in their endless dance.

From the fact that, in modern coven practice the priestess, the

Goddess's representative, is the one who casts the sacred circle and rules all that happens within it, it is sometimes believed that the God is seen as secondary, the subordinate consort of the supreme Goddess. He is not.

As in human society the walls of patriarchy are crumbling in all but a few cultures, the balance naturally changes. The recognition of feminine power, the strength of the Goddess and her identification with the whole Earth and all life upon it spreads and strengthens. It is right and necessary that in the mundane world the woman's contribution in all areas beyond the 'traditional feminine' should grow and be recognised. But this implies no belittling of the masculine in daily life, nor of the male partner of the eternal dance. It is right that the Lady, so long denied and disregarded by the many, should now have centre-stage and spotlight for her solo, and that both men and women should leap up cheering her, but it is the great joy of her Lord to stand and watch, smiling at the honour rightly paid to her.

We cannot tell what element of truth there is in accounts from the time of the witch trials, of mainly female covens under the sole command of a male Magister representing the Horned One, and of course written down as 'the Devil'. No question, he existed, but that he was the absolute boss of a group of adoring or over-awed women seems extremely unlikely. And that these people had totally lost the Goddess, who had undoubtedly been there in much earlier times, is equally unlikely. The persecutors, with their patriarchal minds, would of course say that 'obviously' a man must be in charge, what else? And either the questioners' victims had such love for the Lady that she was never mentioned, or much more likely, if she was, the reaction would have been 'Lies, rubbish — tell us what you did with The Devil.' Just as today with Sunday newspaper reporters! And with very little chance of acquittal, the truth was useless in defence and irrelevant to the prejudged charges. And had the accusers listened, no doubt they would have said, who is your Lady but Lilith, the source of Temptation and Sin!

The Lady, then, is mistress of the circle representing the whole Earth on which we stand, and as the mother of all living it is to her that most petitions are addressed. For the young child, though he or she may turn to Daddy for defence against the frightening schoolteacher (non-loving authority) or the bully next door (hostility for no known reason), turns to Mummy for the unfailing listening ear and the provision of all other needs.

Though she may pronounce the decision and the blessing, it

is a foolish priestess who does not give full weight to her priest's counsel and wisdom to balance her own intuition; her hot line to the Goddess is not immune to all interference from the self, and he sees from a different angle but with no less validity. And at the appropriate moments, she is the first to offer the respect and adoration due to the First Father, the Protector and Champion of life both male and female.

The way in which mankind sees its deities reflects the life of that age and place. As civilisations change, so do the guises in which the God appears. In a hunting society, he is the father of both hunter and prey, responding to the need of the hunters to find the skills to succeed and bringing the prey within their reach, but also holding the balance, stimulating the fertility of the wild herds to maintain their numbers. And of course he is not only in the stag, king of his own tribe but at the mercy of man and of the large carnivores; he is also in the wild boar and those same big cats who can bring down the unwary human hunter.

Where animal husbandry is the dominant activity, his spirit is seen inspiring the seasonal rut of goat, ram and bull. Among a people concerned mainly with crop growing, his is the force of the rising green shoots and (at least in temperate climates) of the benevolent sun ripening the mature grain. From this concept of him as the spirit of the corn comes the idea of his 'death' at harvest time, the so-called Lammas sacrifice, of which more later. (It may be interesting to speculate on what concept of him would be held by peoples primarily dependent on fishing — for the sea is usually seen as the province of the Goddess.)

The next great area of human activity is the fashioning of artefacts; and now the God is seen as the archetypal craftsman, Wayland and Smith. From the forging of sword and ploughshare it is a short step to the machine, liberating man from wearisome hand labour, giving to the many the possibility of time for recreation, creativity and study. So in today's world, what can and should his primary image be the millions now divorced from the forest and the plough, in cities far from the sea? This is not so obvious, and perhaps accounts for the weight of attention now focused on the Goddess. For in every family home she is recognisable, reflected in the woman as carer and provider. The God is not so obvious, though he is still, as always, there in the father, consort and protect. But as he was the Master Smith, now one may see him as the Master Programmer, weaving the patterns of unimaginable numbers to free and extend the mind of man as his muscular strength was extended by the machine.

Some pagans today see science and technology as hostile forces bringing destruction into the life of Earth's creatures, but it is never science itself that is guilty, only greedy or aggressive humans. Like magic, science is a neutral force to be used as man wills, wisely or unwisely. The Master Programmer builds in so many options and possibilities for us to use, but he does not seek to control our use of them. His only law is that in our search for our personal goals we avoid harm to other Earth-dwellers, human or animal. For the follower of the God to withdraw into the forest to listen to him is good and necessary, but to wish to stay there, playing no part in the attempt to build a decent society for one's urban fellows is not service to him.

Today, the Lord of Forests and of the Hunt is best served by the one who devotes his energy to the protection of those forests and of the creatures who dwell in them. No longer need we take the lives of beasts for our survival, though it was always rare that the hunt for food threatened a species. That threat is more recent; the greed for skins, ivory or feathers for the adornment of town-dwellers far away, rather than as honest trophies of a necessary hunt, and the destruction of habitat for roads, dams or timber, bring forth the anger of the God and the tears of his Lady. And do not doubt that angered enough, together they have the power to avenge their beloved creatures, for mankind is not their only care.

Gods come in different sizes. In a Roman home there were the images of the household gods above the hearth, personal to the one family. This process extended through local gods of places felt to be sacred, officially deified emperors (a few remain today!) to the principal pantheon of that society. It seems to be only the religions stemming from the Middle East (Judaism, Christianity, Islam) that have put up the idea of The One True God, and because of the ruling ethos of the time, decided that He must be male. Elsewhere, people have found it more real and more instinctive to live with the gods of natural forces, of a location, of a people, of activities.

The Great Architect of the Universe just cannot be imagined and is rather pointless to address or speak of — certainly not as a He, nor even as a He-She. The Force is perhaps nearer the mark. If we cannot visualise what is going on in the core of a super-cooled Cray computer, created by the ingenuity of mere humans, how can we form any concept of how the Force works or what its intentions are? Wicca concerns itself with deities which personify the highest qualities and powers that we on this planet *can* conceive of, towards which through many lifetimes we may climb a little way. They are the father and mother of all life on this planet. Whether our Lord and Lady serve a higher power which is conceivable to them, cannot concern us. We may look into space, but we will find the God in the eyes of our fellow man, and closest in ourselves, if we can look deep enough.

In most religions the priest's role is to interpret established doctrine to the people, to tell them how they should behave in order to please the deity or avoid his disapproval. It is also to intercede with the deity, to put forward their prayers in some way that supposedly the ordinary worshipper is not to able to do alone. He is the advocate licensed to address the judge, the diplomat seeking concessions from the foreign ruler, and the herald proclaiming his royal master's will. He is consecrated a Special Person, invested with power to administer sacraments, to pronounce divine approval of human acts and formal forgiveness of what are defined as Sins.

In Wicca the priesthood embraces all initiates, and all are in that sense, but only that, special people, because they have offered themselves and been accepted by the Lord and Lady. They take on duties to serve their fellows within and without the Craft, but receive no rights to bless, condemn or forgive. They claim no special power to know the Great Ones' will, and if another is harmed, forgiveness must come equally from the victim and from the doer's Self, with honest restitution where possible. But there is one real power of priesthood which is theirs; to have invoked upon them the presence of the God or Goddess. This is done in the circle at certain festivals, some for the Goddess and some for the God. The invocation asks the deity to 'descend upon the body of your servant and priest(ess)...' using the ritual name of the individual. They are then regarded as indwelt by the deity and in that role pronounce the Charge or message of the God or Goddess to their worshippers. The original Goddess Charge as we use it is well known and has been printed in several places, that of the God less so, though it is no less powerful and beautiful. The words used in my own coven I may not give, but the sense of them is conveyed by the invocation quoted in *The Witches' Way*, pp. 298-299 (J and S Farrar). The overshadowed priest will often speak in a voice quite unlike his familiar one, and may bring through inspired words beyond those of the usual Charges. To convey the atmosphere of this moment, which in our calendar comes at Lammas, nothing comes closer than the chapter called 'The Piper at the Gates of Dawn' in Kenneth Grahame's *The Wind in the*

Willows. The reader may recall this from childhood; if not, a visit to the junior library is recommended!

Around the seasons and events of the year as it is experienced in these latitudes are built the pattern of festivals celebrated by Wicca, and around them a legend of the life and relationship of the God and Goddess. This is a cyclic story which is repeated every year, not unlike the Christian calendar. In this picture the God is seen first of all as a child born of the Goddess, who learns the lessons of a young man. He grows to manhood, follows many pursuits and becomes the lover of the Goddess, now in her maiden aspect. He begets on her the Child of Promise and becomes her consort and protector. He stands in his height and full power at midsummer, and at harvest time, filled with strength by the sun. As autumn and winter approach, he fades into shadow, taking on his other main aspect of the Lord of the Gates of Death, the Comforter, receiving all living at the end of human and animal lifetimes, giving rest and renewal and preparing them to take on life again as he does, coming forth as the Child born at Yule. These are the barest bones of the story, and it is only a story put together by the people of an earlier time, on the patterns of their own lives, and inevitably influenced by other religions.

And just as the picture of the God may be conditioned by human lives, so the birth-life-descent-death cycle can be and has been too literally transferred on to him. To the ancient Egyptians, the sun aged and descended into death each night. He passed through the Underworld and his life was rekindled by magic for him to arise reborn in the new dawn. But they did no know what was beyond their own horizons. Today we know perfectly well that as we say farewell to the sun on his journey, he goes to illuminate the lives of friends we can speak with in the same moment in California, in Australia and India. We do not have to throw away the beauty and symbolism of sunset and dawn, but we *know* that somewhere he is shining at full strength on other humans. So how can we say, as many do, that he himself dies and is reborn with the year of Earth's seasons, any more than does the Lady? For she is not only of the eternal stars, but very much of Earth too, giving birth in due season but eternally renewing herself. He too is in all things and all places and does as he wills, showing us the aspects appropriate to our Earthly seasons. Just as some of his worshippers here see him falling in the cutting of the corn, he is in the same instant sowing his seed in another place, instilling life into green shoots. In the very same field a sick and weary beast lies down, and he is there with another face to take it into his rest. Corn king and holly king may be authentic enough characters of folklore, but they are not the God of the Craft, nor even aspects of him. Sacrificed kings are common enough in the legends of many lands, but kings they are, not gods. True, dying gods are found, again mostly in Middle Eastern beliefs; Osiris, Tammuz, Jesus. The concept of sacrifice is not a part of the central thesis of Wicca, though some traditions hold that the man who represents the god at Beltane should in ritual sacrifice his life at Lammas so that his blood should fertilise the fields for the next year. Sometimes this is acted out symbolically; the man is supposed to be dead and buried. It is said that in England a century or two ago, maybe every few years a man was actually killed in this way. He was always, they say, a volunteer who knew what would happen. All this may well be true, and the idea that if crops failed a sacrifice is called for is understandable, but it has nothing to do with the worship of God and Goddess. For in the charge the Goddess says 'Nor do I demand sacrifice.' The bodies of animals and men come back to nourish the Earth at their natural death, all is used again, so what need is there to offer fresh blood to the Earth, which is the body of the Goddess?

Corn spirits and tree spirits may be cut down to spring up again; men and heroes and kings have their time and are gone and in time may return, but the Lord of Wicca merely turns his head and shows us a different face. He is lord of life and of death at once and always. Though it may suit us in our ritual pattern to show him passing from one to the other, he is always both; he is Pan.

The God by day is the essence of the qualities of the male animal, the intelligent human, and more. He rejoices in the physical and the mental, he runs with horse and stag, he flies with hawk and swallow, he inspires the stonemason and the sculptor, the joiner and the woodcarver, the rugby player and the chess player. He loves best to dance with his Lady, but even alone he always dances. He can be a trickster, making fools of pompous and conceited humans, but without real malice. In everything he finds cause to laugh. Nothing rules or limits him but his own one law, to harm none. All pleasure is his sacrament, blessed for its own sake, needing no purpose or justification. He holds the banner of freedom and proclaims that the freedom of the male to be his own man steals nothing from the female, nor can her freedom to be fully herself take anything from her chosen mate. Pursuit is a game, but happy consent is the only outcome he seeks. Rampant he is, but a rapist he is never. Possession or ownership of the female is hateful to him. He ranges out and follows his will, and returns in time to his Lady. She does not doubt his return, and knows that his nature expects nothing of her but to fulfil her own will in the same freedom.

So the makers of rules and behaviour systems fear and revile him, call him a devil that threatens their tidy patterns. Their fear arises because they know well enough that he is there inside them too, and that at any moment they may let themselves throw off their sober hats and join his dance. And that the dance may turn to a wild laughing chase through the trees, men and women, forgetting all but his command to follow their nature, which is his nature. And his nature is always to reach out for his mate, to complete the dance in joyful union.

The God by night holds the key to pass as he will between the lands of life and of death. He deals in the secret things that make up the part of witchcraft people outside often believe to be sinister and thus threatening. Just as the 'threat' of the lord of bright nature consists in forcing to the attention the instinctive desires too often suppressed, the 'threat' of the Underworld lord lies in revealing ways to gain an understanding, which you fear may upset your neat and tidy, or deliberately untidy, ways of thinking. He may invite you to look into what you see as 'dark' corners of yourself and examine why they seem dark. He may teach the arts of the shamanic quest, of inner journeying, of shape-changing and divination. He may lead you 'down, down, down the dark ladder' and give you a fright, and laugh at the look on your face, but you will wake unharmed! He may put power in your hand, and make you think what you will do with it, which some call temptation. You will have to question your motives and foresee what may happen. All magical enterprises require a certain amount of daring. But you will never stand in danger if you remember the one law: *If it harm none*, do as you will. And that he has no possible wish or reason to harm body or mind of any living thing.

Remembering this, let us view the roles of the God in the seasonal celebrations of the Wiccan year. The Celtic year, on which our British calendar is based, starts from Samhain or Halloween, which marks the end of the agricultural year and the preparation for winter. At the darkest time of winter, the Sun Lord is deeply asleep, renewing his energies for the year to come, and his other self the Dark Lord is in attendance on the Lady, giving his protection, calming her with his gentle presence and diverting her with tales and songs of far past and far future while she awaits the imminent birth of the Child of Promise, which his Sun-self seeded in her some months before. The days start to lengthen once again, the Child comes forth and grows, takes from his mother the weapons of manhood and sets out on his journey. Already he knows that manly pursuits do not hold complete fulfilment, and he senses that somehow there is a Goddess to be sought and found, that only through her will he find completeness.

At the feast of Imbolc or Candlemas we find him striding about as a young and arrogant warrior, demanding that she shall show herself to him. Going to be the first of the four quarter candles, he invokes her presence. Nothing happens. Angry, he strikes out the light. Going to the next quarter, he calls again. Again nothing, and he strikes out the light. At the third quarter, he thinks 'she must be here this time' but again there is silence, and disillusioned, he puts out the candle. He stands before the fourth candle, apprehensive now, but committed to his foolhardy course for he sees no alternative. With hesitant voice he calls for her presence, but is not answered, and he must do as he has threatened and put out the last light. He is in darkness now and for a long time there is silence, as the realisation sinks in that she is not to be commanded. Then out of the dark comes her voice, in the words of the Goddess Charge: 'Know that thy seeking and yearning shall avail thee not, unless you knowest the mystery, that if that which thou seekest thou findest not within thee, thou wilt never find it without thee, for behold, *I have been with thee from the beginning* and I am that which is attained at the end of desire.'

As the young warrior, he continues on his journey of adventure, growing in strength and comeliness, and at the Spring equinox, virile and eager, he finds again the young Maiden Goddess. Wand upraised, he goes from quarter to quarter while she, at the cauldron, now eagerly awaits him. Together they clasp the wand and plunge it into the cauldron:

> *The Spear to the Cauldron*
> *The Lance to the Grail,*
> *Spirit to Flesh,*
> *Man to Woman,*
> *SUN to EARTH!*

In the joyful dance that follows, all are sprinkled with water 'blessed by the seed of the Sun, arising in his strength in the sign of Fire.'

Love is tasted and found good, a child may follow, but that is for the future. The young Sun Lord dances on his way, exulting in his new-found power and fully enjoying his freedom. At Beltane, all people and all creatures, under the symbol of the may blossom, gather in the greenwood for the great festival of celebration of life. He gladly returns to his lady and is welcomed. They dance as accepted lovers, they exchange the wine of light and of shadows, and he willingly accepts the commitment as father and protector of the Goddess's lands, people and creatures.

At midsummer, the height of the Sun God's year, we might expect him to be exulting in his power and all the aspects of his masculine strength. One might expect this to be the time for the greatest emphasis on God-power. But this is not so at all. The young man who was confused and foolish at Imbolc, whose approach was so wrong, now in his full maturity has understood how to find and call on the Goddess, and now at the height of his own power he honours and celebrates her in all her three aspects. In the rite, three priestesses represents her, at first hidden behind leafy branches. With the cauldron containing hot charcoal, the priest, speaking for him, casts the first incense and invokes the Maiden, linking with her earlier awakening of his manhood. The first priestess shows herself. He invokes the aspect of the mature woman, lover and mother, linking it to his own full powers of manhood. He casts the essence of roses, and the centre figure, the high priestess, shows herself. In the third invocation he calls the Crone, and links her to his forthcoming sleep and reawakening, and the last priestess lowers her branch. Then the high priestess, as the synthesis of the three, comes forward and greets him. He has learned well and done well, and she honours him, and they dance together in the noon of the year.

Lammas is 'Loaf-mass', the celebration of the first bread from the grain of the new harvest. It is also the time of honouring Lugh, the god of Light, and therefore of the sun. So it is with us; we honour him now as the leader of his people. He has shown his power as the Lord of Life and the giver of life; later he will show us his face as the Lord of Death just as through the seasons the Goddess shows her different faces. So in the ritual he is invoked upon the priest crowned with the horned headdress, and in the Charge of the God he speaks to his people as the lord of life *and* of death, and accepts their homage. Behind the shining figure who has ruled us since spring we start to see the other shadowy figure who will now come forward and become more solid as summer dies. But with us today is not a man who has fulfilled his purpose, has fathered the child to the Goddess, who has raised and harvested the crop, whose usefulness is now over. This is Pan, of the horns and the hooves, the player of the magical pipe tunes that entrance us all, leading us in a great dance in celebration of the circle of life, love, death and rebirth.

The autumn equinox sees the passing over of power from the summer to the winter aspect of the God. It is not a struggle, an overcoming, but a natural and accepted process. Light and Dark are present together, represented by two priests, both, if possible, horned. The priestess speaks of the balance of the two hands, the left and the right, the dark and the light. The two aspects advance towards her round the circle, speaking in unison — for a moment they are one. She gives a hand to each, sharing her love equally. Then she announces a choice — for the winter months she will dwell under the protection of the Dark One. The Light shall take his rest until he is ready to assume his role again. He retires into the shadows, and the Lady circles in a stately dance with her winter love.

Halloween brings an end and a beginning. As winter closes in and the last leaves fall, the stores are gathered in and all made ready for the dark time. Those of the Craft family who have travelled return for the counting of heads, greeting the newborn, hearing who has passed on, reporting of their travels and contacts made. Guest of honour is the Dark Lord, and honoured he is, now fully in his winter aspect, a faintly perceptible veil between him and the living. With his sword he puts out the altar candle, announcing, 'Summer is dead.' Till that moment it has not been final. Now it is, and we accept his judgement. At his entrance he has opened the gates of his kingdom so that all those newly departed may for this night return and see that all is well with the Family before they resume their road to the Summerland. At the celebration of cakes and wine, the priestess brings him food and drink, which he accepts. His presence has brought a thoughtful silence, penetrated by the words of his message:

> I am the God who waits
> In the dead of the year, in the dark of life,
> In the depths of the wood where no birds sing;
> There will you rest again in my hand.
>
> Be fearless to look upon my deaths' head
> For I have other faces, and another hand
> To give again in that which I take.
>
> Come gladly when I call,
> The Great Mother holds my promise

180

And no thieves shall steal from you,
Or evil ones harm you,
In the compass of my hand.

Remember you trusted me in the spring green child places,
Finding enchantment,
Found me merry in summer attendance when you wed,
Feared not to meet me in the autumn forest hunt —
Shrink not from me in the winter snow.

Have you not seen the return of life to the Earth
Safe from my keeping?
Will I do less for you, my children?

I am the great lord of death who waits for you;
Have faith in life and trust in me.
As the great circle of the year
Brings forth the time of my domain
Take me into your hearts, as you have ever been in mine.

THE WAY OF THE WANDERER

By

PETER TAYLOR

Creation-myth, cosmic parable or visionary statement, this extraordinary text concerns the encounter between the Wayfarer (whom we may think of as Everyman) and the Wanderer (the Norse god Odin) who takes him on an amazing trip across the cosmos, taking in along the way such matters as the nature of the creation, evolution, and the place of mankind within it all. Drawing primarily on the Norse myths, but with an understanding of physics and worldwide spirituality, Peter Taylor skilfully weaves all of these strands into a remarkable visionary whole.

In choosing to write about an aspect of masculine deity which has had more than its share of identification with the more negative aspects of masculinity, the author performs a much needed task of re-alignment for the archetype; by showing that matters such as evolution and creation are not necessarily the sole provenance of the Goddess, he succeeds in restoring a sense of balance to the idea of male/female deity.

Here, then, is a masculine mythology which transcends the gender question entirely, and which reveals a totality of vision seldom encountered in contemporary Western writing. Readers may be unfamiliar with the mythology, but they will certainly find, as they read on, that its message is one which they already know, and which they have been part of from the moment they first drew breath.

9

THE WAY OF THE WANDERER

'Wandrer' heißt mich die Welt;
weit wandert ich schon:
auf der Erde rücken
rührt ich mich viel.
('Wanderer', names me the World;
widely have I wandered:
on the Earth's back
I have travelled far.)
Richard Wagner (*Siegfried*, Act 1; Scene 2)

A certain Wayfarer, having no clear journey's aim, strayed by seeming chance on to a pathway leading away from the World towards the Wild Wood. The pathway, winding and twisting like the spine of a dragon, had evidently not been used for many circlings of the stars; it was thickly overgrown with tangles of unhealthy vegetation and blocked by piles of evil-smelling rubbish and rusting machinery. In places, the way had been deliberately diverted. Yet the Wayfarer was able to follow the true course, even as if remembered from long ago.

After many weary days the pathway gradually cleared, resolving into the dry bed of a river narrowing towards its source. Chill mist, with the faint, sharp odour of yeast and salt, clung to the rime-hard ground. The black edge of the Wild Wood cut across the Land, a terrible guardian weapon forbidding passage beyond.

The first tree of the Wood was a tall Ash crowned with golden flames. It stood beside a milk-white pool — still as ice — from which the river once had flowed. Coiled around the base of the Ash was a white serpent, its eyes gleaming splinters of obsidian. Seated upon a stone beside the frozen pool, a beautiful ancient Lady, clad and hooded all in black, spun with a distaff the hair of a silver wolf.

The white serpent gazed intently at the Wayfarer; the Lady continued spinning, quietly singing a weird old song as she did so. Having finished her work she rose, placed the point of her distaff in the centre of the frozen pool and set it spinning. It remained perfectly upright and moved not a hair's breadth from the centre. The Lady indicated that the Wayfarer should approach, but only so far as the edge of the pool. The distaff continued to spin, the space around it scintillating with rays of ancient starlight drawn from the deeps below.

'Well, Wayfarer, so you wish to enter the Wild Wood; you dare to enter?' She pointed at the spinning distaff. 'None may pass beyond this point unless they are willing to learn and accord themselves with the Rites of the Law of this Land: Rites of Primaeval Law; Rites of Cosmic Law; Rites of Divine Law. Certainly you may not walk in the Wood clad thus! Cast those rags on to the bed of the river — soon will they dissolve away in the mist — and I will weave you a garment fit for a young wolf!'

The Lady seated herself upon the stone and set to weaving the silver thread into cloth, whispering and chanting holy secrets as she did so. The Wayfarer knelt naked before her, gazing into the depths of the pool. The spinning distaff penetrated far into the deeps of space beneath and beyond the surface of the ice, at its point a blue star like a watchful eye. A wise eye in a titanic head, which steadily returned the Wayfarer's gaze.

The beautiful ancient Lady anointed the Wayfarer with three drops of venom, given by the white serpent, blended with her own spittle, and bestowed the new garment of silver hair, chanting as she did so: 'Eye of Serpent; Child of Wolf; Swiftness of Horse; Wisdom of Raven; Countenance of Eagle!'

Thus clad and bearing a staff of Ash, the Wayfarer went forth into the green and golden Halls of the Wild Wood of the Wise.

The stars circled, the rhythmic dance of the seasons turned, and the Wayfarer gradually awoke to an awareness of the subtle and secret life of Nature. The arising and setting of stars and planets; the songs of birds; the voice of the wind in the trees; the fragrance of flowers and of rotting leaves and branches; the iridescence of dewdrops glistening in a spider's web; the elemental faces of the old trees; the subtle colours of moss, lichen and bark; the benediction of sunrays piercing thorugh leaves and moist air — all began to speak with a language of clarity and significance, each element resonating and harmonising with the other to produce the wholly coherent and constantly shifting pattern of planetary life. The keys to the 'Rites of the Law of the Land' were indeed slowly being revealed. And the hidden dwellers in the Wood entered the aware-ness of the Wayfarer, to show how those keys might be used to unlock deep sources of knowledge — knowledge all but forgot-ten in the realms of the World.

It was on a wild day, the wind howling with fury through the swaying treetops, that the Wayfarer neared the far end of the Wood. The waves of the Ocean hurled themselves in a frenzy against the cliffs far below and icy arrows of blinding rain drove through the Wood. Toward nightfall, the Wayfarer took shelter in a hollow and kindled need-fire in a circle of stones. Bright flames soon were crackling merrily, bringing life back to chilled limbs. The Wayfarer prepared soup in a pot, set it on the fire to cook and relaxed contentedly in the warmth.

An icy blast of wind wailed through the hollow, sending showers of sparks spiralling wildly into the air. Rime-stones hissed and spat in the flickering flames. A deep shadow followed the wind through the Wood. A resonant voice stilled the wind, filling the hollow with the calm breath of deep, ancient magic.

'Hail, Wayfarer! Welcome, warmth and wine for the Wayweary Wanderer?'

There emerged from the trees a tall, beared figure clad in a deep blue cloak patterned with stars; upon his head a broad-brimmed hat which all but cast his face into shadow. He bore a spear, with a shaft of Ash fashioned in the form of two spiralling ser-pents — carven with holy runes. A cold wave of terror momen-tarily washed over the Wayfarer, which was almost instantly replaced by a deep feeling of awe, love, respect — and of ancient recognition.

'Welcome indeed, Váfuðr:[1] warmth and wine are yours — you appear much in need of them! I had not thought to receive the good fortune of a guest on so stormy a night — the old roads can be lonely through the long hours of winter darkness.'

Váfuðr leaned his spear against a tree, seated himself on a stone close to the fire and gratefully received a goblet brimming over with blood-red wine. He gazed deep into the heart of the glow-ing embers, chuckled softly, raised his head, pierced the Wayfarer with the direct regard of his one eye: brilliant sapphire-blue, dis-tant golden sparks dancing within.

'Long in count of years are the old ways upon which I have wan-dered the World, watching the deeds of humankind. All too rarely do I receive so open-hearted a welcome as that with which you have gifted me, Child of Wolf. Bölverkr, ill-doer, Bileygr, shifty-eyed; and Glapsviðr, swift-in-deceit, men call me; thus raising barriers wrought of their own fears and prejudices. Yet others know me as Fjölsviðr, Wide-in-wisdom; Sanngetal, Truth-getter; and Thekkr, Much-loved. To all I impart gifts — and not always what they think they need, or wish, to receive! But giving to these latter is an especial joy, which eases somewhat the burden of my tasks.

'Óski Wish-god grants to you, Wayfarer, the gift of threefold wisdom. Here by your hearth three questions ask me; three questions will I answer. And no questions will I ask in return, unless you wish it. Beware now, lose not your head! True wisdom often lies in finding the right question rather than knowing the answer.'

The Wayfarer poured more wine for the Wanderer, placed windfallen branches on the fire, then stood a while regarding the Runespear, deep in thought. The spearhead was tipped with a sharp point of ice-blue starlight, the carven runes on the shaft in constant, spiralwise movement. The Wayfarer slowly reached out a hand, as if to touch the spear, abruptly withdrew it and sat down beside Váfuðr.

'As I journeyed through the Wild Wood,' said the Wayfarer, 'I observed and gradually became aware that everything in existence is part of a rhythmic pattern, a cyclic movement. There is the procession of the constellations of stars; the rising and setting of the Sun; the phases of the Moon; the tides of the Ocean; the passage of the Seasons; the differing activities of animals, birds and insects in accordance with the Seasons; and the stages and growth of trees and plants. It is all rather like a circle dance, which ought to have some sort of centre — otherwise there would not be a proper circle, or a spiral for that matter. Váfuðr, my first question is: what is the centre of the rhythmic dance of life?'

Göndlir Wand-bearer arose swift as lightning, grasped his spear, thrust it deep into the heart of the fire. Thunder roared; the World turned upside-down.

Váfuðr, mantled with gleaming black feathers, stood with the Wayfarer at the top of a high hill; a beacon hill, crowned with the cairn of a barrow, above the Ocean and at the edge of wild moorland. Iring's Way — the Way of the Wanderer — arched across the dome of space, stretching from horizon to horizon; a radiant bridge of stars. Encircling the hill was a spinning ring of fire, the flowing blood of a dragon. Arising from the centre of the barrow at the summit of the hill, a revolving pillar of frozen flame soared to the hub of the sky. Stella Polaria — Nail or Lode Star of the current Polar Epoch — burned at its apex, a glowing golden lamp.

Iđavöllr, the whirling Meadow of Stars, revolved with the pillar — down which flowed a double spiral of sparkling energies.

Váfuđr gazed up at Polaris, whispered into the deeps of the Sea of Space: 'Hrafnásar Raven-god, they used to call me. A thoughtful name; a name to remember!' He plucked two feathers our of his mantle and tied them in the Wayfarer's hair. They settled themselves on a stone before the entrance to the barrow and listened a while to the resonant clarity of the music of the whirling stars. The voice of Hrafnásar emerged from out of the deep, magnetic vibrations emanating from the revolving pillar of burning ice.

'The One Creator of All once fashioned a great vessel or cooking pot, shaped like the head of the oldest ancestor of all. The Creator put certain ingredients into the pot, tightly sealed the lid and set it on the Secret Fire of Divine Love to cook.

'Now the first ingredient the Curator put into the pot was a great void of space; the second ingredient was something rather like a frozen crystal of salt, held together by a pressure so vast that the entire potential matter of Creation was concentrated into no space whatever; and the third ingredient was an egg at the heart of the crystal — containing two embryos — which was exerting an outward pressure equal to the pressure holding the crystal together.

'The One Creator sang gently over the pot, setting up a resonance in the nucleus of the spaceless seed of matter: a Matrix of involutionary movement into space. And responding to the resonance, the twin embryos began to grow, causing the outward pressure to become greater than the inward pressure. The frozen crystal of salt melted into the Great Void. In the same moment — at the farthest possible point from the expanding crystal — the Creator allowed warmth from the Secret Fire of Divine Love to penetrate into the cooking pot.

'The egg at the heart of the crystal cracked open — the embryonic fluid blending with the expanding brine; bringing to birth within the source of outflowing life two primordial beings named Mímir and Urđr. And the womb of their genesis had three names: Mímisbrunnr, the Well of Memory; Urđabrunnr, the Well of Fate; and Hvergelmir, the Roaring Kettle.

'The shell of the egg dissolved in the essence within the Well, precipitating a confused, swirling mass of filaments of potential matter. Mímir and Urđr together gathered up the entire mass, and while Urđr spun all the tangled filaments into eleven shining threads, Mímir sang a song of making; a magic song of love and memory, a song which patterned the resonances of the primal

Matrix into the spinning threads. The outflowing essence carried the threads out into the Great Void in eleven rivers named Elivagar.

'The whirling rivers flowed so far from their source in Hvergelmir that the inward, constricting pressure re-asserted itself. The spin and outward flow of Elivagar gradually became slower and slower, and the essence became colder and denser. A volatile oil, like the sweet venom of a wise serpent, separated out and floated to the surface. Towards the midst of the Void, the venomous oil froze — giving off thick clouds of vapour. The vapour turned to frost which built up a wavefront, in many heavy layers, right across the mouths of the rivers. The flow of Elivagar ceased; the only movement was a terrible icy wind, blasting into the centre of the Void.

'The warmth of the Secret Fire of the Creator moved across the Void as flames, sparks and as a hot breeze — also blowing into the centre. The two winds met, began to interpenetrate. The venomous rime melted in the heat, releasing the vast spin which had built up in Elivagar. The eleven rivers surged forward, spinning into a single entity — a whirling pillar of the first created matter with the interwoven golden threads at its core. The flowing drops of venom re-combined with essence from the rivers, congealing in the heat into a seething mass in the midst of the Void.

'The ice and fire continued to interpenetrate, building up an incredible momentum as their masses combined — the ice also imparting its spin to the fire. When the two principles were wholly conjoined, their opposite forward motions translated into a high frequency oscillation — equalling the rate of the spin.

'Thus came into being the Central Axis of the Vessel of Creation, turning about the still point of the primordial Matrix; the Well of Memory. And the names of the Axis are: Mímameiðr, the Tree or Post of Memory; Irminsul, the World Pillar; and Yggdrasil, the World Tree, whose threefold root draws sustenance from the threefold Well.

'The spinning axis defines all vertical polarities within Creation and imparts its spin to all the worlds, which dance about that centre. One direction only has the Tree of Memory, which is neither up nor down, but always and ever pointing towards the One Creator of All.

'The seething mass in the midst of the Great Void further congealed and quickened in the warmth; took form in resonance with the Matrix. Thus was brought into being the androgynous cosmic titan named Ymir, the Roarer. And the Post of Memory was its backbone.'

Hrafnásar took the Wayfarer's staff of Ash and with a stone knife carved Runes thereon. The spinning pillar of burning ice described an arc across space, pointing in turn towards various stars. Moving away from golden Polaris, the current Pole Star, it pointed to Alderamin in the constellation of Cepheus; next to blue-white Deneb in Cygnus; and then to brilliant blue Vege in Lyra, the Pole Star in 13,000 years time.[2] And each time it pointed towards a star, a vast bell tolled in the deep of space. The hill became an island awash in a rising sea of mist, a sea glowing with starlight.

'Because of the perturbation of the axis of planet Earth,' continued Hrafnásar, 'it marks out in space a cycle of Pole or Lode Stars which takes 26,000 years to complete. Picture this axis as the hand of a cosmic clock, which tells the time in polar epochs rather than earthly hours and minutes. When the hand points towards a particular Lode Star, the bell of the epoch strikes and the principles and energies embodied by that star reach the peak of their influence on Earth. One polar epoch lasts for 3700 earthly years, there being seven epochs in a complete cycle of 26,000 years. In the time it takes for Sol to turn just once around the Galactic Axis, there would be 8000 such cycles of polar epochs.

'This sevenfold cyclic movement is the means whereby different aspects of the Divine Will of the Creator are mediated by the Pole Stars, to be worked out as patterns of destiny on Earth.

'Each star is the physical body of a lordly being known as a Stellar Logos; each having a particular task to perform as an element in the fulfilment of the Divine Plan. When one of the cycle of seven becomes Pole Star for an epoch, the Logos of that star takes on an additional office — sometimes known as the office of the Týrwaz or Shining One. The task of the Týrwaz is to mediate the dynamic of the undivided Spiritual Will in its primal expression; and to maintain awareness on Earth of the Realm of the Creator beyond the Vessel of Creation.

'As I said before, the Axis of Creation — rather than its local expression in Earth's Axis — always points in one direction only. You might do well to imagine this direction as being indicated by an arrow of light reaching from the centre of Earth to the Pole of the Ecliptic, which is the central point delineated by the cycle of Lode Stars.'

Two ravens, their eyes glinting with intelligence and humour, glided down in a broad spiral around the turning pillar and landed on Hrafnásar's shoulders. He greeted them fondly in their own strange old tongue; they in return rowned* to him, whispering holy Mysteries.

'I am Huginn, bearer of Thought,' said one.

'And I am Muninn, bearer of Memory,' said the other. They conversed a while as the Wayfarer absorbed Váfuðr's words — searching for the second question. Muninn spread his wings, rose into the air, circled the pillar thrice, settled on the Wayfarer's left shoulder and uttered a series of nine primal sounds — roots of magic words; words of making; runechants. Muninn's vibrant utterances triggered a subtle pattern of resonance in the body and inner being of the Wayfarer, helping to release the blockages impending the articulation of the second question.

'Much, Váfuðr, do you know about the centre of the dance of life; I thank you for sharing that knowledge. My second question is: what is memory?'

The sea of luminous mist continued to rise until only the cavernous mouth of the barrow was visible, a distant point of icy blue starlight within. Hrafnásar called softly into the mist, and there emerged therefrom the sound of galloping hooves, swiftly followed by a beautiful grey stallion with sparking eyes. Sleipnir lovingly greeted his master and gently acknowledged the Wayfarer. Hrafnásar helped the Wayfarer up on to Sleipnir's back, himself mounted with great agility and whispered a soft command. Sleipnir entered the mouth of the barrow and paused a moment, exchanging energy with the distant source of starlight; instantly shifted from repose into a whirling vortex of movement, down into earth, down toward the blue star.

'Yggr, the Terrifier, men used to call me,' cried Váfuðr. 'And Galdrsfaðir, Master of Magic!'

The swift spiralling movement — down into the earth, down toward the stars — translated into a brilliant chord of sound, an interweaving of stellar transmissions. The voices of the ancient children defined the road within. The spiral chord glowed, radiated, became a spinning wheel of blue starlight — portal to the Country of the Stars beyond.

Sleipnir leaped through the centre of the wheel and came to land in a beautiful flowery meadow beside a swiftly flowing river — wherein danced myriad iridescent, pulsating sparks. Beside the river, a spire of gold and obsidian soared into inner galactic space, a vast blue lamp burning and revolving at its apex. A bridge of stellar flame arched from horizon to horizon, from

---

* Old English: 'to whisper' (as in a holy secret)

source to mouth of the river. And thereupon walked lordly beings, Shining Ones of the First Light.

The riders dismounted and made their way across the meadow towards the spire, leaving Sleipnir contentedly feeding. Galdrsfaðir, clad in robes of sapphire-blue and gold, led the Wayfarer into the spire, which they ascended by way of a steep spiral stairway. As they neared the upper levels, Galdrsfaðir indicated a series of circular windows which gave a wide view of the countries of the inner stars beneath and beyond. The Galactic River flowed from East to West in a broad crescent, shimmering with its own polychromatic radiance; mirrored by the breathtaking arch of Bifröst, the Asgarðr Bridge, which soared toward the Supercelestial Realms beyond. Either side of the river, the star palaces arose like islands of paradise from a slowly shifting, pulsating sea of sound and light.

The Spire of Vega, in which Galdrsfaðir and the Wayfarer stood, was one of a series of seven — the spires of the cycles of Lode Stars — which, arising north of the river, delineated the shape of a great cosmic egg. And ascending through the centre of the egg was Yggdrasil, the Turning Pillar of the Terrible Initiator; Mímameiðr, the Tree of Love and Memory.

Galdrsfaðir led the Wayfarer into a spacious, luminous chamber, just beneath the blue lamp at the top of the spire. The air had a subtle fragrance like the nectar of spring flowers and the atmosphere was alive with highly-charged, spinning energies, which filled the Wayfarer with a feeling of joyous elation and inspired purpose. The chamber — which had been constructed according to the principles of a multi-dimensional geometry, having the effect of stretching the mind well beyond its assumed capabilities — was furnished after the fashion of a scientific laboratory. At its centre stood an athanor — or alchymical furnace — whose radiant blue fire emanated from the heart of the star Vega. Upon the athanor was a great cucurbite, or vessel, of crystal, capped with an alembic. Rising out of the alembic was an elegant structure of gleaming glass tubes in the form of a double spiral. The spiralling tubes fed into a second cucurbite, shaped like an egg, which was suspended from the apex of the domed ceiling. Seven narrower double spirals of tubing descended from the egg and curved down into the floor of the laboratory.

Galdrsfaðir indicated the central cucurbite. 'Within this vessel is placed the Blood of Wisdom and the Nectar or Honey of the Stars. These ingredients are cooked within the apparatus, being many times distilled and circulated. Eventually they marry, conjoin and bring to birth the Mead of Divine Inspiration, which is a medicine of inestimable virtue — of benefit in satisfying the true needs of both angels and men.'

Within the vessel a crystalline blossom growing in the medium of a heavy, pale golden liquid, was very slowly unfolding. Glowing nectar from the blossom ascended the double spiral, fountained into the egg as an incandescent white flame, and divided into seven constituent elements, circulating and flowing down the smaller glass spirals.

Galdrsfaðir and the Wayfarer sat down beside the furnace, from which emanated swirling streams of sparkling blue and golden particles, all resonating to the spiralling measures of a celebratory dance. The two old ravens flew in through a portal and circulated within the pulsating radiance. Muninn reminded his Master — who was intently watching the unfolding of the blossom in the vessel — that he had yet to attend to the Wayfarer's second question. Galdrsfaðir rose, crossed over to the strangely angled portal through which Huginn and Munnin had entered and stood gazing without. Softly he uttered a deep chant, like the tolling of a bell beneath the Ocean. The angles of the chamber shifted, the walls and ceiling became transparent. The rays of the inner stars entered, curving toward the egg-shaped vessel, filling it with a glowing, blood-red liquid. The portals were black mirrors, spinning: gateways to inner realms and dimensions linked to the Stellar Being of Vega. The Wayfarer's inner vision was drawn towards and within one of the spinning portals.

The words of Galdrsfaðir echoed across the starry deeps, unlocking ancient images of Holy Powers to the consciousness of the Wayfarer.

'Ymir, the androgynous cosmic Titan, slumbered for many turnings of the Post of Memory. Because of the warmth of Divine Love, it sweated as it slumbered. The resonances of the primal creative Matrix — the Well of Memory — which had been patterned into the core of Ymir's spine by Mímir and Urðr, became active. The being of Ymir remembered the Song of Creation; the impetus for involutionary movement into space. Thus by the intertwining of Love and Memory, there came to birth within the sweat beneath Ymir's left arm two radiant Shining Ones, male and female: divine twins. Such was the inception of the race known as the Sweatborn which, it should be said, is a lifewave of glorious cosmic Titans which passed through an entire cycle of involution and evolution prior to the manifestation of planetary life as you know it.

'They dwelled in a state of paradisal innocence, within the Eternal Present Moment of Creation. They experienced direct memory of the Matrix, for as yet none by evil will had distorted memory, separating it from love. Of their essence, they embodied the dynamics of spinning and weaving first set into motion by Urđr. Their cycle of growth was but an increasing consciousness of the Will of the Creator; of the Divine Plan. From this shining race was born Bestla, my Mother.

'Having given birth to the divine race of the Sweat-born, Ymir awoke. Because of the great flux of life-force which had flowed out of it at the birth, it was ice-cold and hungry. Now within the seething mass congealing in the midst of the Great Void, there had also come into being a vast nurturing feminine force named Auđumbla, the Rich Hornless Cow. Four rivers of milk flowed from her teats, providing Ymir with sweet nourishment and warmth; and laying down the originating pattern of the spiralling rivers of stars known to you as galaxies. Once more, Ymir slumbered.

'Having fed Ymir, Auđumbla was herself hungry. She gently licked a salty rime stone. So vast were the forces of nurturing and forming that flowed through her, and so clear was the message of the Matrix held within the salt, that as Auđumbla received nourishment, there came into being the first of a second race of lordly Shining Ones. For three turnings of the Tree of Memory, Auđumbla licked the salty rime stone. At the end of the first turn, there emerged from the stone the hair and radiant crown of the Shining One. At the end of the second turn, there emerged a great, beautiful head. And at the end of the third turn, there emerged from the stone the powerful, titanic body of Búri the Producer. The Race of Búri also experienced direct memory of the Matrix, of their essence embodying the pattern-making dynamic set in motion by Mímir. The mysterious objects known to you as quasars are an ancient resonance of these timeless cosmic beings. From this shining race was born Búr, my Father.

'The two races involved through the holy realm of the Eternal Paradise, in total innocence, neither having any conscious awareness of the other. Their involution was a preparation, initiated by Mímir and Urđr, for the nodal point of convergence and emergence at which they would awaken to mutual knowledge. And so they reached the nadir of their cycles of being, the conjunction of two flowing circles of spacetime.'

A pulsation in the fabric of the laboratory; the inner eye of the Wayfarer was drawn through a second portal...into a beautiful, ancient garden. The clear songs of birds fill the air, mediating the language of angels; the colours of flowers are bright chords of bells, their perfume that of the nectar of the stars; and the hum of bees in search of the nectar is a warm chant beneath the chimes. A network of narrow streams flows through the garden, tributary to four rivers rising from a green mound in the centre. The rivers run toward the four directions. The islands of land between the streams are the dwelling places of clusters of growing, sentient jewels and tall trees with sonorous voices. A narrow pathway, bordered with fragrant herbs, winds through the garden — a serpentine maze leading to the green mound at the centre. From the mound grows the oldest tree, its bark pale, glowing gold. The garden is enclosed by three spinning rainbows, intersecting to outline a sphere — with the golden tree as its axis.

The voice of Galdrsfaðir emerges out of the holy song of the garden: 'By the Well of Memory, in the shade of Yggdrasil, Búr met with Bestla. Each was filled with awe and terror at the holy power and beauty of the other. Búr sang a song of making; Bestla drew water from the Well. They shared the draught; awoke to the memory of love; conjoined in holy nuptials; merged in the ecstatic measures of the cosmic dance of life.

'Of their union was brought to birth Xau-xaz, the High One, Father of a third divine race of Shining Ones — those Holy Powers of the One Creator known as Aesir, Cosmocratores, Archons and Dhyani Chohans. They were the Cosmos Builders who, out of the primordial mind-substance, made certain dynamic principles, in order to initiate the process of the evolution of consciousness within the Vessel of Creation. They encoded these principles into a new expression of the Matrix, fashioned of thought and memory; and the pattern of the Matrix is a double spiral, or helix, coiled around the Pole of Memory, which manifests in all modalities of being.'

A pulsation in the fabric of the laboratory; the inner eye of the Wayfarer was drawn through a third portal. . .into a vast, echoing hall; a transparent dome set upon a pinnacle, high above a sea of sparkling blue and golden flames. The music of the circling stars penetrates the dome, creating an inner space of swiftness, clarity and harmony: meeting place of the Star Council of Vega. Crystal thrones are set in a circle about a turning rod of transparent fire, about which plays a complex pattern of radiant, spiralling energies. The Stellar Logoi of many systems cross the Asgarðr Bridge and assemble in the dome, together with Masters of Magic and Wisdom representing the planetary evolutions. The voice of Ebn-Xau-xaz, Just-as-High, who is Hierarch of the Star Council, emerges from the Voices of the Stars.

'The first two divine races entered upon the evolutionary epochs of their cycle of existence, their primary task being the initiation of the Son of Búr and Bestla into the Mysteries of Creation. Vast, slow waves of their sublime consciousness, millions of lightyears in length, pulsed and rippled through the Sea of Spacetime; communicating the elements of the language of the angels to the infant primogenitor.

'For nine turns I hung from Yggdrasil in the midst of the Void: pierced by the Spear of Love and Memory; torn by the raging of the cosmic winds. Thus Xau-xaz, the High One, offered up the entirety of his being to the service of his Creator. The waters of the Well of Memory flowed through me; the pattern of the Matrix was imprinted upon the essence of my being. I knew that Love and Memory are one creating word, that must never be separated: for without love, memory gives birth to nought but abomination.[3]

'I peered downward into the waters of manifestation, saw reflected therein the radiant counternance of Divine Wisdom. In that moment I grasped the Matrix: knew it as an interwoven pattern of shining Runes — whispered Mysteries in the first creating language of the Shining Ones; saw it as a pulsating double helix winding around the Tree of Memory; realised it to be the unified expression of the dynamic behind involving and evolving lives within the Vessel. The Memory of Love of the Creator for all created lives.

'And in that moment was I filled with love for Divine Wisdom. Uttering the word of manifestation, I fell from Yggdrasil — down into the deeps of the Void; down into the waters beneath; down to the Rose of Paradise. My love sat me upon a throne of gold, and there came to us a Shining One of the race of Bestla, my Mother, who taught us nine songs of making, mighty songs for the formation of the worlds.

'My heart was stirred; I was ready for my task. Between us, my love and I, we distilled the holy Mead of Inspiration; the Soma; the Amrita. Of our combined spittle, of the Blood of Wisdom and of the Nectar of the Shining Ones we made the Mead; in the three great vessels which are one we brought it forth. We drank the Mead and between us, my love and I, we conceived the Aesir, the Cosmocratores, the Archons, the Dhyani Chohans.

'The Mead suffused us with the eager fire of creation; we remembered the plans for the birth of stars and the birth of the planetary worlds. We sought for material with which to build and in our seeking remembered the body of Ymir, the androgynous cosmic Titan. Ymir had evolved to other realms in a far distant age, yet its backbone remained as the Cosmic Axis; and the coagulation of primordial life-essence which had been its body was still in the midst of the Void.

'We let flow the blood of Ymir, which we wrought into three vast spinning rings — intersecting to outline a sphere. The first was the Ring of Space; the second the Ring of Time; and the third the Ring of Spacetime. Within the spinning rings we contained and set in order the primal substance, the array of involving forces, of Ymir's body; together with the molten particles which had been dwelling freely in the Void. The backbone remained as the axis of the sphere and of all Creation.

'Thus was brought into being a vessel of reception for the involving Divine Sparks, a coherent space containing all the necessary ingredients for the experiment of stellar and planetary life. All these things were done wholly in accordance with the Will of the One Creator of All; and by loving memory of the information contained in the primal Matrix — the still point of the turning worlds.'

The inner eye of the Wayfarer withdrew from the third portal and returned its attention to the upper chamber of the Spire of Vega. The laboratory was no longer apparent. Ebn-Xau-xaz, clad all in pale, shimmering gold and bearing a sceptre with a jewel of cosmic ice mounted on the end, stood with the Wayfarer in a circular glasshouse. It was situated on top of the green mound in the garden, with the golden tree growing up through the centre. The tree was surrounded by a waterlily-pool, in which were swimming great golden fish with sapphire eyes. A profusion of trees and plants from the tropical regions of the Earth — many with fragrant, brightly coloured blossoms and large, succulent leaves — filled the glasshouse. The air was very warm and humid, with the sharp, musky aroma of fertile soil. All the vegetation was dripping with moisture. Seven glass corridors radiated from the periphery, each with a different temperature and level of humidity.

Ebn-Xau-xaz looked down at the blue lotus with a golden heart, obviously moved by its beauty. For a moment, the sceptre he was holding seemed to become of almost unbearable weight. He recovered himself and turned to face the Wayfarer, who was deeply troubled by his distress.

'Yes, it does sometimes become very heavy,' said Ebn-Xau-xaz. 'But I think you — and others like you — can help me bear it. Look around you. Most of the trees and plants in this glasshouse may well be extinct on Earth in a few years' time. We have the genetic material here, of course. But that's really not much use if there is nowhere for them to grow.'

Ebn-Xau-xaz led the Wayfarer over to a seat by the pool. 'Beyond the stars,' he continued, 'they call me Xau-xaz, the High One. There I am wise Father of the shining Cosmocratores, who builds the dynamics of involution and evolution in accordance with the Will of the One Creator of All.

'Among the stars, they call me Ebn-Xau-xaz, Just-as-High. There I am Stellar Logos and Hierarch of the Star Council of Vega, who mediates the primordial dynamics of the cosmic mind-code, building them into the patterns of divine destiny — of which the shining constellations of holy stars are a living expression — for onward transmission to the planetary worlds.

'On Earth, they call me Thridjaz, the Third. There I am Manu and Planetary Logos, who as Rigden-jyepo — Lord of Shambhala — bears the shining jewel Norbu-rinpoche, which is an active memory of the divine destiny of planet Earth.

'This sceptre is an embodiment of the dynamics of the Tree of Memory — even as is my Runespear when I walk the Earth as Wanderer. The jewel mounted on the end is Norbu-rinpoche, which fell from cosmic space when consciousness first awoke in the World. Its substance is ice from the Well of Memory. See gleaming within a spark from the Secret Fire of the One Creator. Norbu-rinpoche *remembers* what planet Earth is capable of becoming.

'Certain entities — known as the Lords of Evil Countenance or Wielders of Unbalanced Force — try to prevent the Earth from fulfilling her destiny. Their sole aspiration is to impose their own self-directed wills upon all they behold, rather than to serve the Divine Will of the Creator. They take all things unto themselves, as if by right, giving nothing in return. Thus do they pervert the proper flow and circulation of energy in any system, creating massive blockages — cosmic cancers.

'In order to empower the fulfillment of their selfish desires, these evil ones have sought deliberately to distort the cosmic code of the Matrix. The falsification of DNA on all levels of being. The divorce of Love from Memory.

'These distortions are now manifesting in the body of Earth in fundamental ways, particularly through the medium of certain types of scientific research and in the cancerous hoarding of vast quantities of stolen power. It is now officially acceptable to alter the genetic code of a type of yeast, in order to speed up the process of making bread. It is now officially acceptable to carry out genetic engineering experiments on the human foetus. Do those who act thus have any idea of the possible long-term consequences? Do those who act thus know or care about the spiritual realities behind manifest life? Do those who act thus have any realisation of the sanctity of life — indeed, of all created things? The service of false memory rather than the Will of God has become the basis of life on Earth.

'Scientific research and the development of technological artefacts are, in principle, perfectly natural and acceptable activities for certain intelligent species, wholly in keeping with the process of the manifestation of creative energies. They are, however, only acceptable when carried out with love, compassion and with the basis of an innate knowledge of the essential unity of all the seemingly diverse elements of Creation. It would seem to be fairly evident that scientific and technological endeavour on Earth fails to meet these rather obvious requirements. Humankind is still, for the most part, a highly aggressive and greedy species. An increasingly dangerous species. Self-interest and the sophistication to manipulate the building blocks of matter do not lie easily together!

'Despite the vociferous outcry of those with a vision of truth — those who remember that the whole point of humanity involving the Earth was to undertake the stewardship of matter, not to preside over the systematic destruction of the biosphere — despite the endeavours of those wise ones, the upholders of the bent will of man continue to suck the life out of the planet; continue to act out the sterile dynamics of the Fall.

'Awaken; remember! Key words for those who would tread the Way of the Wanderer. No longer is there any excuse for mindlessly maintaining the falsified patterns. Awaken to reality; remember the true Matrix; allow, through yourself, the double helix of Love and memory to emerge and manifest on Earth.'

The prismatic lights of the spinning rainbows were mirrored in the still depths of the waterlily-pool. The angelic songs of the birds in the garden interwove, producing a complex polyphonic chorus. Each melismatic element of this unwilled music was a mediation of the essence of a Divine Principle, having its point of emanation in the archonic realms beyond the stars. It was a multi-dimensional music, a music of Spacetime, delineating the contours of a sonic map of Paradise. A resonance of the choirs of the Holy Powers of the One God.

The lights and the music penetrated to the innermost heart of the Wayfarer, effecting a profound transmutation; an awakening and a remembering. The blood of the dragon stirred, translating the language of the angels. The essential being moved towards an awareness of that which it already is: dwelling in the Eternal Present Moment of Creation. A discovery of the direction of the door to the Paradise Garden.

The Wayfarer turned to Ebn-Xau-xaz. 'Much, Váfudr, do you know about memory; I thank you for sharing that knowledge. My third question is: what is evolution?'

Ebn-Xau-xaz rose from his seat beside the waterlily-pool and gently touched the trunk of the golden tree with the jewel Norburinpoche. A great peal of bells chimed a radiant chord in the deeps of inner space; the waters of the pool arose in a sparkling fountain, full of blue and golden stars. The seven glass corridors spun like the radiating spokes of a wheel and the roof of the glasshouse opened out, even as the petals of an unfolding blossom. The entire edifice underwent metamorphosis, becoming a vast circular ark spinning about a central golden mast.

A fanfare of fiery angelic voices sounded above a deep, thunderous tone — like the pedal trumpet of a mighty cathedral organ. The ark whirled into space; surged on to the almost impossible arch of the spiral arm of the Galactic River; on to Bifröst, the Asgardr Bridge of the shining Aesir; on to Iringes Weg, the Way of the Wanderer.

The spinning curve of Spacetime unfolded about the constantly accelerating ark, a polychromatic sea of stellar consciousness — each individual element of which was forever joyfully exchanging polar energy with all the other individual elements, as well as with the totality of the consciousness. The glad hosts of the Stellar Logoi raised their voices in the ecstatic chant of the Lordly Ones of the First Light. And their eyes burned with the clear flame of the remembrance of Paradise.

'Báleygr, Fire-eye, men used to call me,' cried Xau-xaz, 'and Farmatýr, God of Cargoes! Certainly the cargo stowed in the hold of this vessel is worthy of attention of the High One! For here we have in safe-keeping the genetic material of all the living creatures dwelling in the various phases of the current incarnation of planet Earth. Stellar DNA.

'All planetary species come into manifestation as a vital element in the pattern of the planetary ecology and as a particular expression of the evolving group soul of that species. Because of the inner memory distortions I mentioned before, a proportion of these manifestations is by no means perfect. Even so, every species, intelligent or otherwise, has the divine right to fulfil the purpose of its current lifewave before withdrawing to the inner.

'All species eventually reach the point when it is no longer appropriate or necessary for them to continue in that particular expression of their being — even Ymir withdrew from its body in the midst of the Void, the substance of which was later recycled in a very useful way!

'But any species, having been divinely gifted with intelligence, which deliberately causes the extinction of another species before its proper time, merely for the satisfaction of some temporary desire, is guilty of an evil crime; is breaking cosmic law. And do not forget that any action which is detrimental to the life of the planet will also adversely affect the entirety of evolving life within the Vessel of Creation. The ill-effects of the murder of a species increase exponentially as they resonate through the Inner Hierarchy of Responsibility.

'Evolution by "natural selection" or "survival of the fittest" is, to a certain extent, physically factual. It is, however, a prime example of the manifestation of distorted memory. A specious excuse for selfish aggression, which can be used to justify an entire range of activities — held by a large proportion of humanity, without a moment's thought, to be perfectly acceptable — which abuse the divine gift of spiritual free will to a very high degree indeed.

'An important example is the prevailing attitude towards the disposal of "waste" products. The usual procedure would seem to be: take a quantity of raw material from the Earth, suck out the goodness for profit or pleasure, and discard whatever remains in the cheapest and least time-consuming fashion possible. This is in direct contravention of cosmic law — with no case for the defence! In technologies properly based in spiritual principles, the *whole matter* is always used; nothing whatever is discarded. This ensures the proper circulation of planetary energies, with no build-up of blockages or excess poisons, and maintains an even, harmonious distribution of the elements of substance.

'The reality of the evolutionary process is an entirely different matter, having nothing whatever to do with aggressive dominance or the acquisition of power for self-directed ends.'

The interior of the stellar ark hummed with potent energies, like the chant of the sacred bees in the garden. Quanta of luminescence, visible to the re-opened inner eye, produced a flickering, multi-dimensional pattern: a rapid metabasis[4] through a series of transmissions from inner stellar sources, each appearance of the pattern representing an entire communication in the old language of Vega and the Pleiades. A large convex screen, like an obsidian mirror, filled one side of the ark. It showed the surrounding star field over the entire electromagnetic spectrum —

stretching well beyond both gamma rays and very long radio waves. All the component stars and other celestial bodies were linked by a network of shimmering lines of light, delineating the sea-lanes through inner space and the paths of intercommunication; the gleaming Web of the Star Weaver. A synthesis of the information given by the pattern of photons and the image on the screen produced direct linkage to the Stellar Hierarchy.

Within the ark was a wide variety of simulated planetary environments. Therein dwelled living creatures, two of each species, many of which were close to extinction on Earth. Xau-xaz led the Wayfarer down to the gene banks. They were sealed by bright sigils and energy fields which might only be broken by Xau-xaz together with Frigg, his consort. The keys to the locks were encoded in the Matrix. And before each gene bank stood a terrible guardian angel with flaming sword.

The two voyagers made their way back to the upper levels of the ark and stood watching an orang-utan feed her child. As they did so, Xau-xaz continued with his teachings on the subject of evolution.

'Of the hair which grew from the shining crown centre of Ymir, the son of Búr and Bestla fashioned the trees of the first forest in the World; the scions of Yggdrasil.

'Once, on a wild and windswept day, I was wandering by the shore of the first Ocean in the World. The tide was just on the turn towards the ebb, when I espied two trees from the First Forest lying on the strand. One was a beautiful old Ash; the other seemed as if carven from glowing amber resin — and I rememberd them from the first making. They lay with their branches entwined in a gentle, passionate embrace, with the lonely music of the waves for a nuptial song. I made for them a threefold wedding gift, a love-gift: shaped by the song of the primal Matrix, wholly in accordance with the Will of the Creator — which is the Law of Nature.

'I sang a song of making, a runechant of fashioning and forming — thereby bestowing my threefold gift. Xau-xaz, wise Father of the shining Aesir, brought his gift from the Cosmos Builders beyond the stars: the holy gift of Divine Breath. Ebn-Xau-xaz, Lord of Vega, brought his gift from the Stellar Logoi: the holy gift of consciousness and memory. And Thridjaz, the Planetary Logos, brought his gift from the Green Lord of the Forest: the holy gift of royal blood. In this wise came into manifestation the first man and woman to walk upon the sacred fields of Earth. Askr and Embla: thus I named them, and taught them the magic of speech, the language of making from the stars.

'The dwelled in the Earthly Paradise, full of love and innocence, and daily they spoke with the shining Watchers of the Holy Garden. I, Manu of their race, charged them with the task of helping the Watchers look after the Earth, and imparted to them all those things that they needed to know to enable them to be good stewards of planetary matter.

'This tale — which, believe me, is absolutely true! — is an image of the process known as involution. By this process, which might be seen as a sort of cosmic childhood, the Divine Sparks of created lives are gradually prepared for the time when they will be given the opportunity to take on some measure of responsibility for the World around them, for events beyond purely personal desires. It is the path of least resistance, with minimal expenditure of personal energy, whereupon most of the work is done by those who have gone before. The vessels for the indwelling of the involving Divine Sparks have already been built in the various modalities of being through which they will pass; the laws of life have been laid down; the trials and tests by which they will learn and gain experience are provided.

'The story of Askr and Embla makes it clear that the substance of the vessels for the indwelling of the involving human lifewave proceeded from a very exalted source indeed: no less than the crown centre of the great cosmic Titan! That the hair of Ymir provided the substance of the trees, which in turn provided the substance of humanity, indicates the closeness of the relationship between mankind and the vast old forces of Nature. There is much that you could learn from the Green Lord of the Forest, particularly about the links between Earth and the Stars. For he still directly encounters the Stellar Logoi, knowing them as close and vibrant living beings rather than remote cosmic potencies.

'The evolution of an intelligent species only begins when individual members of that species develop an unselfish attitude to planetary life; when they are filled with an overwhelming desire to assist in the restoration of the Earthly Paradise. The process of evolution is triggered by an awakening to the remembrance of the primal Matrix. This awakening will most usually be a painful one, bringing a keen awareness of the fallen condition of humanity. Childhood and the path of least resistance are left behind; the self-discipline and responsibilities of cosmic adulthood have to be embraced.

'The ideals and spiritual aspirations of the evolving human are not those of the species as a whole — which are based on false memory. This is *not* an excuse for attempting to escape from the conditions of planetary life into some sort of fantasy world. The evolutionary urge demands, rather, than your loving relationship with Earth should become closer and deeper; and that your energies should be put at the disposal of those Holy Powers of the Creator entrusted with the task of enabling the human lifewave as a whole to enter upon the path of evolution.

'The human species is, to a certain extent, a rather uncomfortable symbiosis of stellar and animal natures — a somewhat dangerous experiment in genetic engineering! The physical *body* of the human dervies from genotypes very close to those of certain earthly animals, all arising in a common source. Thus do those animals bear characteristics of appearance and behaviour which demonstrate that intimate bond of flesh. The physical *substance* of all planetary life derives from stellar sources; your body is made of matter that once burned in a star, perhaps at a temperature of millions of degrees. The "natural" condition of elemental substance is liquid or gas: a planet, capable of being inhabited by physical life as you know it, is a highly specialised being wherein the chemical elements are frozen within the vessel of time and space. The stellar *nature* of humanity derives from its involution through the inner countries of the stars, during which process it was divinely gifted with the potential for conscious thought.

'Thus are you both child of the stars and beast of flesh. And although it is the stellar nature that is currently most in need of awakening, both natures are of equal importance; of equal holiness. Indeed, the two natures are, of their essence, one nature. The first stage in the process of evolution, either for an individual human or for the species as a whole, is to allow the harmonious integration of the starchild with the fleshy beast. The celebration of a loving, sacred marriage, which takes place within the innermost chamber of your heart — before the door to the Paradise Garden.'

The ark accelerated beyond the stars; beyond movement; through the portal of the Super-celestial World of the shining Aesir, the Cosmos Builders...to a point of stillness, silence and absolute calm. Beside the Well of Memory stood an ancient throne — set there before the manifestation of planetary life. Seated thereupon, Xau-xaz gazed out over all the worlds within the Vessel of Creation, Huginn and Muninn perched upon his shoulders. He was robed in the blue-grey luminescence of a lambent flame, through which swirled vortices of pulsating rainbow lights; and upon his brow burned his eye of angelic vision — a galaxy of sparkling emanations of the principles of wisdom, love and power. Xau-xaz indicated that the Wayfarer should be seated beside him upon the throne and looked deep into the Well of Memory.

'I remember,' said Xau-xaz softly, his voice echoing across the Void, 'another threefold gift bestowed by the Lord of the Cosmos Builders, the Hierarch of the Star Council, the Planetary Logos of Earth.

'Shambhala: the City of Seven Gates, dwelling-place of the Lords of the Earth. Spinning around the polar axis of the World is a shining golden ring of stars, a hidden serpent-path, stretching from East to West: the Way of the Wanderer. A reflection in Earth of the Milky Way; of Bifröst, the Asgardr Bridge of the Shining Ones. Set into this path of serpent-fire, like jewels in a crown, are the seven portals of Shambhala. Beyond them is the Great Abyss of the Desert, at the secret heart of which is a glowing lake of liquid emerald. In the midst of the lake, upon an island, a celestial city of golden domes and spires of obsidian arises from the Paradise Garden. And therein do Holy Ones ever tread out the ecstatic measures of the dance of the starry cosmos; about a pillar of incandescent flame do they dance, to the music of gongs and bells and the voices of birds.

'Thridjaz, Lord of Shambhala, ascended his Star-tower and gazed into the frosty mirror of the Sea of Intergalactic Space. He elevated the sceptre of his office towards the primal Matrix, towards the Well of Memory. And there entered into the jewel Norbu-rinpoche a glorious ray of light from a new star, from the Hidden Star of the Magi. This sublime luminary, the One Source of all emanations, lights, stars and Divine Sparks, burned within the waters of the Well; had been received into the vessel of the Matrix. The One Creator of All the Worlds penetrated and entered the Vessel of Creation, to be born as a man from the flesh of the Virgin of the World.

'Thridjaz descended from his Star-tower, crossed over the emerald lake, mounted his great golden camel and set out on the Way of the Wanderer, following the light of the Hidden Star. And with him he bore three holy and royal gifts to offer to the infant Redeemer; to the Incarnate Immortal World.

'Thridjaz, he offered Gold from the Earth; Ebn-Xau-xaz, he offered Frankincense from the Stars; and Xau-xaz, he offered Myrrh from the Realm of the Archons. Thus did the Lord of the World lovingly acknowledge the sovereignty of his Creator in all the Worlds of Creation.'

Mímameiðr, the Tree of Memory, turns about the still point of the Matrix; the radiant Halls and Palaces of the shining Aesir pulsate with divine emanations of creative principles; the three prismatic rings of the Asgarðr Bridge spin and whirl, encompassing the deeps of Intergalactic Space; the spiralling Quasars and Galaxies cause the patterns of divine destiny to reverberate across the starry cosmos; the planetary worlds dance to the music of the circling stars.

Planet Earth stretches out through Space and Time a scintillating web of radiant energies flowing and circulating in harmonious resonance with the voices of the stars. A Map of the World before the fall of man; a Map of the Earthly Paradise, showing the old serpent road — shining with swiftly moving iridescent lights — linking the lands of East and West: the Way of the Wanderer.

Xau-xaz robes the Wayfarer in a vortex of rainbow lights and together they step down on to the Earth. The Wanderer leaves his young pupil peacefully relaxing beside a gently flickering fire. A fire in a woodland hollow somewhere on the backbone of the World.

REFERENCES

1 Wanderer
2 The other Pole Stars in the cycle are: Ras Algethi (Alpha Herculis); Alphecca (Alpha Coronae Borealis); Thuban (Alpha Draconis).
3 (Old High German) *minna* memory, love; (German) *minne* love; (Sanskrit) *manas* mind, *man* to think; (German) *Minnesinger*.
4 A transition from one point to another.

RUNAWAY CHILD

By

PETER LAMBORN WILSON

In the final chapter, we reach ahead — beyond the images of God or Goddess, to that of the Child, specifically the 'runaway' child, who has turned his back on the mores of our prohibitive society, abandoned gender, slipped out of the noose of the masculine stereotype. Images of this abound in the mythologies of the world — from the Puer Eternitas to Mabon the Child God of the Celts. Often they have to do with capture and escape — the child is imprisoned by the weight of its inheritance but escapes, often aided by animal helpers, to become stronger. Like Peter Pan, some men never want to grow up — but they are forced to do so by the exigencies of life. They exemplify exactly the freedom of spirit, the refusal to be bound — to have their futures decided for them — which ought to be the basis of the New Man. We should begin to look beyond the old pendulum swing of matriarchy/patriarchy towards something else — perhaps, as some would have us believe, to the next development of humanity — androgny, bisexuality, the partaking of both ways. Certainly, the many images of childhood which occur once the walls of the masculine labryinth are broken down seem to suggest that the Way of the Child is what we really need.

10

RUNAWAY CHILD

(In memoriam Mick L of *Minor Problems*)

Advocates of the New Male Spirituality seem to want to delineate a path for feminist heterosexual men, in opposition to a form of spirituality based on male ascendency in Babylonian-style civilisations (and who in the world does not now live in Babylon?) One mythic paradigm sometimes offered in support of the New Male Spirituality derives from the hypothesis of a primordial matriarchy. Paleopsychology offers some good evidence for this hypothesis. For example, the primordial Chaos-monster, Tiamat, who had to be destroyed by the male god Marduk before Babylonian civilisation could emerge, is distinctly imagined as female. Anthropology offers us a view of hunter/gatherer (ie pre-Babylonian) society under the sign of the female — perhaps the sign of the Tao, both male and female, but over-all somehow more feminine, watery and shadowy.

However, can't we criticise this view of human becoming as itself somehow tainted with the dialectical poison of 'patriarchal' mentality? In other words, must we view pre-history, history and post-history as some sort of tick-tock device in which matriarchy and patriarchy take turns like the figures in a Swiss weather-clock? Primordial matriarchy, as described by certain modern authors, sounds suspiciously like a revenge-fantasy-parody of the patriarchal lie which claims that the world 'began' only when the repulsive Tiamat was destroyed.

I read recently an article by someone who had just discovered a banal truth of anthropology: that you can always find some tribe somewhere who practise a moral code which violates other moral codes. Every sort of 'sin' is somewhere a 'virtue'. The author began to suggest that this cultural relativism might be used as theoretical support for emerging new sexual/gender moralities in our society — but then stopped to warn us that *some* of these tribes possess 'virtues' we consider abominable, even when practising cultural relativism like good liberals. I recall that male chauvinism was mentioned as an example; cannibalism and head-hunting were not...perhaps only out of delicacy. In any case, the author missed the point. Morality is not determined by some genetic/memetic code, much as it may seem so to each isolated tribe (*including ours*). We are, on the contrary, free to imagine any morality; or, indeed, none at all. Nietzsche called this moment the death of God; however, in a late note in *Will to Power* he also envisioned it as the rebirth of Dionysus.

The overbearing macho-Martian Babylonian/patriarchal terror at the heart of *civilisation* has finally begun to reveal itself as empty. The boring old fart, if not quite dead, totters and nods on his greasy throne. Whatever their gender, many now yearn for a strong counter-dose of the spirit of the feminine. (To give this subjective focus, let me mention my own devotion to the Hindu goddess Tara, and the New World goddess of moon and sea, Yemaya, who is very popular in New York.) As an anarchist, however, I am bothered by the word *matriarchy*. Words ending in *iarchy* make me want to reach (metaphorically of course) for little black bombs, incendiary devices against all control-languages and grammars of oppression. I don't believe I'd care for the reign of Queen Mom any more than that of King Dad.

The archetype of the Androgyne (rooted like all such in the *body* and its 'streaming sensations', to quote Reich) might make a better emblem for the flag of the risky Utopia already taking shape in the cracks and interstices of the crumbling Babylonian monolith of 'empty discourse'. Hermes/Aphrodite — precisely the disc of the Tao. Let us also note that a certain occulist logic (to coin a phrase) suggests that the Age of the Mother (Tiamat, Old Stone Age) and the Age of the Father (Marduk, New Stone Age-to-the-present) must be superseded not by the return of the Mother but by the Age of the Child.

In some ways, the Child makes a better symbol than the Mother for the structure of hunter-gatherer societies. Such tribes, where they survive in our world, are invariably treated *as children*, to be punished and civilised — 'brought up'. Their non-authoritarian political structures resemble those of the spontaneous child-gangs that spring into being amongst children everywhere. Such a gang, in our world, can be seen as nothing other than 'juvenile delinquents' — but in hunter/gatherer societies, children often have their own lodges, gangs within the bigger gang of the tribe. American Plains Indians evolved very sophisticated versions of the 'child-gang' social model, in which daring, vision and adventure were considered the highest values, leaders emerged spontaneously and situationally, shamanism was 'democratised', etc. Child-gangs tend to a certain separation of the sexes: girls and boys often have separate lodges and 'mysteries'. This very separateness, however, reflects gender *ambiguity* as much as (or more than) gender *war*. The male or female band moves in a magic realm of cultural homoeroticism. When such bands emerge within a Babylonian-type civilisation they are seen as agents of chaos, wolf packs, *mannenbunden*, shape-shifters, witches, gypsies, hobos, delinquents, marginals, perverts. The Child as demonic Other, sensationalised in countless horror fantasies, or as the archetypal victim of satanic abuse — in either case, *alien*.

By marvellous chance, while writing this article I came across an account in a book on Melanesian Cargo Cults (P Worsley, *The Trumpet Shall Sound*, New York, 1968) of a child-gang which might have been designed by a fantasy novelist just to illustrate my thesis. The material was taken from the memoirs of a British Colonial Officer, A B Brewster, *The Hill Tribes of Fiji* (London, 1922).

The Water Babies (*Luve-ni-wai*, Children of the Water) were not Cargo cultists, nor were they simply a traditional tribal youth group of the sort familiar from Malinowski or Mead. Though based on tribal myth, the cult was something new (1880s and '90s), perhaps a sort of 'pagan revival' in opposition to the growing influence of Wesleyan missionaries (who were the first outsiders to notice its appearance).

Brewster writes that the movement was inspired by *vu-ni-nduva*, 'magicians', who are said to have astonished their followers by making food appear out of thin air and other sleight-of-hand tricks. (The use of 'stage' magic by shamans is not taken as evidence of any hypocrisy by modern anthropologists, however. A healer may 'fool' a patient in the course of treatment, for example, while still believing implicitly in the spirits, levels of being, etc, of the shamantic cosmology.)

Our Colonial observer tells us that although the Luve-ni-wai used occult signs and performed 'strange ceremonies', the group was viewed at first as 'a sort of junior republic' or 'pastime for young people.' The name of cult was taken from the fairy-like 'fauns' who were believed to people the forests and waters, miniature men with long hair in the traditional style, 'and very handsome withal.' Boys claimed to have met these friendly sprites in the forests and to have learnt songs and dances from them. Where they had met, 'fairy rings' were kept swept and magically protected, cleaned and decorated with flowers.

To join the movement, a boy had to acquire his own personal guardian from among these forest creatures. He would pray in the bush, offering *kava*, and wait till a spirit entered his body. Then he would take a new name, usually that of a flower.

Minor tutelary or totemic spirits of nature such as the fairies and undines are often depicted as children, childlike, or associated with children. This is not merely a late decadent sentimentalisation of figures who were 'originally' terrifying, chthonic, shaggy or uncanny. Raven, the trickster-god of the North West Amerindians, appears both as a top-hat-wearing giant black bird with an erection *and* as a young boy (as well as in the reflection of the moon through pines on still water, etc). The child, who grows, is seen as *natura naturans* ('Nature nature-ing') and thus 'wild', as opposed to the non-growing adult, *natura naturata* ('Nature natured'), the 'tame' representative of culture. In anthro-jargon one might also say that the child is *liminal*, a threshold or in-between figure, standing 'between' and 'for' both human and beast, both culture and chaos.

As the Water Babies movement developed, it linked itself with another, more grown-up, more politicised and anti-Colonial neo-pagan sect, the Tuka. By 1884 the movement was said to be getting out of hand in Serea, the largest village in Tholo East. A government official found all the youths and boys assembled in the temple in the presence of the shamans. When they resisted arrest, 44 were seized, including Pita, their leader, taken to Vunindawa and flogged. For six years nothing was heard of Luve-ni-wai in this area. Then in 1890 the local government representative went away for eight months. On his return he found both the Luve-ni-wai and the Tuka movement again 'rampant'. A number of youths were tried and sentenced to three months hard labour.

Brewster thought the early stages of the movement quite innocuous: '. . . in my opinion, it was not really seditious, it led the boys to be cheeky and insubordinate, and to a certain amount of larceny. I think there is not much harm in it so long as the votaries refrain from picking and stealing, and are duly respectful to their elders, and there is certainly a fair element of romance and poetry about it.'

After the suppression of the Luve-ni-wai, Brewster tried to take the lads' minds off their troubles by getting them interested in. . .cricket! He succeeded all too well: his cricket clubs became clandestine fronts for the Water Babies, nascent cells of the anti-

Colonial struggle, and within a few years the leaders were all in jail.

If an anthropologist were to wander through America's malls and discover a band of kids in strange quasi-ceremonial garb, gain their trust and interview them, no doubt all the perennial themes illustrated in the Luve-ni-wai story would re-emerge. The 'republic of children', the secret society, use of intoxicants, vision-quest, identity-quest and ritual self-re-naming, 'romance and poetry' (spontaneous aesthetics), rebellion against adult authority (both the 'elders' of the immediate clan and the distant powers of political oppression) — dance, music, even possession and the occult.

I would prefer, however, that the anthropologist did not publish these findings. Every secret brought to light and exposed to the media somehow becomes a representation of itself, immediately falsified. The delicate and subtle flower of our perception about the free spirit of youth suddenly becomes 'Youth Culture', complete with ads and flowcharts, or else 'Youth in Trouble', with sociological statistics and award-winning photo opportunities. Under the glare of such a gaze, as Foucault noted, the very phenomenon in question somehow mysteriously *disappears*.

However, childlife has not vanished, but rather has 'been disappeared', to borrow a metaphor from South American politics. Childlife has been buried under the empty image of a childlife that meets all expectations — positive and negative — of the consensus institutions. But childlife is organic; it cannot be so easily smothered by culture. Perhaps it has become an invisible empire of the senses.

And who would be the autarch — or rather, what would be the autarchic principle of such a 'dissipative structure'? Where would it find its 'Strange Attractor'? What could it be, outside hospital, family, school, outside the categories predetermined by media? Unmediated childlife? If it eludes all tests, polls, surveys and analyses, how can we feel certain it even exists?

Perhaps it's one of those things that can no longer be discussed in polite society, like racism or God, one of those categories 'we' all pretend to believe no longer really exists — despite the annoying phantoms and lingering traces that sometimes haunt us. It must not be spoken of, since words lend substance to fears, to shameful memories which are better left to moulder, which can written out of our theorems or theories, because there's something dirty about it — messy, erotic, dreamlike, superstitious, magical. Its smell cannot be computed.

It belongs in in-between places, like the edge of town where unplanned bits of second-growth forest blur the margin between urbanity and wildness; or in bed, between waking and sleeping. It exists even in the subjective experience of mediated images, which may undergo certain radical re-interpretations, which may be incorporated into meaning-complexes never intended by their producers, which are no longer passively consumed but rather actively transformed by imagination, by spontaneous ritual, by *being seen*.

To write about it is already to say the wrong thing. It must not be betrayed — but it *cannot* be betrayed, because all portrayal misses it. It is a nuance. It is *latif* (Arabic, 'subtle', as in alchemy). Contemporary occultists do in fact speculate on the emergence of the 'current' of the Child (sometimes named Horus). *Neoteny* — a scientific term designated species which possess no 'mature' form — applies to both the axolotl (who regrows his lost tail) and to human beings, who are capable of overcoming genetic and social 'fate' through the regenerative faculty of imagination.

The wandering dervish never 'grows up'; he is on 'perpetual holiday' (Nur Ali Shah Esfahani) like a 'gypsy girl or beggar' (Fakhroddin Iraqi). Unlike the orthodox Sufi, the dervish (*qalandar, maulang*) refuses the responsibilities of adult life, feeling them as bars to spiritual progress. A true zero-work radical aristocracy — like the hobos of America's railroad age. Moving from city to city, sometimes following a rule of never resting twice in the same place (or no more than 40 nights), the dervishes foreshadow the urban nomadism of today (especially the *dérive*, the conscious poetic 'drift' of the Situationists); in fact, they offer us a spirituality of urban nomadism.

And by the amusing conceit that the science of symbolism can be used to connect anything to anything at all, let's follow some associations: from the Sufis to the Assassins; from the Assassins to the Templars; and now to Baphomet, even Klossowski's Baphomet, a Moor's-Head presiding over a spontaneous rite of mystical pederasty; and from there to William Burroughs and the Wild Boys.

The single-sex utopias of science fiction all feel marred by the *resentment* of one gender for the other. On the positive side, however, these fictions release a certain benevolent power (*mana, baraka*) in the image of *one's own gender*. On the male side I'm thinking of Samuel Delany, or of Storm Constantine's *Wraeththu* trilogy (but Constantine is a woman). On the female side, Angela Carter, Leonora Carrington; a story by Rachel Pollack, 'Burning Sky' (in *Semiotext(e) Science Fiction*) exemplifies the Wild Girls version of the myth Burroughs popularised — the myth of shape-shifting erotic youth, werewolves, jaguar sodalities.

The whole complex of themes can be summed up under the heading of the *aesthetics of chaos*, of Tiamet, rather than the usual aesthetics of the splendour of Order which governs civilisation, the aesthetics of Marduk. But we have moved beyond the mere dualism of male/female which obsesses so many mainstream feminist commentators on history/herstory. We are, remember, moving forward under the sign of the Child, which somehow escapes gender, almost as if our children were a third sex (as H de Montherlandt put it). There are boy gangs and girl gangs — and mixed gangs — but all are androgynous in some sense.

The child-gang disappears. It does not confront 'adult authority', it simple evades the grown-ups. The Amazonian Indians who fire blowguns at helicopters want to remain invisible. Outcast groups, mixed-race groups, heretic communalists, gypsies, Maroons, hippies — all these 'child-gangs' prefer to vanish in the face of Marduk's cop-like rigidity and terror. As pirates they prey on society; as monks, pray for it, but in every case they evade its burdensome banality, including such responsibilities as the sacraments of gender. This kind of disappearance, as Baudrillard says (in *Fatal Strategies*), is itself a kind of insurrection. In the face of the empty discourse of power, the simulacrum which Babylon has become, this counter-power of invisibility possessed by marginal types can assume real tactical vitality; like a sort of *vajra*-weapon; or an *aikido* which 'wins' by *avoiding* power.

The child-gang also wants to avoid *mediation*. It wants *its own* dream. Most of all, it wants its own everyday life to be penetrated by the marvellous (in the dada/surrealist sense or the Sufi sense). The marvellous must not be represented, but *present*. King Arthur's knights, a boy-gang if ever there was one, centred their existence around the single virtue of *adventure*: that whatever happens *is* the marvellous. Once one has disappeared from beneath the fatal gaze of Babylon, the humdrum of Order, only then does one really live.

It will be said (especially by our own Civilisation of Safety) that this is a dangerous idea. Yes it is. That's the point of adventure. Order will have its say in any event; let us speak for the beautiful idea, which is paradoxically also a very traditional idea, of the spirituality of divine disorder; perhaps of the rebirth of Dionysus.

The child-gang can degenerate toward a 'fascist' spirituality, but it can also exemplify what may be called an anarchist spirituality: radically monist, on the side of wildness (and thus 'green'), erotic, spontaneous, playful — and therefore artistic. This artistry tends towards the totemic and the rediscovery of the paleolithic psyche: it is sickness of civilisation, but escapes morbidity by the contemplation of the emblem of its own energy. This energy moves in space rather than time: it is not bound by history. It is 'always young.'

The rediscovery of the Goddess and the New Male Spirituality have both donated great riches of possibility to the complex from which individual paths emerge and move toward 'liberation'. But for some, the whole god/goddess structure carries too much weight, too much oedipal misery, too much representation of the nuclear family and its atomistic discontents. For them the spirituality of Father and Mother are both to be overcome — even 'denied', in the word of a certain wild boy.

Not the New Man or New Woman, but the Child — the runaway child and the moment of the beginning of the adventure. That is the Image.

NOTES ON
CONTRIBUTORS

John Matthews has been a student of the Mysteries since the age of fifteen. The author of more than 20 books on this and related subjects, he gives lectures and workshops worldwide with his life-partner, Caitlín Matthews. He first became interested in the idea of working with men after attending a workshop given by Robert Bly. He is preparing several other books for publication, including *The Celtic Shaman* (Element Books, 1991) and a study of *The Green Man*.

Ean Begg read modern languages at Oxford and studied analytical psychology at the C G Jung Institute in Zurich. After a varied career in education, the wine trade, the Dominican Order and gastronomy, he now practises as a Jungian analyst in London. Author of several books, he has written and presented programmes for BBC television and radio.

Robert Bly is one of America's most celebrated poets and story-tellers. In 1966, he helped found American Writers Against the Vietnam War, and in 1968 he won the National Book Award for his poetry collection 'Light Around The Body'. In the seventies, Bly published renderings of the works of Rumi, Kabir, and Rilke, and eleven books of poetry. In the eighties he turned much of his attention to the question of male identity in the aftermath of the women's movement, becoming the foremost spokesman of the emerging men's movement in the USA.

Peter Lamborn Wilson's contributions to Islamic/esoteric studies include collaborative translations of Nasir Khusraw and Awhadoddin Kermani, and (with W C Chittick) the *Lama'at* or *Divine Flashes* of Fakhroddin 'Iraqi (Paulist Press, 1982). His work has appeared in *Gnosis, Temenos, Parabola, Studies in Mystical Literature, Interzone,* the British Science Fiction magazine, and other periodicals. His latest book is *Scandal: Essays in Islamic Heresy* (Autonomedia, 1988). After fifteen years of nomadism in Central and South-East Asia and India, he is now encamped in the dubious oasis of Manhatten, working for *Semiotext(e)* magazine and doing radio for WBAI-FM.

Robert Lawlor is the author of *Sacred Geometry — Its Philosophy and Practice* (Thames & Hudson) and co-author, with Keith Critchlow, of *Homage to Pythagoras* and *Geometry and Architecture* (Lindisfarne Press). While living in France and London, he translated works of Alain Daniélou and R A Schwaller de Lubicz for Inner Traditions. Lawlor lectured for five years with the Lindisfarne Association in New York and Colorado, has contributed articles to the journals *Parabola* and *Corona*, and is a former painter and sculptor whose artwork has been displayed in the Walter P Chrysler Museum, the Brooklyn Museum, the Pratt Institute, and various private collections. His most recent work includes intensive seminars on the subject of Earth Honouring at New York's Open Center. Currently a writer and producer of films, Lawlor lives on an island between the Australian mainland and Tasmania. There, while active in local conservation issues, he continues writing books and screenplays.

John Rowan is the author of a number of books, including *The Reality Game* (Routledge, 1983), *The Horned God* (Routledge, 1987), *Ordinary Ecstasy* (2nd edition, Routledge, 1988), and *Subpersonalities* (Routledge, 1990). He has co-edited *Human Inquiry* (Wiley, 1981) with Peter Reason, and *Innovative Therapy in Britain* (Open University Press, 1988) with Wendy Dryden. He is a founder member and on the Board of the Association of Humanistic Psychology Practitioners, and on the editorial board of the *Journal of Humanistic Psychology*. He is a chartered psychologist, a qualified psychotherapist and an accredited counsellor. He practises Primal Integration, and teaches psychology and psychotherapy at a number of centres. He also writes poetry, and has taken part in many poetry readings.

Greg Stafford has been practising shamanism for almost ten years, and is president of Cross Cultural Shamanism Network, the publisher of *Shaman's Drum* magazine. He is also president of Chaosium Inc, and author of the experiential roleplaying games, *King*

Arthur Pendragon and *Prince Valiant*. He teaches workshops on Experiential Arthurianism, mythology and shamanism, and is a sweat lodge leader and vision quest leader. He is a single parent, and lives in California.

Bob Stewart (R J Stewart) is a Scots author, composer and musician. His professional career spans over 20 years of touring, recording, writing and composing (from his first television performance in 1968). He has 24 books in publication worldwide (1990), of both fiction and non-fiction, and his work has been translated into French, Dutch, German, Spanish, Portuguese, Italian and Japanese. He has also contributed to anthologies, magazines and many arts projects. As a composer and musician he has written, directed and recorded five LP records, a series of cassettes, and music and songs for feature films, television, radio and theatre productions. Bob Stewart has also appeared on British, European and American stages, television and radio, as a solo performer and as a presenter of material on myths, legends and magical traditions. He lives in England.

Peter Taylor was born in Isleworth, England, in 1954. His guided explorations of inner space led him to experience resonances of the celestial harmonies at a very early age. He is now an exponent of the practical aspects of the Magical Tradition, having a particular interest in the current resurgence of the Starry Wisdom — which, he believes, provides us with the means to return scientific endeavour to a proper basis in spiritual reality. The raw material for his writing comes from experimental magical work carried out in small groups.

Richard Wybold entered the original coven founded by Gerald Gardner, which met at Fiveacres, north of London, in 1967. During the 1970s he moved to become high priest of a daughter coven in Surrey, but in 1976 returned to the mother coven, which he still attends, though he now lives in the West of England. Besides strictly Craft activities he is an active member of several high magic groups and believes the cross-fertilisation of ideas between the strains of natural and ritual magic to be a constructive tendency. Though his early training scorned 'interference' with the ritual forms of Gardner and the pioneers, he welcomes the poetic and exploratory work of more recent contributors such as Vivienne Crowley.

He has had a successful professional career as an electronics engineer, still practises as a consultant, and derives huge pleasure from world travel whenever possible.

FURTHER READING

OTHER WORKS BY THE CONTRIBUTORS

Robert Bly

A Little Book of the Human Shadow. San Francisco, Harper & Row, 1988
The Kabir Book. St Paul, Minnesota, Ally Press, 1985
Loving a Woman in Two Worlds. San Francisco, Harper & Row, 1987
Men and the Wound (cassette). St Paul, Minnesota, Ally Press, 1988
The Naive Male (cassette). St Paul, Minnesota, Ally Press, 1988
The Pillow and the Key. Commentary on the fairy tale of Iron John (Part One). St Paul, Minnesota, Ally Press, 1987
Selected Poems. San Francisco, Harper & Row, 1987
When a Hair Turns Gold. Commentary on the fairy tale of Iron John (Part Two). St Paul, Minnesota, Ally Press, 1989

Robert Lawlor

As on the First Day. Vermont, Inner Traditions International, 1991
Earth Honoring: The New Male Sexuality. Rochester, Vermont, Park Street Press, 1989
Geometry and Architecture (with Keith Crichlow). Lindisfarne, West Stockbridge, Mass. Press, 1981
Homage to Pythagoras (with Keith Crichlow). Lindisfarne Press, 1982
Sacred Geometry: Its Philosophy and Practice. London, Thames & Hudson, 1982

Greg Stafford

'Labryinth and Tor of Glastonbury' (in) *Shaman's Drum*, 1987

Pendragon (role-playing game). Albany, California, Chaosium Inc
Prince Valiant (role-playing game). Albany, California, Chaosium
    Inc
'Sir Thomas Malory' (in) *The Household of the Grail* (ed John Mat-
    thews). Wellingborough, Aquarian Press, 1990

John Rowan

The Horned God. London, Routledge & Kegan Paul, 1987
Ordinary Ecstacy. London, Routledge & Kegan Paul, 1988
The Reality Game. London, Routledge & Kegan Paul, 1983
Subpersonalities. London, Routledge & Paul, 1990

Ean Begg

The Cult of the Black Virgin. London, Arkana, 2nd edition 1989
Myth and Today's Consciousness. London, Coventure Press, 1984
On the Trail of Merlin (with Deike Rich). Aquarian Press, 1991

Peter Lamborn Wilson

Angels. London, Thames & Hudson, 1980
'Cave Pirates of the Hollow Earth' (in) *Tarot Tales* (ed Caitlín Mat-
    thews and Rachel Pollack). London, Legend, 1989
Divan. London, Crescent Moon Press, 1978
The Drunken Universe (with Nasrolla Pourjavady). Grand Rapids,
    Phanes Press, 1987
'Glatisant and the Grail: An Arthurian Fragment' (in) *At the Table
    of the Grail* (ed John Matthews). London, Arkana, 1987
Heart's Witness (with B M Weischer). Tehran, Imperial Iranian
    Academy of Philosophy, 1978
Kings of Love (with Nasrolla Pourjavady). Tehran, Imperial Iranian
    Academy of Philosophy, 1978
The Winter Calligraphy. Ipswich, Golgonooza Press, 1975
Scandal: Essays in Islamic Heresy. New York, Autonomedia, 1988

John Matthews

The Aquarian Guide to British and Irish Mythology (with Caitlín Mat-
    thews). Wellingborough, Aquarian Press, 1988
The Arthurian Book of Days. London, Sidgwick & Jackson, 1990
An Arthurian Reader. Wellingborough, Aquarian Press, 1988
The Arthurian Tarot: A Hallowquest. Wellingborough, Aquarian
    Press, 1990

At the Table of the Grail. London, Arkana, 1987
Boadicea: Warrior Queen of the Celts. Poole, Firebird Books, 1988
Celtic Battle Heroes (with Bob Stewart). Poole, Firebird Books, 1988
El Cid: Champion of Spain. Poole, Firebird Books, 1988
Elements of Arthurian Tradition. Shaftesbury, Element Books, 1989
Elements of the Grail Tradition Shaftesbury, Element Books, 1990
Fionn mac Cumhail: Champion of Ireland. Poole, Firebird Books, 1988
Gawain, Knight of the Goddess. Wellingborough, Aquarian Press, 1990
The Grail: Quest for the Eternal. London, Thames & Hudson, 1981
The Grail Seeker's Companion (with Marian Green). Wellingborough, Aquarian Press, 1986
Hallowquest: Tarot Magic and the Arthurian Mysteries (with Caitlín Matthews). Wellingborough, Aquarian Press, 1990
Household of the Grail. Wellingborough, Aquarian Press, 1990
Legendary Britain: An Illustrated Journey (with R J Stewart). London, Cassell, 1989
Legendary London (with Chesca Potter). Wellingborough, Aquarian Press, 1990
Richard Lionheart: The Crusader King. Poole, Firebird Books, 1988
Taliesin: The Shamanic Mysteries of Britain (with additional material by Caitlín Matthews). London, Aquarian Press, 1991
Warriors of Arthur (with R J Stewart). London, Blandford Press, 1987
The Western Way: vol I The Native Tradition (with Caitlín Matthews). London, Arkana, 1985
The Western Way: vol II The Hermetic Tradition (with Caitlín Matthews). London, Arkana, 1986

Forthcoming Books
Celtic Book of the Dead (with Caitlín Matthews). Aquarian Press, 1992
A Celtic Reader. Aquarian Press, 1991
The Celtic Shaman. Element Books, 1991
A Glastonbury Reader. Aquarian Press, 1991
Ladies of the Lake (with Caitlín Matthews). Aquarian Press, 1991
Song of Taliesin. Aquarian Press, 1991

R J Stewart

Waters of the Gap (2nd edition). Bath, Arcania Books, 1989
The Underworld Initiation. Wellingborough, Aquarian Press, 1984
The Prophetic Vision of Merlin. London, Arkana, 1986
The Mystic Life of Merlin. London, Arkana, 1986

Music and the Elemental Psyche. Wellingborough, Aquarian Press, 1987

Living Magical Arts. London, Blandford Press, 1987

Advanced Magical Arts. Shaftesbury, Element Books, 1988

The Book of Merlin (ed). London, Blandford Press, 1987

The Second Book of Merlin; Merlin and Woman (ed). London, Blandford Press, 1988

Warriors of Arthur (with John Matthews). London, Blandford Press, 1987

The Merlin Tarot vol. 1. Wellingborough, Aquarian Press, 1988

Legendary Britain (with John Matthews). London, Cassell/Blandford Press, 1989

Elements of the Creation Myth. Shaftesbury, Element Books, 1989

Magical Tales; The Storytelling Tradition. Wellingborough, Aquarian Press, 1990

Elements of Prophecy. Shaftesbury, Element Books, 1990

Robert Kirk; Walker Between Worlds. Shaftesbury, Element Books, 1990

Music, Power, Harmony. London, Blandford Press, 1990

Celtic Gods, Celtic Goddesses. London, Blandford Press, 1990

Psychology and Spiritual Traditions (ed). Shaftesbury, Element Books, 1990

Cuchulainn. Poole, Firebird Books, 1987

Other Authors

Only a handful of the many new books beginning to appear on the subject of men's mysteries, together with some primary works on mythology.

Berman, M *The Re-enchantment of the World.* New York, Bantam Books, 1984

Bolen, J S *Gods in Everyman.* San Francisco, Harper & Row, 1989

Campbell, J *The Hero With A Thousand Faces.* London, Paladin, 1986

Farrell, W *Why Men are the Way They Are.* New York, MacGraw Hill, 1986

Levinson, D *The Seasons of a Man's Life.* New York, Ballantine Books, 1978

Moore, R and Gillette, D *King, Warrior, Magician, Lover.* San Francisco, Harper & Row, 1991

Pearson, C *The Hero Within.* San Francisco, Harper & Row, 1989

Tigner, L *Men in Groups.* New York, Vintage Books, 1970

Of further interest

TALIESIN

Shamanism and the Bardic Mysteries in Britain and Ireland

JOHN MATTHEWS

Taliesin is the *'Primary Chief Bard of the Island of Britain'* — a real figure who lived in Wales during the latter half of the sixth century and who wrote a number of works which may still be read with reward.

The writings of Taliesin, lost and forgotton for many years and still virtually unknown, fall into two groups: poems composed by the bard himself and a vast body of mythical allusion, story and song which constellated around him as the last of the Celtic Shamans — living embodiment of a racial memory stretching back thousands of years.

From this remarkable body of authentic material John Matthews, drawing on nearly thirty years of research and an in-depth reading of every available text, has reconstructed what may be seen as the original Shamanic and Bardic mystery teachings of Britain and Ireland. There are references to methods of divination, to a secret poetic language which kept the ancient mysteries in coded form, and to the rites, rituals and beliefs which formed an essential part of the worship of major Celtic deities. With the assistance of Caitlín Matthews there are completely new translations of Taliesin's major poems and those of his contemporary, Merlin. Throughout, the original mystery teachings are set forth in both a scholarly and exciting manner.

Of interest to all who share a belief in the power of Shamanism, and who love and respect the ancient traditions of these lands, this revolutionary study should prove to be one of the most challenging for many years on the subject of Celtic mythology and the Mystery Religions of Britain and Ireland.

SOPHIA — GODDESS OF WISDOM

CAITLIN MATTHEWS

Honoured as the transcendent wisdom that inhabits the heavens as Bride of God, but also feared as the Black Goddess upon Earth, Sophia has been one of the few active manifestations of the Divine Feminine for the last two millennia. Now, in response to the ecological, social and spiritual needs of the twentieth century, the Goddess is re-emerging from her long eclipse, along the pathways that Sophia has kept open.

Sophia — Goddess of Wisdom is a major new book that takes the reader on a journey through time, seeking out the presence of the Goddess from pre-Christian spirituality to the present day. Drawing mainly on sources from the Western tradition the many faces of the Goddess are revealed. She is shown as the primeval Black Goddess of the earth, as Saviour Goddess, the Gnostic Sophia, World Soul, Apocalyptic Virgin and as Mother of God. We see how the foundation mysteries of the Goddess underlie the esoteric streams of orthodox religions, and trace her hermetic presence in Qabala and alchemy. Finally, we track her appearance in the realms of Goddess religion, feminist theology and the New Age movement.

This definitive work gives Sophia a voice that will be welcomed by all who seek to reaffirm the Goddess as the central pivot of creation and as the giver of practical and spiritual wisdom.

TO BE A WOMAN

EDITED BY CONNIE ZWEIG

A new era in women's self-awareness is about to emerge. With the fruits of feminism and individual development, women now have the opportunity to imagine and to live a kind of femininity that is consciously chosen — and that contains the benefits of our hard-won independence as well.

In this ground-breaking collection, women from many walks of life describe the key insights and experiences that can provide entry to this new level of consciousness.

This book explores what it means to be a woman in a man's world for those of us who do not wish to stay at home and 'become like our mothers' or to strive aggressively and 'become like men'; why women in conventional marriages are initiating divorce in greater numbers than ever before; why women are expressing deep disillusionment with the promises of feminism and the reality of career success; why women are leaving careers and rushing to have babies late in life, and why women are exploring feminine spirituality and the Goddess.

The answers can be found in a woman's longing to be authentically feminine, to experience herself fully as a woman and, at the same time, to be a strong, independent individual whose power and authority are rooted within her. At a time when feminine values are on the rise, this book offers a vision of renewal.

Contributors include Marion Woodman, Jean Shinoda Bolen, Riane Eisler, Linda Schierse Leonard, Merlin Stone, Sylvia Brinton Perera and June Singer.